YOUR STRATEGY NEEDS A STRATEGY

YOUR STRATEGY NEEDS A STRATEGY

How to Choose and Execute the Right Approach

MARTIN REEVES : KNUT HAANÆS : JANMEJAYA SINHA

HARVARD BUSINESS REVIEW PRESS

BOSTON, MASSACHUSETTS

Copyright 2015 The Boston Consulting Group, Inc.
All rights reserved
Printed in the United States of America

10 9 8 7 6 5 4 3

No part of this publication may be reproduced, stored in or introduced into a retrieval system, or transmitted, in any form, or by any means (electronic, mechanical, photocopying, recording, or otherwise), without the prior permission of the publisher. Requests for permission should be directed to permissions@hbsp.harvard.edu, or mailed to Permissions, Harvard Business School Publishing, 60 Harvard Way, Boston, Massachusetts 02163.

The web addresses referenced in this book were live and correct at the time of the book's publication but may be subject to change.

Cataloging-in-Publication data is forthcoming.
    ISBN: 978-1-62527-586-8
    eISBN: 978-1-62527-587-5

The paper used in this publication meets the requirements of the American National Standard for Permanence of Paper for Publications and Documents in Libraries and Archives Z39.48-1992.

CONTENTS

YOUR STRATEGY NEEDS A STRATEGY

CHAPTER 1

INTRODUCTION

Your Strategy Needs a Strategy

How to Select and Execute the Right Approach to Strategy

Strategy is a means to an end: favorable business outcomes. When we think about strategy, we tend to think about planning: study your situation, define a goal, and draw up a step-by-step path to get there. For a long time, planning was the dominant approach in business strategy—in both the boardroom and the classroom. But effective business strategy has never really consisted of just this one approach. The multidecade plans that oil companies make would feel inappropriate to the CEO of a software firm that faces new products and competitors every day and that therefore adopts a more fluid and opportunistic approach to strategy. Neither would such long-term plans feel natural to an entrepreneur creating and bringing a new product or business model to market. What is this broader set of ways in which we can approach strategy, and which approach is the most effective in which situation? That is the central question of this book, and we will show that getting the answer right can deliver demonstrable, significant value.

Today, we face a business environment that is faster changing and more uncertain than ever because of, among other factors, globalization, rapid technological change, and economic interconnectedness. Perhaps less well known is that the *diversity and range* of business environments that we face have also increased. Large corporations, in particular, are stretched across an increasing number of environments that change more rapidly over time (figure 1-1), requiring businesses not only to choose the right approach to strategy or even the right combination of approaches, but also to adjust the mix as environments shift.

One size *doesn't* fit all.

Prompted by the increased uncertainty and dynamism of business environments, some academics and business leaders have asserted or implied that competitive advantage and even strategy more broadly is less relevant.[1] In fact, strategy has never been more important. The frequency and speed with which incumbents are being overthrown and the performance gap between winners and losers have never been greater (figure 1-2). Many CEOs are looking over their shoulders for the upstart competitor that may undermine their company's position, and many upstart companies are aspiring to do just that. It has never been more important, therefore, to choose the right approach to strategy for the right business situation.

FIGURE 1-1

Increasing diversity of environments

Heat map of range of strategic environments faced by companies

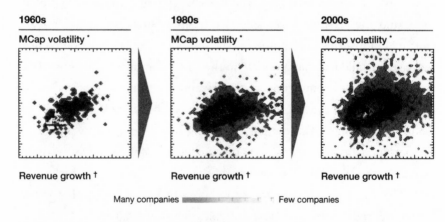

Source: Compustat (US public companies); Martin Reeves, Claire Love, and Philipp Tillmanns, "Your Strategy Needs a Strategy," *Harvard Business Review*, September 2012.

Note: MCap, market cap.

* Standard deviation over ten years of annual growth in market capitalization (MCap) (log scale).

† Absolute percent revenue growth averaged over the decade (log scale).

FIGURE 1-2

Increasing gap between winners and losers for US companies

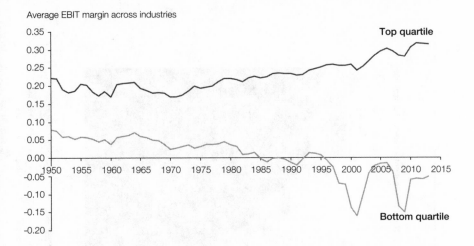

Average EBIT margin across industries

Source: BCG analysis (August 2014), Compustat.

Note: EBIT: earnings before interest and taxes. EBIT margin across industries is based on an analysis of approximately 34,000 publicly listed, mainly US companies in years when net sales were greater than $50 million; computing quartile average within six-digit GICS industry (unweighted), then averaged across industries (weighted by number of companies per industry per year); excluding outliers (higher than 100 percent margin or lower than minus 300 percent margin) and industries in years with insufficient data points.

Unfortunately, it has also never been more difficult to choose the right approach. The number of strategy tools and frameworks that leaders can choose from has grown massively since the birth of business strategy in the early 1960s (figure 1-3). And far from obvious are the answers to how these approaches relate to one another or when they should and shouldn't be deployed.

It's not that we lack powerful ways to approach strategy; it's that we lack a robust way to select the right ones for the right circumstances. The five-forces framework for strategy may be valid in one arena, blue ocean or open innovation in another, but each approach to strategy tends to be presented or perceived as a panacea. Managers and other business leaders face a dilemma: with increasingly diverse environments to manage and rising stakes to get it right, how do they identify the most effective approach to business strategy and marshal the right thinking and behaviors to conceive and execute it, supported by the appropriate frameworks and tools?

FIGURE 1-3

Proliferation of strategy frameworks

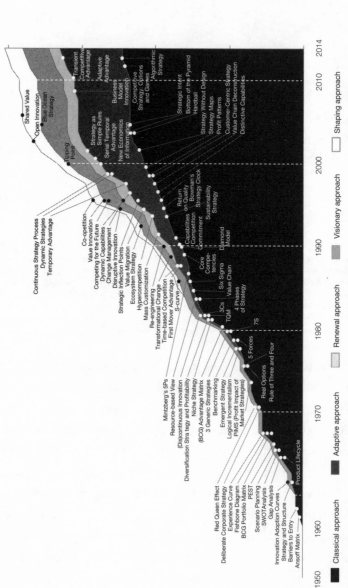

Number of salient strategic frameworks

Source: Pankaj Ghemawat, "Competition and Business Strategy in Historical Perspective," *Business History Review* 76 (Spring 2002): 37–74; Lawrence Freedman, *Strategy: A History* (New York: Oxford University Press, 2013); research by The Boston Consulting Group Strategy Institute.

Note: 3Cs, Customer, Competitors, Corporation; 5Ps, Plan, Ploy, Pattern, Position, Perspective; 7Ss, Strategy, Structure, Systems, Shared Values, Skills, Staff,

In researching and writing this book, we spoke with many business leaders, and our conversations confirmed their dilemma. Some opined that strategy as a discipline had been made less relevant by changing circumstances. Others explained how traditional approaches to strategy needed to be replaced by new and more effective ones. One executive even warned that the word *strategy* had been banished from use in his company. Many told us that in businesses as large and diverse as theirs, they couldn't conceive of using a single approach to developing and executing effective strategy.

To address the combined challenge of increased dynamism and diversity of business environments as well as the proliferation of approaches, this book proposes a unifying choice framework: *the strategy palette*. This framework was created to help leaders *match* their approach to strategy to the circumstances at hand and execute it effectively, to *combine* different approaches to cope with multiple or changing environments, and, as leaders, to *animate* the resulting collage of approaches.

The strategy palette consists of five archetypal approaches to strategy—basic colors, if you will—which can be applied to different parts of your business: from geographies to industries to functions to stages in a firm's life cycle, tailored to the particular environment that each part of the business faces.

EVIDENCE ON WHICH THIS BOOK IS BASED

This book is built on a broad body of evidence. *Your Strategy Needs a Strategy* is the result of half a decade of research within The Boston Consulting Group (BCG) Strategy Institute, numerous conversations with our clients, and a detailed survey of 150 firms from industries as diverse as banking, pharmaceuticals, high tech, and agri-food across major industrial nations in 2012. We also analyzed the conditions in different industries across a sixty-year period to understand how business environments have changed over time.

To supplement these observations, we conducted more than twenty in-depth interviews with CEOs about their experiences and perspectives on developing and realizing winning strategies. We also leveraged joint research with our academic collaborators, especially Simon Levin of Princeton University, with whom we explored insights from biological and evolutionary strategies, which are often associated with complex, diverse, dynamic, and uncertain environments.

Finally, we have explored the strategy palette mathematically, by developing a computer model that simulates business strategies and their performance in different business environments. The resulting model is at the heart of a companion iPad app, which will enable readers to experience and develop a more intuitive understanding of each approach. To download the iPad app, visit Apple's App Store and search for "Your Strategy Needs a Strategy." You can also find it by visiting our website: www.bcgperspectives.com/yourstrategyneedsastrategy.

Five Strategy Environments

The Strategy Palette

Strategy is, in essence, problem solving, and the best approach depends upon the specific problem at hand. Your environment dictates your approach to strategy. You need to assess the environment and then match and apply the appropriate approach. But how do you characterize the business environment, and how do you choose which approach to strategy is best suited to the job of defining a winning course of action?

Business environments differ along three easily discernible dimensions: *Predictability* (can you forecast it?), *malleability* (can you, either alone or in collaboration with others, shape it?), and *harshness* (can you survive it?). Combining these dimensions into a matrix reveals five distinct environments, each of which requires a distinct approach to strategy and execution (figure 1-4).

- **Classical:** I can predict it, but I can't change it.

- **Adaptive:** I can't predict it, and I can't change it.

FIGURE 1-4

The strategy palette: five environments and approaches to strategy

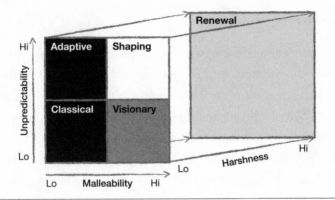

- **Visionary:** I can predict it, and I can change it.

- **Shaping:** I can't predict it, but I can change it.

- **Renewal:** My resources are severely constrained.

Five Strategy Archetypes

Each environment corresponds to a distinct archetypal approach to strategy, or color in the strategy palette, as follows: predictable *classical* environments lend themselves to strategies of position, which are based on advantage achieved through scale or differentiation or capabilities and are achieved through comprehensive analysis and planning. *Adaptive* environments require continuous experimentation because planning does not work under conditions of rapid change and unpredictability. In a *visionary* setting, firms win by being the first to create a new market or to disrupt an existing one. In a *shaping* environment, firms can collaboratively shape an industry to their advantage by orchestrating the activities of other stakeholders. Finally, under the harsh conditions of a *renewal* environment, a firm needs to first conserve and free up resources to ensure its viability and then go on to choose one of the other four approaches to rejuvenate growth and ensure long-term prosperity. The resulting overriding imperatives, at the simplest level, vary starkly for each approach:

- **Classical:** Be big.

- **Adaptive:** Be fast.

- **Visionary:** Be first.

- **Shaping:** Be the orchestrator.

- **Renewal:** Be viable.

Using the right approach pays off. In our research, firms that successfully match their strategy to their environment realized significantly better returns—4 to 8 percent of total shareholder return—over firms that didn't.[2] Yet around half of all companies we looked at mismatch their approach to strategy to their environment in some way.

Let's delve a little deeper to see how to win using each of the basic colors of strategy and why each works best under specific circumstances.

Classical

Leaders taking a classical approach to strategy believe that the world is predictable, that the basis of competition is stable, and that advantage, once obtained, is sustainable. Given that they cannot change their environment, such firms seek to position themselves optimally within it. Such positioning can be based on superior size, differentiation, or capabilities.

Positional advantage is sustainable in a classical environment: the environment is predictable and develops gradually without major disruptions.

To achieve winning positions, classical leaders employ the following thought flow: they *analyze* the basis of competitive advantage and the fit between their firm's capabilities and the market and forecast how these will develop over time. Then, they construct a *plan* to build and sustain advantaged positions, and, finally, they *execute* it rigorously and efficiently (figure 1-5).

FIGURE 1-5

The classical approach to strategy

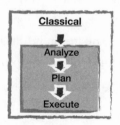

We will see how Mars, the global manufacturer of confectionery and pet food, successfully executes a classical approach to strategy. Mars focuses on categories and brands where it can lead and obtain a scale advantage, and it creates value by growing those categories. This approach has helped Mars build itself into a profitable $35 billion company and multicategory leader over the course of a century.[3]

Classical strategy is probably the approach with which you are the most familiar. In fact, for many managers, it may be the approach that defines strategy. Classical strategy is what is taught in business schools and practiced in some form in the majority of strategy functions in major enterprises.

WHAT YOU MIGHT KNOW IT AS

Most readers will be familiar with at least a handful of strategy concepts. So that you can relate your existing knowledge of strategy with the five colors of the strategy palette, we will highlight the main related schools of strategy and their associated frameworks and tools in sidebars like this one in the chapters detailing each approach.

For example, we will show how the classical approach is exemplified by Bruce Henderson's experience curve and growth-share matrix or by Michael Porter's celebrated five forces model. For the adaptive approach, we will describe Kathleen Eisenhardt's simple rules-based approach to strategy or Rita McGrath's work on strategies of agility. Similarly, we will discuss how the visionary approach underpins Gary Hamel and C. K. Prahalad's book *Competing for the Future*, and how the shaping approach is connected with the growing body of work on platform businesses and business ecosystems.

The aim is not to be comprehensive but rather to show how well-known approaches relate to each other and to the strategy palette, to clarify which should be used when, and to give readers some points of departure for further investigation.

Adaptive

Firms employ an adaptive approach when the business environment is neither predictable nor malleable. When prediction is hard and advantage is short-lived, the only shield against continuous disruption is a readiness and an ability to repeatedly change oneself. In an adaptive environment, winning comes from adapting to change by continuously experimenting and identifying new options more quickly and economically than others. The classical strategist's mantra of sustainable competitive advantage becomes one of serial temporary advantage.

To be successful at strategy through experimentation, adaptive firms master three essential thinking steps: they continuously *vary* their approach, generating a range of strategic options to test. They carefully *select* the most successful ones to *scale up* and exploit (figure 1-6). And as the environment changes, the firms rapidly iterate on this evolutionary loop to ensure that they continuously renew their advantage. An adaptive approach is less cerebral than a classical one—advantage arises through the company's continuously trying new things and not through its analyzing, predicting, and optimizing.

Tata Consultancy Services, the India-based information technology (IT) services and solutions company, operates in an environment it can neither predict nor change. It continuously adapts to repeated shifts in technology—from client servers to cloud computing—and the resulting changes that these shifts cause in their customers' businesses and in the basis of competition. By taking an adaptive approach that focuses on monitoring the environment, strategic experimentation, and organizational flexibility, Tata Consultancy Services has grown from

FIGURE 1-6

The adaptive approach to strategy

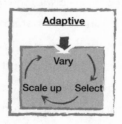

$155 million in revenue in 1996 to $1 billion in 2003 and more than $13 billion in 2013 to become the second-largest pure IT services company in the world.[4]

Visionary

Leaders taking a visionary approach believe that they can reliably create or re-create an environment largely by themselves. Visionary firms win by being the first to introduce a revolutionary new product or business model. Though the environment may look uncertain to others, visionary leaders see a clear opportunity for the creation of a new market segment or the disruption of an existing one, and they act to realize this possibility.

This approach works when the visionary firm can single-handedly build a new, attractive market reality. A firm can be the first to apply a new technology or to identify and address a major source of customer dissatisfaction or a latent need. The firm can innovate to address a tired industry business model or can recognize a megatrend before others see and act on it.

Firms deploying a visionary approach also follow a distinct thought flow. First, visionary leaders *envisage* a valuable possibility that can be realized. Then they work single-mindedly to be the first to *build* it. Finally, they *persist* in executing and scaling the vision until its full potential has been realized (figure 1-7). In contrast to the analysis and planning of classical strategy and the iterative experimentation of adaptive strategy, the visionary approach is about imagination and realization and is essentially creative.

Quintiles, which pioneered the clinical research organization (CRO) industry for outsourced pharmaceutical drug development services, is a prime example of a company employing a visionary approach to strategy.

FIGURE 1-7

The visionary approach to strategy

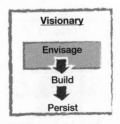

Though the industry model may have looked stable to others, its founder and chairman, Dennis Gillings, saw a clear opportunity to improve drug development by creating an entirely new business model and, in 1982, moved first to capitalize on the inevitabilities he saw. By ensuring that Quintiles moved fast and boldly, it maintained its lead and leapt well ahead of potential competition. It is today the largest player in the CRO industry which it created and has been associated with the development or commercialization of the top fifty best-selling drugs currently on the market.[5]

Shaping

When the environment is unpredictable but malleable, a firm has the extraordinary opportunity to lead the shaping or reshaping of a whole industry at an early point of its development, before the rules have been written or rewritten.

Such an opportunity requires you to collaborate with others because you cannot shape the industry alone—and you need others to share the risk, contribute complementary capabilities, and build the new market quickly before competitors mobilize. A shaping firm therefore operates under a high degree of unpredictability, given the nascent stage of industry evolution it faces and the participation of multiple stakeholders that it must influence but cannot fully control.

In the shaping approach, firms *engage* other stakeholders to create a shared vision of the future at the right point in time. They build a platform through which they can *orchestrate* collaboration and then *evolve* that platform and its associated stakeholder ecosystem by scaling it and maintaining its flexibility and diversity (figure 1-8). Shaping strategies are very different from classical,

FIGURE 1-8

The shaping approach to strategy

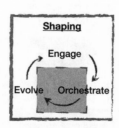

adaptive, or visionary strategies—they concern ecosystems rather than individual enterprises and rely as much on collaboration as on competition.

Novo Nordisk employed a shaping strategy to win in the Chinese diabetes care market since the 1990s. Novo couldn't predict the exact path of market development, since the diabetes challenge was just beginning to emerge in China, but by collaborating with patients, regulators, and doctors, the company could influence the rules of the game. Now, Novo is the uncontested market leader in diabetes care in China, with over 60 percent insulin market share.[6]

Renewal

The renewal approach to strategy aims to restore the vitality and competitiveness of a firm when it is operating in a harsh environment. Such difficult circumstances can be caused by a protracted mismatch between the firm's approach to strategy and its environment or by an acute external or internal shock.

When the external circumstances are so challenging that your current way of doing business cannot be sustained, decisively changing course is the only way to not only survive, but also to secure another chance to thrive. A company must first recognize and *react* to the deteriorating environment as early as possible. Then, it needs to act decisively to restore its viability—*economizing* by refocusing the business, cutting costs, and preserving capital, while also freeing up resources to fund the next part of the renewal journey. Finally, the firm must pivot to one of the four other approaches to strategy to ensure that it can *grow* and thrive again (figure 1-9). The renewal approach differs markedly from the other four approaches to strategy: it is usually initially defensive, it involves two distinct phases, and it is a prelude to adopting one of the other

FIGURE 1-9

The renewal approach to strategy

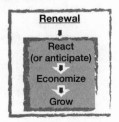

approaches to strategy. Renewal has become increasingly common because of the number of companies getting out of step with their environments.

American Express's response to the financial crisis exemplifies the renewal approach. As the credit crisis hit in 2008, Amex faced the triple punch of rising default rates, slipping consumer demand, and decreasing access to capital. To survive, the company cut approximately 10 percent of its workforce, shed noncore activities, and cut ancillary investment. By 2009, Amex had saved almost $2 billion in costs and pivoted toward growth and innovation by engaging new partners, investing in its loyalty program, entering the deposit raising business, and embracing digital technology. As of 2014, its stock was up 800 percent from recession lows.[7]

Applying the Strategy Palette

The strategy palette can be applied on three levels: to match and correctly execute the right approach to strategy for a specific part of the business, to effectively manage multiple approaches to strategy in different parts of the business or over time, and to help leaders to animate the resulting collage of approaches (figure 1-10).

FIGURE 1-10

Three levels of application for the strategy palette

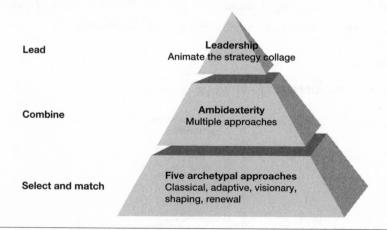

Lead — Leadership / Animate the strategy collage

Combine — Ambidexterity / Multiple approaches

Select and match — Five archetypal approaches / Classical, adaptive, visionary, shaping, renewal

The strategy palette provides leaders with a new language for describing and choosing the right approach to strategy in a particular part of their business. It also provides a logical thread to connect strategizing and execution for each approach. In most companies, strategizing and execution have become artificially separated, both organizationally and temporally. Each approach entails not only a very different way of conceiving strategy but also a distinct approach to implementation, creating very different requirements for information management, innovation, organization, leadership, and culture. The strategy palette can therefore guide not only the strategic intentions but also the operational setup of a company. Table 1-1 summarizes the key elements of the strategy palette and includes specific examples of companies using the five approaches.

TABLE 1-1

The five approaches of the strategy palette

			Approaches		
Key elements	**Classical**	**Adaptive**	**Visionary**	**Shaping**	**Renewal**
Core idea, or what it takes	• Be big	• Be fast	• Be first	• Be the orchestrator	• Be viable
Type of environment	• Predictable, non-malleable	• Unpredictable, nonmalleable	• Predictable, malleable	• Unpredictable, malleable	• Harsh
Industries where approach is most visibly applicable	• Utility • Automobile • Oil and gas	• Semiconductors • Textile retail	• Not industry specific (create new, disrupt existing)	• Some software • Smartphone apps	• Financial institutions in the 2008–2009 crisis
Indicators of the approach	• Low growth • High concentration • Mature industry • Stable regulation	• Volatile growth • Limited concentration • Young industry • High technological change	• High growth potential • White space, no direct competition • Limited regulation	• Fragmentation • No dominant player, platform • Shapable regulation	• Low growth, decline, crisis • Restricted financing • Negative cash flows

(Continued)

TABLE 1-1   *(Continued)*

The five approaches of the strategy palette

	Approaches				
Key elements	**Classical**	**Adaptive**	**Visionary**	**Shaping**	**Renewal**
How	• Analyze, plan, execute	• Vary, select, scale up	• Envisage, build, persist	• Engage, orchestrate, evolve	• React (or anticipate), economize, grow
Measures of success	• Scale • Market share	• Cycle time • New product vitality index (NPVI)	• First to market • New user customer satisfaction	• Ecosystem growth and profitability • NPVI	• Cost savings • Cash flow
Related approaches	• Experience curve • BCG Matrix • Five Forces • Capabilities	• Time-based competition • Temporary advantage • Adaptive advantage	• Blue ocean • Innovator's dilemma	• Networks • Ecosystems • Platforms	• Transformation • Turnaround
Key examples	• P&G under Lafley • Mars under Michaels	• Tata Consultancy Services under Chandrasekaran • 3M under McKnight	• Amazon.com under Bezos • Quintiles under Gillings	• Apple under Jobs • Novo Nordisk under Sørensen	• Amex under Chenault • AIG under Benmosche
Key traps	• Overapplication	• Planning the unplannable	• Wrong vision	• Overmanaged ecosystem	• No second phase

The palette can also help leaders to "de-average" their business (decompose it into its component parts, each requiring a characteristic approach to strategy) and effectively combine multiple approaches to strategy across different business units, geographies, and stages of a firm's life cycle. Large corporations are now stretched across a more diverse and faster-changing range of business contexts. Almost all large firms comprise multiple businesses and geographies, each with a distinct strategic character, and thus require the simultaneous execution of different approaches to strategy. The right approach for a fast-evolving technology unit is unlikely to be the same as for a more mature one. And the approach in a rapidly developing economy is likely to be very different for the same business operating in a more mature one.

UNPREDICTABILITY, MALLEABILITY, AND HARSHNESS AS AXES IN THE STRATEGY PALETTE

Why are unpredictability, malleability, and harshness the right dimensions for characterizing the business environment and choosing the right approach to strategy? By considering the fundamental underlying assumptions of the most familiar and historically appropriate approach, the classical one, and examining what has changed in the circumstances of business, we can demonstrate that these are indeed the right axes to inform the choice of the appropriate approach to strategy.

Leaders taking a classical perspective assume that the world is essentially predictable. Here, it makes sense to draw up long-term plans and invest in analysis and prediction. Additionally, classical leaders don't believe that they can markedly change the rules of their game, since they consider their environment a given: it is stable and therefore not malleable. Instead, they make the best of the given conditions by positioning themselves optimally.

However, in a rapidly evolving world, these assumptions are challenged in three fundamental ways. First, because of the increased *unpredictability* in today's business environment, long-term planning is often no longer viable. Second, because of technological change, globalization, and other drivers, existing industry structures are constantly being disrupted. Consequently, industry structure and the basis of competition have become increasingly *malleable*, and individual firms have more opportunities to shape market development. Finally, mismatches between strategy and environment, because of either protracted strategic drift or sudden crises, are increasingly severe and frequent. We therefore need to consider the *harshness* of the environment, which can require companies to economize and focus on short-term survival.

Inevitably, any business or business model goes through a life cycle, each stage of which requires a different approach. Businesses are usually created in the visionary or shaping quadrants of the strategy palette and tend to migrate counterclockwise through adaptive and classical quadrants before being disrupted by further innovations and entering a new cycle, although the exact path can vary (figure 1-11). Apple, for example, created its iPhone using a visionary approach, then used a shaping strategy to develop a collaborative ecosystem with app developers, telecom firms, and content providers. And as competitors jostle for position with increasingly convergent offerings, it is likely that their strategies will become increasingly adaptive or classical. As we will see, Quintiles also employed such a succession of approaches to strategy as it developed.

Leaders themselves play a vital role in the application of the strategy palette by setting and adjusting the context for strategy. They read the environment to determine which approach to strategy to apply where and to put the right people in place to execute it. Moreover, business leaders play a critical role of selling the integrated strategy narrative externally and internally. They continuously animate the *strategy collage*—the combination of multiple approaches to strategy—keeping it dynamic and up-to-date by asking the right questions, by challenging assumptions to prevent a dominant logic

FIGURE 1-11

Different approaches to strategy required across the business life cycle

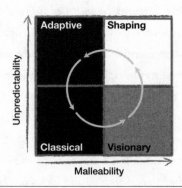

from clouding the perspective, and by putting their weight behind critical change initiatives.

Traps: Where It Can Go Wrong

Most leaders we surveyed understand the need to differentiate their approach to strategy according to the environment: some 90 percent agreed that this is important. But at the same time, there are a number of challenges to doing so effectively. Three types of traps were observed to derail good intentions.

Environmental Perception

Though some leaders correctly estimate the degree of malleability and unpredictability in their environments, we saw that many executives perceive their environments to be significantly more predictable or malleable than they actually are. There is perhaps a human tendency to believe that we can predict and control our environment—but in many cases we can't, and as we have seen, this inability has important ramifications for our approach to strategy. In fact, in our survey, environments were most often perceived as predictable and malleable (visionary), irrespective of their actual measured characteristics. Consistent with this bias, environments were least often perceived as unpredictable and nonmalleable (adaptive), again irrespective of the actual measured environment. Additionally, we have consistently found that firms delay recognition of when they are in a harsh environment that requires a renewal approach. In principle, a renewal strategy could be preemptive, but in practice, most companies trigger transformations or turnarounds only when financial or competitive performance has already begun to deteriorate.

Selecting the Right Approach

We also saw mismatches in the firms' selection of their approach to strategy. While the declared approach was most commonly in line with the perceived environment for classical, visionary, and adaptive approaches, companies often declared styles that were logically incompatible with their perceptions of the environment. The firms also tended to confuse adaptive and shaping approaches when declaring their strategic approach, which is not surprising given the relative unfamiliarity of the latter. The firms also declared an intention to use an adaptive approach much more often than either their own assessment of the environment or an objective assessment of its degree of unpredictability would seem to warrant. This discrepancy may be the result of the recent prominence and popularity of the concepts of agility, speed, and experimentation—an outlook biased toward an adaptive approach, irrespective of the actual business conditions.

Applying an Approach Correctly

Finally, many leaders choose the right approach to strategy for their business environment, but their organizations often stumble in its application. Our survey showed a strong tendency for organizations to hold on to the familiar and comfortable practices associated with the visionary and classical approaches even when the leaders have declared an intention to execute a different approach. Take planning, for example. Most companies create a strategic plan. Furthermore, nearly 90 percent of companies surveyed said they develop these plans on an annual basis, regardless of the actual pace of change in their business environments—or even what the companies perceive it to be.

How to Use This Book

This book begins by exploring the five core approaches to strategy—the basic colors of the strategy palette. We then look at how to use these basic colors in combination—applying different approaches simultaneously or sequentially in different parts of the business—and the role of leaders in dynamically orchestrating the resulting strategy collage.

Case studies and interviews are used to illustrate each approach, and each chapter begins with a major case study. Additionally, sidebars in each chapter examine the strategy palette's theoretical underpinnings and illustrate how each approach works, by showing the results of simulations of different environments and strategies. The book ends with a short epilogue dealing with how to develop individual mastery of the strategy palette.

Chapters 2 through 6 each deal with one approach to strategy in depth, exploring

- **What** defines and characterizes the approach

- **When** to use it

- **How to** apply it successfully, including both how to formulate a strategy and how to execute it, and the implications for information management, innovation, culture, organization, and leadership

- **Tips and traps** to guide the practical application of the approach

You will be able to observe each approach in action in case examples and CEO discussions. A note of caution: our examples feature successful and respected leaders and companies—but our intention is not to hold them up as comprehensive or eternal examples of excellence. Conditions change, competitive advantage fades, and the fortunes of companies rise and fall. In fact, that is precisely why firms need to shift their approaches to strategy over time. Rather, we intend to present the firms we feature as clear examples of the applications of each approach to strategy in a particular business at a particular point in time.

After we explore the five basic colors in the strategy palette, we look at more sophisticated ways of using the palette. Chapter 7 shows how firms can use multiple approaches to strategy successively or simultaneously, for instance, across geographies, business units, or life-cycle stages. We refer to this ability to take a multidimensional approach as *ambidexterity*. Four techniques can be used to achieve ambidexterity and are optimal in different situations:

- **Separation:** firms deliberately manage which approach to strategy belongs in each sub-unit (division, geography, or function) and run those approaches independently of one another.

- **Switching:** firms manage a common pool of resources to switch between approaches over time or to mix them at a given moment in time.

- **Self-organization:** each unit chooses the best approach to strategy when it becomes too complex to select and manage this in a top-down manner.

- **Ecosystems:** firms rely on an external ecosystem of players that self-select the appropriate approaches to strategy.

MATHEMATICAL BASIS OF THE STRATEGY PALETTE

Why did we select these five approaches—classical, adaptive, visionary, shaping, and renewal—and what is the evidence that they are the best ones for each environment? In fact, the different approaches to strategy have sound mathematical underpinnings, which we demonstrate by simulating the environments of the strategy palette. These environments range from highly predictable ones that resemble classical environments, to highly unpredictable and malleable environments that resemble shaping ones. We then simulated different approaches to strategy and allowed these to compete with each other across a range of environments, noting which approaches performed best through many iterations (figure 1-12). The simulations fully validated the match between the five archetypal approaches to strategy and the business environments that make up the strategy palette (our model is described in more detail in appendix C). In separate sidebars in each chapter, we use this model to show why a particular approach to strategy is the fit best for a specific environment.

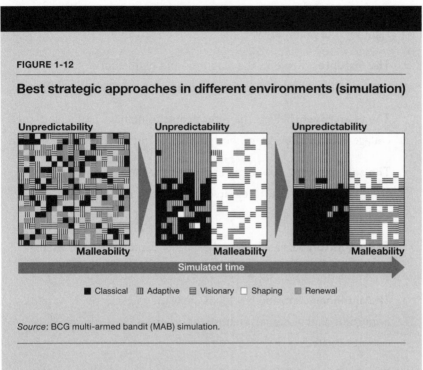

FIGURE 1-12

Best strategic approaches in different environments (simulation)

Legend: ■ Classical   ▥ Adaptive   ▤ Visionary   ☐ Shaping   ▦ Renewal

Source: BCG multi-armed bandit (MAB) simulation.

We used the same simulation model as the platform to develop an iPad app, which is built around a business game in which you can explore which approaches to strategy work well in which environments. You do this by operating the simplest of businesses—a lemonade stand. The app should enable readers not only to understand how to choose and deploy different approaches to strategy but also to experience and develop a more practical feel for each approach.

Chapter 8 shows what your role as a leader is in creating and animating the collage of strategic approaches. We identify eight critical roles that leaders play in this respect.

- **The diagnostician:** Looks externally to assess the business environment and then match it with the right strategic approach.

- **The segmenter:** Matches the approach to the organization at the right level of granularity.

- **The disrupter:** Reviews the diagnosis and segmentation on an ongoing basis, modulating or changing approaches when necessary.

- **The team coach:** Selects the right people to manage each cell of the collage and develops them, both intellectually and experientially.

- **The salesperson:** Advocates and communicates the strategic choices in a coherent, integrated narrative, both internally and externally.

- **The inquisitor:** Sets and resets the correct context for each strategic approach by asking the right questions.

- **The antenna:** Continuously looks outward and selectively amplifies important change signals that might otherwise be overlooked or underestimated.

- **The accelerator:** Puts weight behind select critical change initiatives to speed up their implementation or to increase their traction to overcome resistance or inertia.

Finally, the epilogue details the four steps by which individual managers can develop their understanding and mastery of the strategy palette.

As you familiarize yourself with the different approaches, it can be helpful to try to apply them to your own business: to assess the environment where you do business, to decide the best approach to strategy, and to assess the actual practices that your organization deploys. The short survey in appendix A will provide a simplified but directional view; a more detailed version is also available online: bcgperspectives.com/yourstrategyneedsastrategy. Appendix B lists further reading for those who wish to delve deeper into the different approaches to strategy. Appendix C gives additional background and details of our simulations of different environments and approaches to strategy.

Let's begin our exploration of the strategy palette.

CHAPTER 2

CLASSICAL
Be Big

Mars, Inc.: Winning Classically

If you want evidence that Mars, Inc., operates in a relatively stable environment, just take a look at the dates when its iconic chocolate bars were introduced: the Milky Way, 1923; Snickers, 1930; the Mars Bar, 1932; M&M's, 1941; Twix, 1979. What were the biggest-selling candies in the world in 2014? Snickers and M&M's.[1] After so many years, these brands continue to underpin the success of the company founded by Frank Mars more than a hundred years ago. As of 2014, Mars has revenues of around $35 billion and eleven brands worth more than $1 billion, and it ranks among the largest privately held companies in the United States.[2]

Mars has earned and maintained market leadership through scale and capabilities—being the biggest and best at what it does. Scale is an important factor in the success of Mars, according to Paul Michaels, president of Mars: "Scale is critical in our business—to drive manufacturing scale and utilization, costs and value." Mars is the largest player in the chocolate business and enjoys leading positions in five others—including pet food, with brands such as Pedigree, and chewing gum, with brands such as Wrigley's Spearmint Gum.

Stability and, as a consequence, predictability, underpin Mars's approach to strategy. It means that Mars can plan. "Brands, once established in the minds of consumers, are very durable," said Michaels. "We plan because we operate in relatively stable markets and because it is important to operate our assets efficiently." Michaels develops plans with a one-year and long-term term horizon. "We eliminated a somewhat complex medium-term planning process about a decade ago, as it really wasn't useful," he said.

Michaels says that the key to successful planning is to ensure that it is a simple process, focused on generating insights on essential issues: "The focus is on things we can control—namely, costs and profitability. The job of strategy for a segment leader like us is to drive category growth, and that's the thing you should be thinking about all the time."

The strategy is set from the top, he said: "It's me, the CFO, and a few others in consultation with the family board." But then it is widely shared—and communicated in a way that can be easily digested. "We do lots of town hall meetings, and we expect to be able to explain the strategy in an understandable way in twenty minutes."

In setting the plan, Michaels is guided by five principles, which permeate the culture of the company: quality, responsibility, mutuality, efficiency, and freedom. Efficiency, in particular, is apparent as you walk into the company headquarters in McLean, Virginia. Worldwide, there are more than seventy thousand employees, or "associates" as Mars prefers to call them. But at headquarters, the offices of the tiny corporate staff reside on just one floor of a small, inconspicuous two-story building. As Michaels wryly noted to us: "A senior executive from Nestlé came here and thought he was in the wrong place."

The company prizes discipline and efficiency. For instance, even Michaels himself has to clock in.

The headquarters structure reflects the broader approach to organization, which is relatively flat and relies on few but experienced people. "It's important to keep it simple," Michaels said. "Extra layers and steps weaken and filter the insights. Strategy is important, but it doesn't come out of an elaborate planning process."

After the acquisition of the William Wrigley Junior Company in 2008, Mars was restructured into business units rather than along geographical lines as previously. Michaels explained that the restructuring was meant to "deepen our ability to generate insights and build deep capabilities in each area of the business."

As a private company, Mars is not inhibited by the quarterly reporting cycle, and its decisions can focus on long-term consequences. It invests in incremental rather than radical innovation to keep its production processes and brands updated. The one dimension where Mars looks to shape the external environment is by innovating to stimulate end-user demand, for instance, by designing its Big Night In initiative to push chocolate sales during historically slower summer months.[3]

In short, Mars is an exemplar of classical strategy. The company drives scale economies through category and brand leadership in a stable business, rigorous if lean planning, and building deep knowledge and capabilities, business by business.

The Classical Approach to Strategy: Core Idea

The classical approach to strategy—strategic planning—will be highly familiar to most readers: it's probably what you learned in business school and a process you may participate in annually. The process might be so familiar, in fact, that it may be applied as a default rather than a deliberate choice. Therefore, in this chapter, we will focus on a few questions that often go unasked. For example, when should the classical approach be applied, and when should it be substituted by another approach? What is the difference between a strategic planning process that drives insight and impact and one that is a mere ritual preceding the budget process? What is the link between having a great classical strategy and having it effectively implemented? First, though, let's examine the core idea of classical strategy (figure 2-1).

FIGURE 2-1

The classical approach to strategy

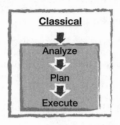

Like Michaels at Mars, leaders taking a classical perspective face an industry that is relatively stable and predictable. Therefore, the basis of competition is also stable, and advantage, once obtained, is sustainable. Hence, the classical strategist's mantra is *sustainable competitive advantage*. Since classical firms cannot easily change the basis of competition in their industry, they win by striving to position themselves optimally in attractive markets where they are advantaged. Advantage can be based on superior scale, differentiation (or, equivalently, scale within a narrower market segment), or superior capabilities.

Like each of the colors of the strategy palette, the classical approach has its own characteristic logical flow. Classical firms deploy rigorous *analysis* to determine market attractiveness, the basis of competition within a given market, and their own firm's current and potential competitiveness, all of which help them to determine their targeted position and strategic direction. They then construct a *plan* to achieve that targeted position. The plan need not change too often and reflects both how the environment is forecast to evolve and the action steps required to build and sustain advantage. Finally, classical firms *execute* the plan thoroughly, focusing every part of the organization on efficiently striving toward the well-defined goals.

Extending our art analogy, the classical approach is rather like creating a still-life painting. Since you have in front of you a clear, unchanging image of what you wish to paint, you need not create multiple sketches or change things on the fly. Rather, you methodically execute each detail until you have completed the masterpiece.

When applied correctly, a classical strategy can be very impactful and create durable and valuable leadership positions. In a stable environment, size, differentiation, or capabilities—being good at what you do—can be stable sources of competitive advantage. There are no penalties for changing only gradually, because the environment is predictable and develops only gradually, without major disruptions. Constant, small improvements in performance can accumulate into a significant and sustainable competitive advantage.

Size, for example, becomes a self-reinforcing benefit. The larger a firm, the lower its costs compared with competitors. As a company accumulates scale and experience, the lower costs can then fund price cuts that increase volumes, completing a virtuous circle, as succinctly outlined by BCG's founder Bruce Henderson: "The payoff for leadership is very high indeed, if it is achieved early and maintained until growth slows. Investment in market share during the growth phase can be very attractive . . . increases in share increase the margin . . . The return on investment is enormous." [4]

Why Scale Matters: UPS and FedEx

The US express freight and parcel market in the early 2000s is an excellent case study of the merits of scale in the classical approach. That market was dominated by two large players, UPS and FedEx, both of which achieved sustainably lower costs and higher margins than did their smaller competitors DHL and TNT. [5] FedEx and UPS were able to maintain their leadership because competitors would have to make prohibitively large cash investments to replicate the scale of these incumbents.

In fact, when DHL entered the US market with its acquisition of local player Airborne Inc., then a subscale competitor, DHL invested nearly $10 billion in the unit. Even that was not enough to buy the scale necessary to sustainably compete with the local giants, however. In 2008, DHL closed its domestic operations to focus on international delivery to and from the United States. [6]

For industry leaders in classical environments, size offers protection: because the industry is stable, they can continue to build incrementally on their scale advantage.

WHAT YOU MIGHT KNOW IT AS

Most leaders are familiar with the classical approach to strategy. In fact, this is generally what they mean when they refer to strategy. The approach has long been dominant in both business itself and business school curricula, since the term *corporate strategy* was coined by Igor Ansoff in the late 1950s.[7] Many of the concepts, frameworks, and tools that managers use today have developed out of the classical approach to strategy. Here are some of the better-known ones.

Competitive strategy was further developed and disseminated in the 1960s by The Boston Consulting Group (BCG), at first predominantly for its large manufacturing clients operating stable, relatively predictable businesses. BCG's founder Bruce Henderson proposed the *experience curve*, the idea that accumulated experience, and therefore overall size, can be a source of durable advantage.[8] The experience curve has been an important tool in guiding companies on how to manage costs and prices for long-term advantage. The *BCG matrix* combined scale advantage with the identification of attractive high-growth markets where leadership can and should be established; in the 1970s and 1980s, this tool was used by the majority of *Fortune* 500 companies to allocate resources across their portfolios of businesses.[9] The *environments matrix*, developed by Richard Lochridge, generalized how the relationship between returns and scale depends on the number and strength of sources of advantage (figure 2-2).[10] The tool explained how competition and advantage work in fragmented, localized, and stalemated markets as well as the more familiar volume markets.

Porter developed perhaps the most comprehensive and best-known perspective on classical strategy.[11] His *five forces framework* explained how industry attractiveness is determined by the interplay of five competitive forces (suppliers, customers, substitutes, complements, and rivals).

FIGURE 2-2

Forms of classical competitive advantage

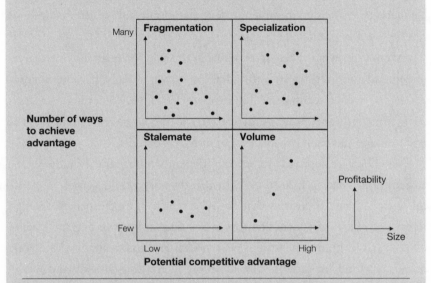

Companies need to pick attractive industries and win with either differentiation or cost—or, equivalently—position and scale.

Birger Wernerfelt, Jay Barney, and C. K. Prahalad and Gary Hamel later focused on how some firms can also achieve superior positioning by building and leveraging distinct capabilities or competences—somewhat confusingly known as the *resource-based view* of the firm.[12] The resources that confer advantage need to be valuable, rare, inimitable, and nonsubstitutable. BCG's Philip Evans, George Stalk, and Lawrence Shulman further explored how firms can build advantage through building capabilities.[13]

But why did the classical approach to strategy become the predominant one, to the point of near ubiquity? It was long the approach that best fitted the environments most large companies faced. For much of the latter half of the twentieth century, most business environments were relatively predictable and nonmalleable—analyzing, planning, and executing was logically the best way to win.

When to Apply a Classical Approach

Firms should deploy a classical approach in relatively stable and predictable markets with an established, stable basis of competition. In such nonmalleable markets, there is no imminent risk of disruption and industry conditions can be taken as given.

An environment is likely to be stable in this way if the underlying drivers of demand and industry structure develop only gradually, because of entry barriers or limited technological or regulatory change. For a range of industries, from insurance to consumer staples to the automotive industry, the environment has been largely classical in recent decades.

The choice of approach to strategy depends on accurately judging the circumstances facing a firm. So which indicators would suggest a classical environment? Industries that are relatively well established, with high returns to scale; infrequent changes in the size ranking among the leading players; stable, homogeneous business models and core technologies; strong brands; and modest growth rates are more likely to experience the sort of predictable, nonmalleable environment where a classical strategy can thrive. Conversely, new industries with low barriers to entry, low returns to scale, fragmented industry structures, frequent or disruptive technological change, high growth rates, and rapidly evolving regulation are likely to require a different approach to strategy.

The household products space largely fits the classical pattern, in which end-user demand can be roughly predicted by changes in demographics and purchasing power. In that industry, the competitive dynamics have remained relatively stable because of high entry barriers created by strong brands, scale advantage, and limited fundamental technological change. Positional volatility is low, and a few companies, like P&G and Unilever, have stayed on top for decades.[14] Returns to scale for consumer staples are as large now as they were three decades ago. Hence, a firm can decide how and where to position its products, according to its current brand scale and positioning; those of its competitors; its capabilities in product development, manufacturing, and marketing; and its prognosis for the evolution of the market. And unless there is a fundamental shift in consumer demand drivers, these plans can be stable and reliable.

Before the 1990s, many industries adopted the classical model of strategy. While numerous industries have since been disrupted by technology and globalization, many others find that classical conditions still hold true. It is therefore a dangerous and misleading exaggeration to claim, as some have, that sustainable competitive advantage and the classical approach to strategy are no longer relevant.

Nevertheless, some traditionally stable industries do need to adopt new approaches to strategy. Consider electrical utilities, a stronghold that historically exhibited deep-seated classical characteristics: demand developed predictably with economic growth, industry structure remained stable because of high barriers to entry and regulation, and even major oil shocks failed to fundamentally change the structure or basis of competition. But with protracted fluctuation in input prices, the rise in alternative-energy sources, increasing regulatory flux on emissions, and governmental crackdowns on nuclear energy after the Fukushima disaster, utilities now need to supplement their classical approach with a more adaptive one.[15] For instance, players increasingly try to diversify their sources of energy, rolling out new technologies like solar panels and evolving their business models to add more services, like smart-home technology.[16] Many other industries have similarly moved away from a classical approach—or need to.

We have seen the power in a classical approach to strategy, but the firm needs to choose its approach to strategy only after carefully observing the specific business circumstances it faces. The decision should not be based on either history, familiarity, general trends in other businesses, or fashions in management thinking. You cannot say a classical approach is valid today just because it was valid yesterday, but neither is it necessarily invalid today because of a general shift toward more-dynamic approaches in other industries.

Nevertheless, we will see that a classical approach to strategy is often applied, or *not* applied, for the wrong reasons.

ARE YOU IN A CLASSICAL BUSINESS ENVIRONMENT?

You are facing a classical business environment if the following observations hold true:

✓ Your industry's structure is stable.

✓ Your industry's basis of competition is stable.

✓ Your industry's development is predictable.

✓ Your industry is not easily shapable.

✓ Your industry displays moderate but constant growth.

✓ Your industry is marked by high concentration.

✓ Your industry is mature.

✓ Your industry is based on stable technologies.

✓ Your industry's regulatory environment is stable.

The Classical Approach in Practice: Strategizing

Jack Welch once observed: "In real life, strategy is actually very straightforward. You pick a direction and implement like hell."[17] Is it as straightforward as Welch claims? Let's find out by examining the classical approach in practice.

Strategy is often thought of as the product of a cerebral exercise carried out by planners and later implemented by others. This separation of thought (strategizing) and action is unfortunate. A strategy cannot succeed unless it is implemented effectively. We will see that there is an intimate connection between strategizing and execution and furthermore that the relationship depends on the approach to strategy taken. We will therefore look at both steps for each approach and how they relate to each other.

Strategizing at Quintiles

Drug development takes years—from preclinical work, through clinical trials, to production. So for a company like Quintiles, the world's largest clinical research organization, which provides drug development services to pharmaceutical companies, the business is highly plannable.[18]

"We are able to adopt a classical approach to strategy because the business is predictable," said Tom Pike, the chief executive of Quintiles. "We can know the pipelines of biopharma companies with some certainty several years out. There are some changes due to the cancellation of drugs in trials, but that's a manageable risk that we can plan for. And outsourcing relationships are quite sticky: customers don't tend to chop and change too much, because both parties invest heavily in building a long-term partnership."

To develop the plan—a formal document—Pike leads an annual planning process. Since he arrived as CEO in April 2012, he has encouraged a more systematic and more forward-looking approach, running the process in a way that "keeps one foot in today and one foot in the future." Pike has strengthened the classical disciplines of focus, efficiency, planning, and accountability in a company that has grown very rapidly, ensuring a clear foundation for its continued success. He explained that the goal of the plan is to support "a scale and portfolio game, so we are advantaged through our scale and our diversification across therapeutic areas, clients, and geographies. Quintiles has tremendous assets and competitive advantages, such as our global workforce, our processes and technology, our scientific and therapeutic knowledge, and our quantitative and analytics expertise. We look at how we can best leverage these capabilities to meet our customers' needs. Our size has enabled us to scale investments faster than competitors and to maintain our leadership." The strategic plan is focused on articulating incremental opportunities, Pike said: "Our main business is doing well, so it's a question of making it even better where we can."

In addition to reinforcing existing sources of advantage, Pike also encourages Quintiles executives to look to the future and to think how industry developments will affect customers. In an industry where the confluence of genomics, big data, personalized medicine, value-based health care, and other trends are driving accelerating change, this view to the future may eventually require a more adaptive or shaping approach to strategy and an increasing emphasis on information, collaboration, and innovation. Pike sees opportunities where the company's capabilities can support the changing needs of a broader range of health-care stakeholders. He acknowledges, "This has to be done at the same time as maintaining the strength that comes from a focused, accountable organization." The CEO is beginning to layer these new considerations on top of the classical approach.

Classical strategizing is a two-part process consisting of analysis—of the attractiveness of a market, the basis of competition, and the firm's competitiveness—and the construction of a plan that forecasts those factors, articulates the targeted position, and maps the steps required to achieve it.

Sound very familiar? It should—in our survey, we found that almost 90 percent of firms intending to employ a classical approach use detailed forecasts and that 80 percent translate those into long-term plans. But that's the risk. Familiarity can breed contempt, and the procedures of strategy can become mechanical, ritualized, or overly complex to such an extent that perspective is sacrificed. Following due process or applying the right techniques can easily become a comforting substitute for insight generation. To generate powerful plans and real impact, the classical strategizing process needs to use its familiar tools to achieve *new, unfamiliar, uncomfortable, and unanticipated* insights that allow you to outsmart competitors. The possibility of discomfort, surprise, and deviation from last year's plan are therefore the hallmarks of a good strategy process. In other words, as our Mars example shows, clear procedures cannot replace clear thinking.

Analysis

Market Attractiveness: Where to Play

Given that the goal of a classical strategy is to identify an attractive position in a given market, the first step toward success is to correctly identify an attractive market. This determines where your firm will play and, just as critically, where it will not. As Michael Porter wrote: "Strategy requires you to make tradeoffs in competing—to choose what not to do."[19] This observation may feel trivial or obvious. Nevertheless, firms need to thoughtfully identify their market, divide it into appropriate segments, and determine the segments' attractiveness. A firm should avoid the inclination to stick with familiar but possibly unattractive markets or to neglect unfamiliar but attractive ones. The worst thing that a firm can do is to pursue growth indiscriminately by not making any choices at all—growth *per se* is not a strategy.

To determine where to play, you need to follow a few essential steps. First, delineate your market, examining established market boundaries with a skeptical eye. A thorough industry analysis may lead to surprising insights that immediately affect a firm's strategic direction. For example, Deutsche Bahn, the German railway company, can now compete more effectively with airlines because it correctly reidentified its market as medium-distance travel, which included not only high-speed trains, but also short-haul flights.[20]

Next, identify and understand industry segments. Many firms default to segmentations based on easily obtainable data, existing product categories, business unit boundaries, or demographics, but a good analysis will go beyond these convenient alternatives to surface the true drivers of demand or natural competitive boundaries. Multinational alcoholic-beverages company Diageo, for instance, segments customers by occasion of use, from high-energy occasions with many people (e.g., parties, nightclubs) to low-energy occasions or individual use, rather than by BU or basic demographics. The resulting segmentation lets Diageo position its brands more accurately and effectively: for instance, its premium Scotch brands are often positioned to address low-energy social occasions or individual use, while vodka brands like Smirnoff address the higher-energy, social end of the spectrum.[21]

The last step is to establish an objective view of which segments are attractive. For a holistic and forward-looking picture, the analysis should combine metrics like profitability and growth with more qualitative indicators like entry barriers, competitive intensity, and the bargaining power of suppliers and customers. Avoid being swayed by the data that just happens to be at your disposal or collecting confirmatory information on segments where you already play. Otherwise, you risk merely perpetuating the status quo.

Positioning Play at Huawei

Huawei Technologies, one of the world's leading telecom equipment companies with annual revenues of approximately $40 billion, has grown consistently through a succession of very deliberate choices about where to do business.[22] Guo Ping, one of Huawei's rotating co-CEOs, told us that the firm's strategy is "absolutely a positioning play." At first, Huawei sought to gain a dominant position in China's rural markets, where it faced less competition from bigger rivals. Then, as it grew stronger, it moved into the country's fast-growing, but more competitive, urban centers. Only when the firm was sufficiently powerful did it expand abroad—first to emerging markets such as Brazil, Russia, and Thailand and then to first-world countries like the United Kingdom, France, and Canada.[23] Guo Ping explained: "We depend on scale, so we built it in large, low-competitive-intensity markets before entering more developed markets." Using the same logic, Huawei originally concentrated on telecom equipment—serving the big telecommunications companies such as Vodafone, British

Telecom, T-Mobile, and Bell Canada.[24] Only recently, Huawei broke into consumer goods, providing handsets for underserved markets where it can attain a dominant position—not only in China but also in several countries in Africa.[25]

Basis of Competition: How to Play

In any given classical market, advantage comes from one of three sources: size, differentiation, or superior capabilities. Even though a market may be attractive for one group, does that mean it's attractive for yours? The attractiveness of a market for your company depends on the fit between the basis of competition in that market and the competitiveness of your firm on that dimension. Consequently, you need to determine the basis of competition.

To understand this basis, look at the relationship between the market share and profitability across all companies in the market. This relationship helps you understand how the game is played. If there is a strong positive correlation between market share and profitability, then the market is probably volume- or scale-driven. If not, the market can be attacked through differentiation in specialized areas or through local scale in geographically constrained, fragmented markets. In the worst case, the market suffers from a stalemate, with commoditization but high exit costs, in which case, it is attractive to no one (figure 2-2).

Volume, fragmented, and specialized markets can all be profitable and therefore, superficially seem attractive. However, they each require different approaches to win. Firms need to understand how profitability is generated in order to decide whether it's a game they, or anyone, can win.

Competitive Position: How to Win

In the final step of analysis, the firm determines its potential for advantage over the competitor. In other words, you decide how your firm will compete, by either scale, differentiation, or capabilities.

Emphasize scale if you are currently already among the biggest in your market. If your business is not in the top three in your industry, winning could be an uphill battle, even with significant investments to buy market share. Underdogs do sometimes win, for instance, if competition is distracted, but Bruce Henderson advocated selling "pets," low-share businesses in low-growth markets. He showed that stable, competitive industries tend to converge toward an end state in which only three generalist players can be profitable.[26] GE's Jack Welch set an even higher bar, insisting that GE had to be number one or two in the industries in which it played.[27]

To maintain a size-based competitive advantage, the firm needs to ferociously defend market share. Striving for size just for size's sake is a questionable approach, though, since sustainable advantage from scale is not inevitable. Size leaders are not always cost leaders if they fail to proactively extract the potential benefits of scale by driving operating efficiencies hard. Henderson said: "These observed or inferred reductions in costs as volume increases are not necessarily automatic. They depend crucially on a competent management that seeks ways to force costs down as volume expands. To this extent the relationship is of normal potential rather than one of certainty."[28]

In the absence of scale, differentiation can be an attractive alternative, particularly when the targeted niche segment is sizable and when the firm can make its products distinct enough to avoid competition from cost-leading mainstream players. Successful differentiation necessitates offering customers in a niche segment a product that is sufficiently valuable and distinctive. Distinctive doesn't mean novel for its own sake, since unwanted extra features can raise complexity and costs. It means uniquely and valuably addressing a specific consumer preference. Niche players need to excel at uncovering, distinguishing, and addressing these latent segment-specific needs in defensible ways. Consider, for example, outdoor clothing companies. Because they make clothes with specialized functions for outdoor enthusiasts, these firms can compete effectively in the highly competitive fashion and clothing industry.

Finally, firms can sometimes win even if they are at a scale disadvantage in hard-to-differentiate categories by focusing on building and deploying superior capabilities that are valuable to customers across multiple markets.

Those capabilities need to be hard to replicate (inimitable, non-substitutable), meaningfully differentiated (rare), and relevant to customers (valuable). A good example of a capabilities-based approach is Procter & Gamble's direction under A. G. Lafley. In leveraging its core capabilities in marketing and supply-chain management to position itself robustly in categories new to P&G (e.g., air fresheners and razors), the firm realized years of high growth and high returns across units.[29]

Positioning to Win at Mahindra

Mahindra, the $16.7 billion Indian diversified multinational company with operations in eighteen sectors, pursues competitive advantage through a rigorous classical approach which focuses on scale and position.[30] In some instances, such as in its tractor business, Mahindra is the outright global leader and reaps scale advantage accordingly. But in other business units, the firm wins through specialization and niche positioning. Anand Mahindra, Mahindra's chairman, explained: "We don't have one monolithic view of how we're going to play. We like to be leaders in our segments, but the question is, 'How do you define your segment?'"

For example, in its auto business (and many of its other units), Mahindra adopts a niche strategy, leading in a well-defined segment of the market. Mahindra told us: "We are the second-largest auto player in India, but we are minnows globally. So globally we have chosen to be only in the SUV and off-road segment, where we differentiate and also create scale by leveraging back-end operations across mobility businesses." Likewise, Mahindra said, in its IT business, "absolute scale is not the game: we want to find three to four verticals where we can be the dominant player, like the telecom segment, and win there."

Planning

Planning and Challenge at Mahindra

Mahindra's novel multistage challenge-based approach to planning allows the firm to create robust, detailed plans and budgets that support the implementation of each business unit's strategy. All eighteen units, from the established tractor business to the newer logistics segment, participate in the Mahindra annual planning cycle. First, in October, each sector goes through "strategy war rooms." Sector leadership presents a strategy proposal, and Mahindra's Strategy Group, which functions as an internal consultant, plays opponent, using a framework of eleven challenge questions. Then at the Blue Chip Gathering later that month, Mahindra takes its top five hundred managers through an exploration of coming trends, themes, and challenges—an exercise that stimulates and reinforces the strategy setting process. Next, each unit goes through "budget war rooms" in February, where central leadership works with unit management to set metrics and milestones and to develop balanced score cards. Anand Mahindra emphasized clarity and account-ability: "These plans are drilled down into incredible detail, where even the shop floor can see their link into the overall business plan for the year." Finally, in "operation war rooms" throughout the year, the leadership checks how the business unit is preceding along the budget and plan.

Importantly, the firm recognizes, and uses varied approaches for, differences between businesses. Specifically, Mahindra modifies its planning recipe depending on the life-cycle stage of the business. For more predictable, mature businesses, the plans may be relatively fixed, but in newer segments, the emphasis is on refining plans more frequently according to cumulative learning. And other newer businesses are managed more autonomously, through an internal venture model. We will explore further these various approaches to developing strategy in the upcoming chapters on adaptive strategy and ambidexterity.

Leveraging their market and competitive analysis, firms can set the strategic direction and goals by forecasting how conditions will evolve, fixing their aspiration, and generating a detailed action plan to achieve their goals. Firms can then cascade the plan down into the operational milestones required to realize it. Because most managers are likely to be very familiar with classical business planning—or think they are—we'll focus on what can make these ubiquitous planning exercises either more, or less, effective.

Set Strategic Direction

Planning processes have a common tendency to become complex, ritualized, and ineffective. Sound planning should not merely be a prelude to annual budgeting that affirms and incrementally adjusts the previous year's plan. Rather it should be insight centered, tailored to the specifics of the business, and flexible to changing circumstances.

Successful classical firms do not let short-term performance become the main emphasis of their planning. A weak process lets managers focus on and commit to short-term targets while bypassing a coherent, long-term view of the company's direction. Conversely, a good plan's short-term targets and commitments flow naturally and inextricably from the long-term view.

As we saw in the Mahindra example, challenge is a key part of a strong strategic planning process and ensures that new, divergent perspectives are surfaced and incorporated. Live discussion and a culture that values challenge are therefore essential elements of success. Rigid templates and routine procedures cannot substitute for these opportunities for live challenge, and process complexity should not crowd out or dilute these opportunities.

The planning process should not default to a fixed annual cycle and a three- or five-year planning horizon but should instead reflect the specific environment of the firm and how fast it changes. Consider how petrochemical giant Shell approaches planning. The firm employs a specialist team of forecasters that plan as far as eighty years ahead. Ollila Jorman, company chairman, explained: "We naturally pay close attention to short-term economic conditions, but we take a long-term, strategic view of the company's development."[31] However, even Shell updates its plans promptly if circumstances materially change, as it did in 2013 after learning about difficulties in arctic and shale gas exploration. As its 2012 sustainability report puts it: "We are incorporating the lessons learned from these events into our future plans."[32]

The main value of a plan is that it creates a predictable path toward competitive advantage. But as the following Mylan example shows, a plan can also, paradoxically, serve as a good basis for managing moderate uncertainty in two main ways. First, by recognizing and structuring what can be planned, it can create the latitude to focus on less predictable or more dynamic elements of the business. Second, thinking deeply through the assumptions in a strategic plan can prime management to respond effectively to unexpected developments. Such *emergent strategies* may even contradict a plan, even though they draw on the thoughtfulness that went into constructing it.

Planning with Discipline at Mylan

Mylan, a US-based pharmaceutical company, is an example of a company that plans with rigor, but without rigidity.[33] In 2007, the firm had annual revenues of $1.6 billion and operated predominantly in the United States. Today, it is one of the largest generic- and specialty-drug providers in the world, with annual revenues of $6.9 billion. Mylan looks to capitalize on relatively gradual, predictable, demographically driven growth trends in the health-care industry, as well as on changes in the way health-care is delivered. Heather Bresch,

Mylan's CEO, explained: "Despite the inherent volatility of our industry, it's still feasible and important to construct high-quality strategic plans. This not only allows us to plan but also to be prepared to respond to a variety of scenarios."

Critical to Mylan's success is a disciplined strategic planning process built on deep market analysis and designed to maximize known opportunities while also highlighting new ones, and to avoid ritualization—doing things the same way just because that's how they've always been done. "We bring discipline to the process by allowing our various business owners and their key partners to frame the discussion by presenting detailed analysis and recommendations," said Bresch. "However, we encourage an active dialogue and a back-and-forth amongst our entire team in order to challenge the status quo and the conventional way of doing things. [This planning process] results in greater clarity around why we do what we do, and really defines everyone's individual roles within the plan and their accountability and ownership for specific results."

Mylan develops both five-year strategic plans and one-year budget plans focused on protecting and growing its core business. The company meanwhile explores and executes on the drivers of future growth and prepares transformative initiatives necessary for long-term sustainability.

Bresch believes that adhering to a disciplined plan has many benefits—but only if the process is flexible enough to allow the company to think more expansively where and when it needs to. "Discipline gives us stability, which gives us flexibility," she said.

Cascade Direction and Goals into Action Plans

A clear destination is insufficient by itself—the plan should also include the map of *how* to get there. The plan serves to make the strategy executable, by creating milestones and metrics that detail the targets the company needs to hit *and* the actions needed to hit these targets.

Good operational plans also link strategic initiatives directly to the overall direction of the firm. They ensure that precious resources are only assigned to projects that are both financially attractive and in line with the company's direction. Too often, the initiative portfolio is only loosely linked to the strategic plan. In other words, a good plan is a map of the straightest route possible to winning and a means of aligning all employees' efforts toward that goal, with lots of checkpoints along the way.

SIMULATING STRATEGY IN A STABLE ENVIRONMENT

In a stable environment, managers can simply analyze up front what the best strategic option is and plan their way toward it. This often involves a brief period of analysis or exploration of all known options, followed by a longer period of optimization and exploitation.

FIGURE 2-3

Classical strategies perform well in stable environments (simulation)

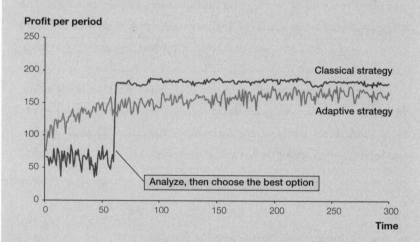

Source: BCG Strategy Institute multi-armed bandit (MAB) simulation.
Note: Results averaged over thirty simulations in noncompetitive environment with thirty investment options.

Our simulation of a variety of approaches to strategy in a stable environment bears out the effectiveness of this approach. You explore, or analyze, your options for a limited time until you are sure you have found the best option. The precise duration of the initial period of exploration mainly depends on the number of options and the degree of difference between them.

Once you find the right option, you should plan to exploit it for the foreseeable future. More exploration would be wasteful given that the optimal strategic option does not materially change in a stable environment (figure 2-3). The lemonade-stand equivalent of this approach would be to analyze which location would attract the most customers, open your stand there, and stay put, while optimizing the operations and realizing scale advantages in that position.

The Classical Approach in Practice: Implementation

Each approach to strategy reflects an important and distinctive relationship between strategizing and execution, or thinking and action, and therefore a very different set of requirements for executing successfully. While these requirements may seem clear and familiar for the classical approach, it's worth explicitly exploring them since (1) many CEOs we interviewed told us that execution is at least as hard as strategy to get right and 2) it's critical to make deliberate choices about the approach to implementation. We will see that these choices vary considerably across different approaches to strategy. That is, implementation does not consist of one universal way, but rather it varies according to the approach to strategy. Consequently, our conception of "strategy" needs to be expanded to encompass both thought and action, as well as culture, organization, leadership, and other business elements that enable thought and action.

For a strategy to work, it needs to penetrate beyond the management committee and cascade down and inform coordinated action throughout the organization. This diffusion is particularly necessary for classical strategy, since although the plan—usually conceived at senior levels—is important, advantage and value are unlocked by execution at lower levels in the organization. Therefore, everything about the organization, from information management to culture, should be focused on supporting the translation of the plan.

Information

Information plays a critical and distinctive role in classical strategy: it informs the analysis and planning process and allows firms to track execution. Superior competitive and market information, analysis, and performance tracking can be game changers in the struggle for competitive advantage. By managing information better, the classical firm can make a better plan than its competitors, react quicker to changes in competitive dynamics, and execute more efficiently.

Successful classical firms invest in mining new sources of information, or consider existing information in new ways, to derive novel insights to drive their plans. Alcoholic-beverage multinational Diageo, for instance, runs many market studies at any time to deeply understand the evolution in customer needs, demographics, and purchasing patterns. It invests heavily in analytic capabilities, for example, in its Customer Collaboration Centre, a state-of-the-art facility to bring consumer, shopper, retailer, and distributor insights together into an integrated perspective.[34]

Classical firms can also derive advantage from superior performance-tracking. As management guru Peter Drucker said, "What's measured improves."[35] Effective performance measurement links the high-level strategic plan with individual initiatives and actions via appropriate key performance indicators that, at each level, roll up to larger goals. Transparent tracking keeps employees accountable, provides early warning signals of plans going off track, and highlights when and where intervention is required or assumptions need to be reexamined.

Companies can put too much faith in complex standardized reports, however, instead of focusing on detecting anomalies that could precipitate either redoubled efforts against the plan or an update in the strategic direction.

P&G, which primarily operates in predictable, stable household goods categories like laundry detergent and toothpaste, provides a good example of how a company can gain advantage through improved performance tracking. In the late 1980s and early 1990s, the firm implemented a new inventory tracking system that monitored stocks across its entire value chain. With this improved information, P&G could reduce buffer stocks and billing errors and could proactively spot and fix potential supply-chain inefficiencies. Even more important to the top line, P&G reduced stock-outs at retailers by analyzing sales patterns more holistically and adjusting shipments in line with promotional activity, seasonal patterns, and shifts in customer preferences. Improved information management helped P&G achieve market-share increases of up to 4 percent in the categories it served.[36]

Innovation

Innovation in a classical strategy is typically occasional, incremental, and cumulative. It helps firms to gradually realize the *potential* advantages of scale, differentiation, and capabilities on which they predicate their plans. Classical innovation is very different from the disruptive innovation of the visionary approach or the continuous experimentation of the adaptive approach. Because innovation in classical firms enables the improvement of a known, unchanging source of advantage, progress tends to be linear and incremental, and permits a defined end state and precise milestones. As such, the innovation process itself can be disciplined and lean.

A classical firm needs to manage its innovation process with as much rigor as it applies to its operating costs. Expected return on investment should guide decisions. Classical firms often overinvest in low-growth cash-cow businesses at the expense of providing capital and attention to more promising, but less familiar growth businesses or initiatives where innovation may be required. Some of the best-known classical tools, like the BCG matrix, are designed precisely to address this challenge of allocating resources across a changing portfolio of opportunities that are varied in potential and stage of development.

Organization

Since classical strategy relies on a relatively static source of advantage, the organization needs to be geared toward excelling at what it does repeatedly. Therefore, the design principles for classical organizations are specialization, delegation (the subdivision of tasks), and standardization to support deep capability-building. Standard operating procedures, a high level of top-down oversight, minimal process variance, and attention to detail are all important attributes of a classical organization. This may sound like common sense for all large firms, but we will see that the requirements for an adaptive or a shaping approach, which need to facilitate continuous experimentation toward unknown or changing ends, are in fact completely different. What we may regard as universal aspects of good organization turn out to depend on the approach to strategy we adopt.

Classical organizations often display a high degree of specialization so that employees can accumulate expertise over time. In this way, the firm benefits from the potential of the experience curve in each area of the business. Training and skill-building tend to focus on enhancing and reinforcing expertise in limited, firm- and function-specific areas so that employees can do their current jobs better.

For classical firms, the devil is in the details, since neglected opportunities for improving cost efficiency can build over time into competitive disadvantage. Classical organizations therefore emphasize discipline and structure to ensure that execution is flawless and efficient. As a result, classical firms are often relatively hierarchical with clear operating procedures. They promote standardization and minimize variation to reduce costs, often supported by frequent internal and external benchmarking exercises.

A classical organization poorly executed may suffer the side effects of these same design choices—conservatism, factionalism, poor horizontal communication, lack of collaboration, rigidity, and high overall complexity. No organization—classical or otherwise—can function effectively if these side-effects are too pronounced. Hence, leaders need to closely monitor for and address these potential negative side-effects.

Organization at Quintiles

Quintiles exemplifies the classical organizational imperative of excelling at a known task. As Tom Pike, the CEO, explained to us, it is a very action-oriented company, focused on "doing," and continually refining and reapplying to customer programs the knowledge and insights from its people and processes.

Quintiles demands functional excellence from its twenty-nine thousand employees in more than one hundred countries around the world.[37] The company provides extensive training and allows employees to specialize, because the company's fortunes ultimately rest on their ability to deliver "consistent performance flawlessly and efficiently." Pike explained that the firm hires for expertise: "We need people who can run industrialized processes, we need people who can manage data and advanced analytics, and we need scientific and therapeutic experts."

To avoid the rigidity that is often a downside of classical organizations, Quintiles sometimes undertakes Jack Welch–style "management work-outs," intensive problem-confrontation meetings where pressing issues can be raised so that they can be solved.[38] "It is sobering to think that Jack had his managers spend twenty-five days a year in work-outs just to eliminate bureaucracy," mused Pike.

Culture

Because a classical firm needs to support the pursuit of excellence in relation to a static advantage, the culture needs to disciplined, focused, analytically minded, goal oriented, and geared toward accountability. A classical culture reflects the mentality of *doers*: it rewards the systematic and energetic pursuit and achievement of known goals and reflects a strong shared sense of a singular purpose.

Classical cultures are analytical and goal oriented; they respect and stick to the plan. For instance, Mars is refreshingly transparent internally. The company displays large, flat screens in its headquarters with its current financials: sales, earnings, cash flow, and factory efficiency. The data disclosure is designed to motivate employees, whose bonuses are partly based on the performance of their respective divisions. And the motivation seems to be working—the workforce turnover at Mars is a low 5 percent.[39]

Classical firms are sometimes portrayed as impersonal and bureaucratic. But companies such as Mars manage to achieve a culture that encourages people to work together to achieve a defined goal in a purposeful, collaborative, and rewarding way. There are no moving targets: it is clear where to focus, so employees can concentrate on getting the job done. Classical cultures often recognize and value small increments in, or specialized contributions to, performance on the way to achieving larger goals. For this reason, a well-articulated classical culture creates a workplace that offers many opportunities for personal achievement and that allows employees to feel a sense of contribution and ownership in the company's goals.

Culture at Pfizer

Ian Read, the chief executive at one of the world's premier innovative biopharmaceutical companies, Pfizer, said that the corporate culture is its critical differentiator.[40] In a classical business, multiple similar firms are competing with one another. "Scale is comforting," said Read, pointing to one of the key elements of the classical approach, "but the key competitive weapon isn't scale—it's culture." He went on: "All our competitors have great people; all our competitors have access to capital. The only way to differentiate is [to have] a better culture so that people will come here and give everything they've got."

Pfizer promotes a holistic firmwide (versus individual) performance view, which, for instance, can make it easier for R&D employees to retire projects into which they've put massive time and energy but which are not promising enough to justify continued investment. The culture is built on discipline, accountability, clarity, and focus and, according to Read, is a significant contributor to the firm's recent performance. Pfizer's market cap has roughly doubled between 2010 and the beginning of 2014.[41]

Leadership

Focus—the exploitation of a well-defined and unchanging goal and path—pervades a classical firm's organization and culture. And, not surprisingly, in a classical firm, that focus comes from the top. Leaders need to set the high-level goals, clarify where and how to win, oversee the development of a granular plan, and encourage the achievement of that plan with relentless focus. At the same time, the leader needs to take a step back to check that a relentless focus on execution and efficiency does not result in dysfunctionality through excess.

The CEO plays a critical role in avoiding the ritualization of the strategy process. Classical leaders must be at the forefront in stimulating their firms to think differently about their market to reach to new insights. They have both the latitude and the perspective to question long-held assumptions, existing market definitions, or an overreliance on easily available information.

During the planning cycle, you as a leader should be taking the 30,000-foot view of strategy. Rather than drowning in short-term financial deliberations, ensure that your managers create and commit to a long-term, coherent plan. Often, this requires pushing your organization to make difficult choices, since the best long-term decision may appear at odds with short-term performance.

Once the plan is set, classical leaders turn their focus to detail and execution. They need to ensure adherence to—and reverence for—the plan, until and unless new information arises and necessitates an update.

Finally, leaders need to be on guard against letting focus become an obstacle to necessary change. An organization that is focused on a fixed goal and methods can fail to spot or react to external changes and its functional silos can encourage a local instead of firm-level perspective, thus obstructing change. Leaders can prevent such dysfunction by maintaining an external perspective and ensuring that the organization is able to flex and change when required.

Leadership at Walmart: Sam Walton

Sam Walton, the founder of Walmart, lived the leadership traits of encouraging both focus and openness to change: he was willing to challenge his own and others' view on retailing and was gifted with a meticulous eye for detail. He was so meticulous that he was once thrown out of a local grocery store in São Paolo, where the local police found him crawling on hands and knees, measuring the aisle widths of competitors.[42] CEO in Aisle 3? That kind of maniacal attention to challenging every aspect of his own business model while pursuing a relentless scale game has enabled Walmart to realize a string of innovations that have protected and extended the retailer's positioning against competition.

Tips and Traps

As we've seen, the essential elements of a successful classical strategy are to analytically define a competitively advantaged position, develop a plan to achieve it, and create an organization which supports the rigorous execution of the plan. Implementing these three elements is, of course, no trivial matter.

Our research shows that when leaders perceive a predictable, nonmalleable environment, they are understandably most likely to turn to a classical strategy approach. However, in many cases, the malleability of classical environments is overestimated and leaders consequently declare a visionary approach. The classical practices of strategic planning, emphasizing ends

ARE YOUR ACTIONS CONSISTENT WITH A CLASSICAL APPROACH?

You are employing a classical approach if you observe the following actions:

✓ You are deliberate and precise about where your firm plays.

✓ You analyze the attractiveness of markets and segments.

✓ You analyze the basis of competition.

✓ You analyze your firm's competitiveness.

✓ You determine your firm's optimal positioning based on scale, differentiation, or capabilities.

✓ You predict market developments.

✓ You set precise short- and long-term goals.

✓ You develop long-range, stable plans.

✓ You establish detailed milestones and performance metrics.

✓ You execute with great discipline.

(goals) rather than means (process, capabilities), and prioritizing accuracy over speed appear to be so widespread and entrenched that they are deployed almost irrespective of the actual or perceived business environment. We also noted that leaders surveyed sometimes tend to declare an adaptive style in classical environments, even though this may not be reflected in the organization's actual practices. This tendency to inappropriately declare an adaptive approach is probably influenced by the current popularity of adaptive ideas in the management literature. Clearly, even for the classical approach, the best-known approach to strategy, there are many opportunities for misperception and misapplication.

Table 2-1 contains some practical tips to consider and some common traps to avoid when you are trying to deploy the classical approach.

TABLE 2-1

Tips and traps: key contributors to success and failure in a classical approach

Tips	Traps
• *Be open to surprise:* Pursue new, unfamiliar insights that allow you to outsmart competitors and may require a level of discomfort and surprise.	• *Ritualization:* Some firms apply classical tools and a complex planning process for their own sake and tolerate a lack of both insight and surprise if due process is followed.
• *Make the tough call:* Use your ability to predict to make the best choices for your company's strategic position. Strategy is not just about where you play, but also about where you don't.	• *Replacing strategy with budgeting:* Allowing short-term metrics and budgets to become the focus of your planning process. A bad strategic plan lets managers focus and commit to short-term targets without committing to a coherent, long-term view of the business.
• *Set the right time horizon:* Align the planning cycle to the industry, and adjust plans when materially new insights become available. Once a year? Three times? Once every two years? Make a *deliberate* choice.	• *More of the same:* Letting "the way it's always been" beat "the way it should be" is bound to keep you in a strategic slump. Being classical doesn't mean not changing.
• *Be in the top three:* When pursuing size-based positioning, starting from a small market share position makes it hard to create sustainable value.	• *Segmentation for convenience:* Segmenting according to known and existing categories, such as current business unit boundaries, rather than attempting a more in-depth analysis, can prevent a deep understanding of customer needs.
• *Chase the experience curve:* Cost improvements don't come automatically; proactively realize and pocket them when volumes grow.	• *Rigid planning cycle*: If you stick to annual planning when your industry's cycle shortens, or if you build your plans around Wall Street instead of the business itself, you may fail to adjust to your firm's specific environment.
• *Be meaningfully different:* Differentiate according to capabilities that are valuable to consumers and hard to imitate, rather than on those that are easy to build.	• *Relying on perpetual advantage:* Focusing only on existing sources of advantage can sometimes lead to problems. While incrementalism is inherent in classical strategizing, large jumps may occasionally be necessary.
• *Innovate rigorously:* Apply the same rigor to your decisions about innovation resource allocation as you do to your operating costs.	• *Assuming a classical approach by default:* Many firms declare or deploy a classical approach because it is most familiar. Don't let familiarity be your guide in choosing the right approach for your firm.
	• *Fashionably nonclassical:* Other firms reject a classical style because of the lure of the latest management fad or because of general trends of dynamism and uncertainty in the economy. Following a trend is not the best rationale for choosing an approach to strategy.

CHAPTER 3

ADAPTIVE

Be Fast

Tata Consultancy Services: Adapting to Grow

Tata Consultancy Services (TCS), the largest Indian company by market cap as of 2014, has grown into one of the most successful technology services firms by evolving rapidly in response to waves of technological change through an ongoing stream of small business-model innovations.[1] This adaptive approach enabled TCS to grow from a small player to a leading global one. TCS's revenue growth is impressive: $20 million in 1991, $155 million in 1996, $1 billion in 2003, and more than $13 billion in 2014. From establishing India's first dedicated software R&D center in 1981 to developing India's first offshore development center in 1985 to entering the bioinformatics market in 2005 and then cloud computing in 2011, TCS has continually evolved by responding to changes in the technology environment and the changes' impact on corporate customers.[2]

TCS, while large, is just one of many firms competing in the fragmented space of technology services, an area that includes software solutions and services, consulting, engineering services, and business process outsourcing. Most players in this area have just single-digit market shares, so no firm can definitively shape the direction of the market, and rapid technological change makes for a high level of unpredictability.

In spite of its size, TCS is very externally oriented so that it can capture and harness change. The firm has grown with the environment, as the world economy has shifted from a physical to a digital economy.

With over two decades at TCS before he became CEO in 2009, Natarajan "Chandra" Chandrasekaran has overseen many of the evolutions in its service offering. "From an IT architecture point of view," Chandra told us, "we started during the mainframe environment and have, over the years, adapted to a client-server environment, after which came the internet environment and today's digital or hyperconnected environment." Chandra sees digital technologies fundamentally affecting companies in many, often unpredictable ways: "Every business process will get reimagined. Every business model will get reimagined. How the company works internally will get reimagined. It is our job to engage with customers on how they think about digital . . . and we will shape our delivery model accordingly." TCS therefore has to doubly adapt to both changing technologies and changing customer usage environments.

As technology and customer needs change, TCS has responded quickly and appropriately. For instance, the firm recognized early client demand for a business division devoted to proliferating online channels.

This need to adapt requires an external orientation that cascades throughout the organization, from strategizing to organization to innovation. For instance, in setting direction, TCS balances a rough top-down approach with bottom-up challenge, whereby a central group provides critical market information on each industry vertical—industry size; growth; and competition, technology, and demand trends—then challenges each business to come up with its own approach to best meet specific customer needs. This way, the eventual strategic direction emerges from a collection of individual initiatives that address the specific environmental changes and other new situations that each business segment faces.

Because the future can't be planned, Chandra does not take a classical portfolio-management approach: "We don't want to have [segment-level] cash cows or stars . . . This is about creating opportunities for each business to evolve and grow." TCS places many small bets and then, depending on the success of each initiative, can reallocate resources quickly across businesses. The approach to innovation is experimental and rapid: TCS runs rapid cycles of what it calls the 4E Model—explore, enable, evangelize, and exploit. The model focuses on proactively promoting research across diverse areas, building prototypes, testing, launching, and scaling up.[3] Because vast troves of information from disparate sources are critical for varied, rich exploration, TCS has invested heavily in its analytic capabilities to support these efforts.

Chandra told us that "customer-centricity" is the most important part of TCS's innovation model: "Understanding and often preempting what the customer needs . . . is at the core of our strategic innovation, helping us innovate in our business solutions, delivery, and service models." Several innovations have paid off for TCS. For example, the MasterCraft suite of tools leverages TCS's expertise in the automation of the software development process to deliver quicker and higher-quality client support. And the Just Ask product, a social Q&A platform that enables a client to tap into the client's own tacit individual or crowd knowledge, enables greater collaboration and reduction of time to market.

In addition to innovating in its products and services, TCS embeds innovation at two other levels in the business. At the engagement level, leadership encourages each business unit to think of every engagement as an opportunity for innovation, since each IT services project has unique characteristics. Finally, Chandra fosters an innovation-oriented, experimental mind-set at the individual employee level. He explained: "With three hundred thousand employees, we have tremendous intellectual horsepower within the company." For instance, the firm's Realize Your Potential program runs contests and hackathons around specific issues faced by customers or by some of the Tata group companies; any employee can participate in these events.[4]

TCS has achieved the rare feat of being both large and nimble by building a modular organization that is empowered to experiment.

Since Chandra took over in 2009, the firm has grown from 140,000 employees to twice that.[5] He said: "The company is very large, but we cannot get rigid, so we created twenty-three units, each addressing a specific group of clients. [The units] have common elements and, at the same time, are able to run with their own strategy. We don't want hierarchy; we want network." TCS's attempts to reimagine how the firm works and collaborates include the Vivacious Enterprise, a social collaboration platform aimed at fostering engagement across TCS's large and distributed workforce.[6] Scale certainly helps TCS—it operates in almost fifty countries, is able to collaborate credibly with large global clients, and is the second-largest pure IT firm after IBM.[7] But unlike a classical firm, TCS doesn't win because it is big; it is big because it wins by taking an adaptive approach.

The Adaptive Approach to Strategy: Core Idea

When the business environment is unpredictable and nonmalleable and advantage may be short-lived, firms have to be ready to adapt quickly to succeed. As Chandra realized in the incessantly shifting technology services industry, an adaptive approach can drive growth and advantage by continuously adjusting to new opportunities and conditions (figure 3-1).

FIGURE 3-1

The adaptive approach to strategy

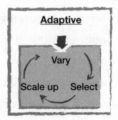

Like the classical approach, the adaptive approach has its own character-istic thought flow. Adaptive firms continuously *vary* how they do business by generating novel options, *selecting* the most promising, which they then *scale up* and exploit before repeating the cycle.

In terms of our art metaphor, the adaptive approach is like painting a landscape under changing light conditions. You need to keep your eye on your subject, work fast, and repeatedly layer brush stroke upon brush stroke until you have captured the fleeting moment—and then move on to captur-ing the next scene.

Strategy emerges from the continuous repetition of this *vary, select, scale up* thought flow, rather than from analysis, prediction, and top-down mandate. By iterating more rapidly and effectively than rivals do, adaptive firms out-perform others, but the classical notion of sustainable competitive advantage is replaced by the idea of serial temporary advantage. As Rupert Murdoch, the chairman of News Corporation, noted: "The world is changing very fast. Big will not beat small anymore. It will be the fast beating the slow."[8]

An adaptive approach is therefore fundamentally different from the clas-sical one: it does not center on a plan, there is no one "strategy," the emphasis is on experimentation rather than analysis and planning, advantage is tem-porary, and the focus is on means, not ends. We will explore some of these differences and their implications in the following sections, but first let's look at another example of adaptive strategy in action.

Why Speed and Learning Matter: Zara

Zara, the Spanish fashion retailer, is a prime example of a company that has become very adaptable in an extremely unpredictable indus-try.[9] On the eve of a new season, fashion retailers can hardly predict whether black is the new black or whether some other color is. In fact, even within a season, customer tastes frequently change. Historically, however, most retailers effectively relied on predictions of what customers would want to wear. And most retailers usually got it wrong and suffered the consequences, having to discount as much as half their stock each year.

Inditex, the holding company of Zara, was no longer happy to bear these kinds of costs and decided to take an adaptive approach to manufacturing and retailing. The holding company introduced *fast fashion*, in industry parlance, with Zara's launch in 1975. Instead of trying to predict what customers might want, Zara opted to react faster to what they actually buy.

Zara achieved this in two ways. First, it shortened its supply chain, moving production facilities closer to customers and willingly accepting the trade-off of slightly higher manufacturing costs to gain more agility. Among other measures, the firm relocated production facilities for United States and European markets from East Asia to countries closer to end markets—countries like Mexico, Turkey, and North Africa. Proximity sourcing has been a success factor for Inditex's model since its origination. The shortened supply chain reduced the time it took to deliver products from the design studio to the main street store to a mere three weeks—an extraordinary five months less than the industry average.[10]

Second, Zara produces only small batches of each style. In effect, these are real-time, in-market experiments, and the successful styles, those that flew off the racks, were selected for scaling up. The retailer tests many more items than its rivals, thereby keeping its customers engaged and ready for more. In fact, Zara commits six months in advance to only 15 to 25 percent of a season's line and locks in only 50 to 60 percent by the start of the season, versus an 80 percent industry average. Consequently, up to 50 percent of Zara's clothes are designed and manufactured right in the middle of the season.[11] If harem pants and leather are suddenly the rage, Zara reacts quickly, designs new styles, and gets them into stores before the trend has peaked or passed.

The impact has been significant: in 2010, Zara marked down only 15 to 20 percent of its inventory, in contrast to the industry average of 50 percent.[12] Also, even though its direct production costs are higher

FIGURE 3-2

Zara's adaptive approach in the fashion industry generates high returns

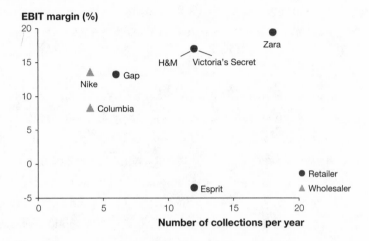

Source: Capital IQ, BCG estimates; BCG project experience; company annual reports.

Note: EBIT, earnings before interest and taxes.

than those of competitors that mostly center production in the Far East, Zara's profit margins in that period were consistently double the average for the industry, and the retailer achieved significantly higher inventory turns to boost its return on capital (figure 3-2).

WHAT YOU MIGHT KNOW IT AS

The advantage of adaptability is not a new notion. Charles Darwin first recognized the power of evolutionary processes, or adaptation, in the biological world. And adaptive business approaches—the notion that strategy cannot always be planned and that speed and flexibility can produce competitive advantage—owe a huge debt to biological thinking.

In the late 1970s, Henry Mintzberg argued that companies sometimes unintentionally end up capitalizing on *emergent strategies*. These strategies are not the result of deliberate top-down plans, but rather emerge serendipitously while the intended plan is being pursued.[13]

In the 1980s, Richard Nelson and Sidney Winter developed the theory of evolutionary economics, suggesting that economic progress is essentially adaptive. BCG leaders Tom Hout and George Stalk around this time pioneered the concept of *time-based competition*, which held that advantage could be created by reducing cycle times in processes like new product development and production. Time-based competition centered on executing *existing tasks* faster, whereas adaptation also requires firms to learn how to do *new things* faster and more effectively too.[14]

In the late 1990s, Charles Fine developed the notion of *temporary advantage*, arguing that advantage is increasingly short-lived and that firms need to match their strategy cycle to the industry's "clock speed." Around the same time, Kathleen Eisenhardt argued that under high uncertainty, organizations and strategies can become agile by using *simple rules* that serve as guidelines and principles in place of complex rules and instructions. Rita McGrath also pioneered the idea of *discovery-based planning*, where plans are not treated as output forecasts against which performance is assessed but rather as plans for discovery that maximize learning while minimizing cost.[15]

Finally, BCG developed and commercialized the *adaptive advantage* concept in the early 2010s to help its clients react to increasing change and uncertainty. This concept detailed how firms can practically realize bottom-up strategic experimentation to replace top-down planning.[16]

When to Apply an Adaptive Approach

An adaptive approach to strategy is appropriate when—and only when—your company is operating in an environment that is both hard to predict and hard to shape.

So how can you recognize an adaptive environment? Essentially, an adaptive strategy is called for when forecasts are no longer reliable enough to produce accurate and durable plans because of ongoing, substantial change in technologies, customer needs, competitive offerings, or industry structure. Such an environment manifests itself in volatile demand, competitive rankings, and earnings; large forecasting errors; and short forecasting horizons.

By these measures, turbulence and uncertainty are now strikingly more frequent and intense in many industries and persist for longer than in previous periods (figure 3-3). Until the 1980s, less than a third of business sectors regularly experienced turbulence. But because of globalization, accelerated

FIGURE 3-3

Increasing unpredictability of returns

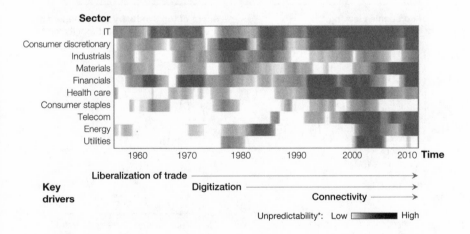

Source: Compustat, BCG analysis.

Note: Volatility based on all public US companies.

*Average five-year rolling standard deviation of percent firm market capitalization growth by sector, weighted by firm market capitalization.

technological innovation, deregulation, and other forces, roughly two-thirds of the sectors now do.[17]

Over the past thirty years, the turbulence of business operating margins, largely static since the 1950s, has more than doubled. Also, the percentage of companies falling out of the top three revenue rankings in their industry each year rose from 3 percent in 1961 to 17 percent in 2002 and was around 8 percent in 2013. The value of incumbency has also diminished: the probability that the top three market-share leaders are also among the top three profitability leaders declined from 35 percent in 1955 to just 7 percent in 2013 (figure 3-4).

Some industries have been especially hard hit by the turbulence; they include software, internet retailing, semiconductors, and, as we saw with Zara, the fashion industry. Most companies in these sectors should be contemplating an adaptive approach to strategy—for part, if not all, of their business.

FIGURE 3-4

Sources of traditional competitive advantage are eroding

Position

% of companies leaving
top 3 ranking position

Returns to scale

Share of top 3 industry scale leaders that
are also among top 3 profitability leaders[*]

Source: BCG Strategy Institute analysis, September 2014, Compustat.

Note: Cross-industry analysis based on thirty-four thousand companies in seventy industries: unweighted average. Industries excluded in years where less than six ranks; companies were excluded in years where only sales or earnings before interest and taxes (EBIT) were reported, or if sales were less than $50 million, or whose margins were less than –300% or greater than 100%.

*Scale is calculated as net sales, profitability as EBIT margin (on net sales).

Indeed, such is the prevalence of turbulence today that even some companies from capital-intensive industries more typically associated with a classical approach might also need to consider deploying an adaptive one. Take mining and metals, for instance. The volatility of metals and minerals prices from 2000 to 2010 was more than six times that of the previous decade.[18] Most mining and metals firms find it hard to make their operations flexible and adaptive because of the long cycle, large-scale capital investments involved. Nevertheless, they are increasingly compelled to find new ways to increase flexibility because even moderate volatility in prices or demand against a high-fixed-cost base can wreak havoc with earnings. As a result, several firms in that sector are trying to shorten their capital cycles, spread investments over an increasing number of smaller assets, share ownership risk, make their operations more flexible, and *exploit* uncertainty by establishing asset-backed trading arms. As Jac Nasser, CEO of BHP Billiton, said in September 2013: "All resources companies will need to improve productivity and be flexible enough to adapt to change in this more challenging market."[19]

Accurately assessing the environment is therefore critical. But it is clear from our research that many companies that objectively face an adaptive

ARE YOU IN AN ADAPTIVE BUSINESS ENVIRONMENT?

You are facing an adaptive business situation if the following observations hold true:

✓ Your industry is dynamic.

✓ Your industry's development is unpredictable.

✓ Your industry is not easily shapable.

✓ Your industry displays high growth.

✓ Your industry's structure is fragmented.

✓ Your industry is immature.

✓ Your industry is based on changing technologies.

✓ Your industry is subject to changing regulation.

environment fail to perceive it as such, because they tend to overestimate the degree to which they can predict or control it. Conversely, even though turbulence is on the rise overall, the adaptive approach is not a panacea and must be applied selectively, when appropriate. As we saw in chapter 2, for many situations, a classical approach is still the right one.

The Adaptive Approach in Practice: Strategizing

Because adaptive strategy emerges continuously from iterative experimentation that is deeply embedded in the organization, thinking and doing converge. The simultaneous nature of these two activities differs from the classical approach, which is composed of two sequential phases of (1) analysis and planning and (2) execution. These activities are performed by different parts of the organization. In the adaptive approach, such a separation between strategizing and implementation would be fatal, slowing down and blunting the learning process. In this chapter therefore, the section on strategizing covers the entire process from capturing change signals to managing a portfolio of experiments. The implementation section of this chapter then deals with the broader organizational context that supports and enables this process to take place.

Applying an adaptive approach is easier said than done. Leaders increasingly use the vocabulary of adaptation, referring to VUCA environments (those with volatility, uncertainty, complexity, and ambiguity) and extolling the virtues of agility and adaptability.[20] However, as we will see later, many of these same firms continue to cling onto the top-down, slow-cycle, planning-centered practices associated with the classical approach.

The adaptive approach involves reading and digesting change signals to manage a portfolio of experiments focused on areas of highest opportunity or vulnerability. The goal is to run the cycle of vary, select, and scale up more quickly, economically, and effectively than rivals do, to build and renew temporary advantage.

Unlike classical strategy, adaptive strategy does not have predefined ends, because these are unknowable in an unpredictable environment. Strategy emerges and evolves iteratively. Leaders using an adaptive approach would therefore be missing the point by talking about *the* strategy. Leadership can define a domain of focus, a rough direction, or an aspiration, but the specific strategies are emergent and dynamic. In contrast, the approach to experimentation can be very deliberate. The risk taking and creativity required by an adaptive strategy may look undisciplined compared with a classical approach. But adaptive strategy requires an equal level but different sort of discipline throughout—from generating new options, to determining how promising ones are tested and selected, to establishing how to reallocate resources from less promising projects toward those that show potential.

Reading Change Signals

As Niels Bohr, the Danish Nobel Prize–winning physicist once put it: "Prediction is very difficult, especially if it's about the future." So what should a firm do when it cannot set its direction through prediction?

To react to and harness change, firms need first to observe and to try to make sense of it. When observing change, firms need to capture the right information and decode it to discriminate between trivial and significant changes (the latter changes being those that might be threatening or constitute opportunities) and between forecastable, knowable factors and currently unknowable ones that require exploration and experimentation. To understand the *significance* of change, firms need also to question and challenge what they think they know by uncovering and reconsidering blind spots and hidden assumptions. External change signals might therefore point directly at an opportunity or a threat or more indirectly at an area of uncertainty where the firm needs to gather more information through experimentation. In this way, experimentation need not be blind, but rather can be more of a guided learning process.[21]

Capturing the *right* data can be immensely valuable to continuously generate new insights about changes in demand or competition. In Japan, global grocery chain 7-Eleven gained a significant information advantage in the early 2000s by leveraging its point-of-sale systems to track not just sales, but also other variables, such as customer demographics and even the weather and time of the day. With this data, the firm could test hypotheses about how these variables drive sales in real time, allowing 7-Eleven to identify promising or less promising items in a particular context. Thus, pricing, assortment, promotions, and layout could be optimized to local conditions on a daily or even multi-hourly basis by location. For example, the 7-Eleven systems could track the altered demand for lunch boxes from a new nearby building site and rapidly adjust the assortment on a store-by-store basis.[22]

Often the relevant information is already available and right under a company's nose, originating, for instance, from interactions with consumers, suppliers, and other stakeholders, but the information may need to be properly captured and decoded through the use of data mining and analytics. Firms must be able to decode hidden patterns in large data sets and to react to changes rapidly before someone else does. The days when companies could secure an advantage by merely *possessing* information are dwindling: the information they possess may quickly lose relevance or may harbor hidden patterns that need to be teased out.

To understand the significance of change, firms must foster self-awareness about what they really know and must uncover their own hidden assumptions. This information map can shift constantly in a changing environment. In some cases, firms underleverage new information available to them—what we might call *underexploited knowns*, or *elephants*. There is also much that you may erroneously think you know—*false knowns*, or *unicorns*—and may need to challenge. Most challengingly, some things cannot be known at the time, without a change of perspective or further experimentation—*double question marks*, or *unknown unknowns*, to borrow an expression from Donald Rumsfeld, the former US secretary of defense (figure 3-5).[23]

Understandably, large companies find it hard to identify and address these three types of blind spots, since most operate with a classically biased world view. Firms assume they have a high level of knowledge about the market or competitive landscape and expect to see only a modest degree of change.

The story of big US car manufacturers and hybrid cars offers a lesson on underexploited knowns. In the early 1990s, the Clinton administration challenged the big automakers to design cars that were more fuel-efficient, against the backdrop of a growing ecological awareness among consumers.

FIGURE 3-5

Tool for segmenting sources of uncertainty

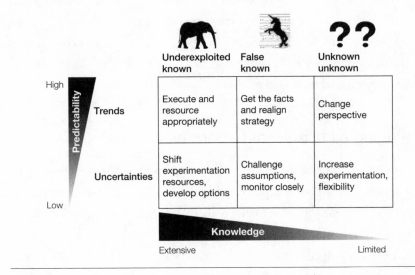

GM, Ford, and Chrysler did develop prototypes—but few reached the production line.[24] This left a gap for Toyota. Its Prius became the first mass-produced hybrid car and was extremely successful. Cumulatively, Prius passed the one million vehicles sold mark in 2008 and reached three million in 2013. In 2009, it was the best-selling car in Japan.[25]

In other cases, firms may neglect to challenge a false known, a dominant but increasingly obsolete world view, in spite of abundant signals of change, because they underrate or ignore information at their disposal. An example of a false known is the apparently reasonable assumption that to at least some significant degree, people use smartphones for making phone calls! It is easy to imagine both how challenging it is for a long-standing tele-communications provider to question this belief and the significant strategic consequences of doing so. Telenor, a Norwegian telecom company, in fact did question this belief, as we will explore later in this chapter.

Of course, there are always things that a company may not or simply can't know—unknown unknowns—without experimenting or a changing its vantage point. Therefore, adaptive companies need to build a culture of self-challenge, one that encourages the questioning of a company's dominant logic to uncover and employs techniques aimed at highlighting blind spots. For instance, they try to look at their own firm through the eyes of an imaginary or real enemy, engage in war gaming against their own business model, or try to make an opposing business case or mandate a compulsory dissenting opinion for each new investment recommendation, in order to deliberately expand their field of vision.

Managing a Portfolio of Experiments

In a turbulent business environment, a company's products, services, and business models can become obsolete very quickly. At the same time, firms cannot predict which new elements will replace the old ones. Luckily, leaders have a viable alternative to prediction: running a portfolio of strategic experiments managed with an eye on the twin imperatives of speed and economy. To do so successfully, firms set the perimeter for experimentation by reading change signals and generating a sufficient volume of new ideas to test in areas of interest. Promising opportunities emerge quickly through disciplined experimentation, with clear rules for selecting and pushing projects forward. Finally, firms scale up successful experiments by rapidly and cleanly reallocating resources.

Companies should first decide what to test. They should leverage change signals to focus on the areas that suggest the highest growth potential, the biggest threats, or the most important blind spots. Even where you lack a clear hypothesis, more experimentation yields more information, which yields more options. Unlike the classical firm, the adaptive firm leans toward taking action first rather than analysis.

Adaptive firms tap into two sources to make sure that they have sufficiently large numbers of new ideas to test. Either they embrace the natural variance inherent in the way the company operates, or they proactively introduce variance by creating a range of experiments and testing them. Passive works well in activities like trading or selling, where there is significant natural variance to tap into. Variance gives the adaptive firm a wide option set to explore. Interestingly, it is precisely this variance that classical firms try to eliminate from their processes in the pursuit of ever-higher efficiency levels. For this reason, it can be extremely difficult for a classical firm to really embrace an experimental approach even when such an approach becomes acutely necessary.

Google is not yet twenty years old and operates in a ferociously unpredictable market. Its cofounder and CEO Larry Page couldn't make the point more strongly: "Many leaders of big organizations, I think, don't believe that change is possible. But if you look at history, things do change; and if your business is static, you're likely to have issues."[26] As a consequence, Google experiments on a wide range of options close to and distant from its core business—from AdWords to more exploratory investments through Google Ventures or speculative projects such as Google Glass. Many of these ideas come from the much celebrated 20 percent time program, which lets some employees spend as much as 20 percent of their time working freely on new projects of their choice.[27]

To ensure that experiments function quickly and cheaply, firms need clear rules for framing, executing, and assessing experiments, applying a principle of freedom within a disciplined framework. On a portfolio level, adaptive firms should strictly monitor their economics of experimentation. They should measure and optimize the number of experiments, the costs, the success rates, and the speed of progression. Typically, experiments should be individually small, large in overall number, and quick to come to a conclusion. Rather than investing a lot of time to evaluate and attempt to predict the success of each project before it is launched, adaptive firms continuously validate what is working in practice and iterate frequently on their portfolio. As management writer Tom Peters has urged: "Test fast, fail fast, adjust fast."[28]

To return to Google: the firm actively measures experimentation outcomes so that, in light of the results, Google can rapidly reallocate resources among projects. Over the past ten years, Google has both launched and killed roughly ten to fifteen products annually without major customer or organizational resentment.[29] While a classical strategist could think that the adaptive strategy sounds like "try something and see what sticks," objective data—rather than disputable gut feel—governs each decision.

SIMULATING STRATEGY IN AN UNPREDICTABLE ENVIRONMENT

Classical strategies perform well when an environment is stable, because the attractiveness of the option chosen after careful analysis doesn't change. However, when we add environmental dynamism and uncertainty to our computer simulation, classical strategies underperform strategies that invest more in continuously exploring new options.

In an uncertain environment, it is likely that the rewards from a currently exploited option will decrease or that new, potentially better options will arise. Therefore, strategies that continuously invest a proportion of resources in exploring new options, or adaptation, should yield improved performance.

Our simulation confirms this relationship. Increasing the degree of uncertainty of rewards per option over time requires a proportionally higher degree and continuity of investment in exploration (figure 3-6).

FIGURE 3-6

Adaptive strategies perform well in turbulent environments (simulation)

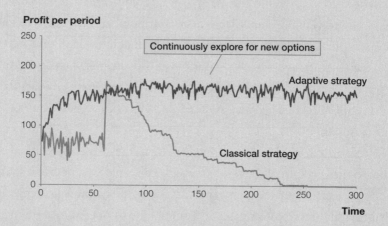

Source: BCG Strategy Institute multi-armed bandit (MAB) simulation.

Notes: Results averaged over thirty simulations in noncompetitive environment with thirty investment options.

Strategizing at Telenor

The telecom industry is a prime example of an industry whose environment has undergone a rapid shift from a relatively stable classical environment to a more rapidly shifting adaptive one. Jon Fredrik Baksaas, CEO of the Norwegian telecom operator Telenor, described the change through analogy: "I call it the 'concrete phenomenon.' You used to be able to plan: how many houses will be built, how much cement will you need, and you produced that much. And then you did it for the next year. And that is fundamentally different today. In our traditional fixed-line business, we have that degree of certainty, to some extent, but that's where it stops."[30]

Telenor's advantage in the historically stable telecom industry came from its scale and cost competitiveness in operating fixed-line and mobile-phone network businesses in Norway, Sweden, and Denmark. However, in the late 2000s, Telenor faced new challenges with the maturation of its network businesses, the accelerating switch in revenue contribution from voice to data, and the flurry of new internet-based services introduced by both tech giants and start-ups like Netflix and WhatsApp. In a short period of time, competition became more fragmented, consumer preferences and segmentation changed, and the industry became much less predictable.[31]

Telenor has succeeded, locally and in emerging markets, by implementing an adaptive approach to strategy, especially in the new areas of its businesses. For instance, it adjusted the speed and horizon of its planning to be more iterative, with a focus on seeing what's happening and responding quickly, and added quarterly updates and revisions to the plan. "Minimizing delays in getting products to market is more important than hitting pre-set targets," Baksaas said.

Additionally, Telenor has adjusted its approach to innovation. Baksaas gave us an example of why speed to market and novelty are so important: "I was speaking to an audience and asked how many had smartphones—ninety percent raised their hands. How many had iPhones? Seventy percent. And of those, how many had used the phone that morning to make a voice call? Only five percent. Everyone else had used their phone, but they had been using data and apps. So we must adapt our model accordingly." In practice, that means that Telenor protects and funds innovation through a trial-and-error process in the innovation's early stages before integrating it into the broader business. Telenor closely manages its experimentation engine, paying attention to adaptive metrics like cost per experiment, time to market, and percentage of sales from new products. It then scales up successfully piloted products rapidly, like appear.in, an in-browser group video conversation service. After a test-and-learn period, the appear.in service is now fully global, serving customers in 175 countries.[32]

Telenor has also updated its approach to talent management to "nurture and appreciate the risk-takers and innovators." The firm, for example, developed a forty-person global leadership program that draws from across the organization and works to generate new business ideas; from this diverse, cross-functional group, eight novel ideas are in the development phase.

Baksaas emphasized that "in an era of unpredictability, the incumbent has the most to lose." To combat the natural inertia that comes from comfortable positions of monopoly or scale, Telenor systematically leverages learning and experience from business in areas where the rate of change is the quickest, like Asian markets. There Telenor focuses on reaching and connecting the most consumers the fastest, for example, by driving the development of mobile phones placed at a price point below $20.

The Adaptive Approach in Practice: Implementation

Let's look at the broader organizational context that supports and reinforces the adaptive approach to strategy. The approach must be embedded in every aspect of the organization, with an eye to promoting signal capture, experimentation, and selection by promoting external orientation, bottom-up initiative, and an agile and flexible organization.

Information

As we've seen, information management is critical for both signal capture and effective management of a portfolio of experiments. Therefore, adaptive firms must continuously refresh their data on external change and must have the analytic capabilities to uncover hidden patterns. These functions and capabilities need to be broadly embedded in the organization. To manage experimentation, information is needed on two levels: information to manage individual experiments (i.e., data on outcomes and controls for each experiment) and information to manage the overall portfolio (such as overall success rate, costs, speed, and aggregate return on investment).

Since the firm that first deciphers and acts on change signals gains advantage in an adaptive environment, the firm's intelligence about the industry, the competition, and customer and consumer trends must be excellent. Adaptive firms, therefore, must invest in developing advanced analytics capabilities that can capture and leverage disparate, real-time data. Since the precise applications of patterns cannot be foreseen, the information needs to be easily and broadly accessible and visualized in a way that makes it easy for all parts of the organization to tap into it.

Car insurance company Progressive is a good example of a firm that built competitive advantage by using novel real-time signals to understand risk in a very segmented fashion. In the late 1990s, Progressive became the first US insurer to build capabilities in telematics, a technology that reads and reports data in real time from remote objects. In 2011, the firm introduced Snapshot, a small telematic device that drivers place in their cars. The device reports data on driver behavior such as mileage and acceleration and braking patterns. With that information, Progressive can create an individualized dynamic risk profile and offer savings of up to 30 percent to low-risk customers.[33] Additionally, the firm uses the knowledge gained to continuously refine and update its customer and product segmentation. As a result of this,

Progressive has improved on all major dimensions—sales volumes, retention, and loss ratio on its customer base. Progressive's CEO, Glenn Renwick, said, "I consider Snapshot to be one of the most important things I've personally seen in my career."[34]

Good results require accurate data for both the experiment and the corresponding control to determine whether the outcome meets the criteria for advancing or stopping the experiment. Effective experimentation also requires monitoring and management of overall idea generation, success rates, experimentation costs, speed of progression and resource allocation across the portfolio to maximize the yield on experimentation.

The firm needs to extract as much learning as possible from each of its experiments—including those that don't work. Failures are critical for adaptive firms, since these experiments could contain valuable information not only on what specifically works and what doesn't, but also on the effectiveness of the experimental approach itself. Caesars Entertainment, a casino operator, leverages the information from the dozens of experiments it conducts in parallel not only to identify the best products for its customers, but also to fine-tune the experimentation process itself. Experiments are undertaken in separate, controlled parts of a casino so that each test can be properly assessed and, if appropriate, rolled out across the company.[35] It is a rigorous process. As Gary Loveman, the CEO, joked: "There are two ways to get fired from Caesars: stealing from the company or failing to include a proper control group in your business experiment."[36]

Innovation

Continuous innovation is quite obviously the lifeblood of an adaptive organization. Since adaptive companies experiment without a predefined goal, they need a disciplined and iterative innovation process to ensure that the best initiatives surface fast and economically. Therefore, adaptive innovation needs to be informed by external signals, built on small, low-cost bets, and iterated upon frequently. And, on a higher level, the process needs to be tolerant of failure and managed for overall economic optimality. This is certainly not to say that innovation and novelty are maximized for their own sake: experimentation is expensive and risky. So the adaptive firm also needs to adjust its rate of exploration to the circumstances and clock speed of its environment and then makes sure that the firm also fully exploits its successes, albeit for short periods.

We dealt with many of the key features of adaptive innovation in this chapter's section on strategizing, so let's now look at some essential differences with how innovation is normally conceived and implemented. Innovation in a classical firm is often somewhat detached from regular business activities, consisting of occasional leaps driven by an entirely separate R&D department. In an adaptive approach, innovation is the opposite: small steps, continuous, and operationally embedded. And unlike the visionary or classical approaches, you may not initially know what "new" thing you're looking for, so you will inevitably have failures, setbacks, and surprises. Therefore, adaptive firms manage individual projects for speed, incentivizing progression and enforcing short timelines to push teams to converge quickly on whether something is worth progressing further, requires a change of direction, or needs to be aborted. For instance, Google requires that project specs be no longer than one page, a limit that helps reduce any reluctance or regret about changing course or winding down.[37]

Organization

The adaptive approach needs an organization that is able to capture and share external signals and to generate and manage a portfolio of experiments effectively. The necessary organization design principles, therefore, are to be externally oriented, information enabled, decentralized, and flexible to reallocate resources quickly as the focus of experimentation evolves.

An external orientation allows firms to capture external signals effectively. Often, this means that a firm embeds customers into its processes by building strong feedback mechanisms or by creating user communities as part of its organizational model. Sometimes, customers are even a main source of innovation ideas.

Adaptive firms are typically broadly information-enabled and make data visualization and analytics available throughout their organization, so that employees can spot change and formulate an immediate, fast response. This is different from the classical approach, where the analytical tools used for strategizing are usually concentrated among a small group of expert professionals.

Because of the need to stimulate bottom-up learning and individual creativity, adaptive organizations often foster a high degree of autonomy and are relatively flat and decentralized. The organizations are often characterized by the existence of informal, temporary, or horizontal structures, like internal forums, task forces, or councils that break down traditional functional silos to allow for sharing of information and flexibility in mobilizing around promising opportunities. Multiple layers, strict hierarchy, and a thick rule book would greatly reduce a company's ability to execute a quick about-face in light of new signals from the environment.[38]

Safe Innovation Space: Organization at Intuit

Intuit is what its president and CEO, Brad Smith, calls a "30-year old start-up."[39] Despite being an "old"—that is, pre-internet—software company, Intuit has continuously rejuvenated its fortunes by retooling its innovation and experimentation processes to design cutting-edge financial software. Senior leaders at Intuit designed an organization that functions as a safe innovation space by reducing friction in new-product development and encouraging a philosophy of speed, guided by simple rules.

For instance, Intuit's organization fosters openness, flexibility, and bottom-up contributions by empowering small, diverse teams of four to six people to identify problems and to prototype solutions rapidly. When an internal task force determined that too many managers were involved in new software releases, making the process inefficient, unclear, and sometimes demoralizing, the group rolled out a new decision process that grants far more authority to the small scrum teams that best know the product and target customers. Management's role in each decision is limited to a pair of approvers: one sponsor to remove roadblocks and one coach to provide vision.[40]

Intuit's organizational rules and processes serve less to constrain the organization than to empower and focus it. Faced with possible commoditization from free internet services, Intuit has maintained its leadership through a combination of new products and smart acquisitions, including the personal-finance aggregator Mint .com. Since Smith became CEO in 2008, Intuit stock has more than doubled.[41]

The adaptive organization is typically modular and flexible, which means that its units can be recombined quickly, depending on shifts in the environment or the decision to scale a particular experiment. Standardized (plug-and-play) interfaces enable the organization to morph to address changing needs by rapidly shift resources. Take Corning, the maker of Gorilla Glass, which has been used as a cover material for iPhones through 2014, along with nearly twenty-five hundred other devices across thirty-three major brands.[42] As we will explore in chapter 7, Corning doesn't know far in advance when device manufacturers will begin to build a new product or what the specs will be. But the company's flexible organizational structure, lack of silos, and common incentives allow it to adjust roles and reallocate resources quickly to mobilize around new opportunities.

Culture

An adaptive firm's ability to read and act on market signals and conduct experiments is underpinned by its culture. Adaptive cultures are therefore externally oriented and means focused. The culture creates the context for the generation of new ideas and rapid learning by allowing for a diversity of perspectives and encouraging constructive dissent, rather than compliance with a single mandated direction.

In contrast to the expressly goal-oriented, disciplined culture in the classical firm, the adaptive approach requires a culture of openness and playfulness to encourage the generation of new ideas. The culture promotes challenge by allowing constructive dissent and promoting cognitive diversity. And because adaptive organizations rely on individual creativity and initiative, they articulate a set of common behaviors and a common purpose in the place of precise endpoints.

Netflix, for instance, is unique in the way it first codified an explicit set of adaptive management beliefs and principles. Here is an example from its "Reference Guide to Freedom and Responsibility Culture": Process-driven companies are "unable to adapt quickly, because the employees are extremely good at following the existing processes . . . we try to get rid of rules when we can. We have a culture of creativity and self-discipline, freedom and responsibility" that benefits from "highly aligned, loosely coupled teamwork . . . the goal is to be big and fast and flexible."[43]

The culture at Netflix has underpinned sustained viability and superior operational and financial performance in a highly turbulent industry. As Netflix has evolved from providing mail-order DVDs to streaming digital media to developing independent content, its stock price rose tenfold from 2009 to 2014, and Netflix became the largest source of internet traffic in North America in 2013.[44]

Leadership

Adaptive leaders lead through setting context, rather than goals. They do this by orienting the organization externally, creating an experimentation-friendly culture, specifying the rules under which experiments are conducted, and highlighting the areas where experimentation is to be focused. Reed Hastings, CEO and founder of Netflix, summarized this important quality of leadership: "The best managers figure out how to get great outcomes by setting the appropriate context, rather than by trying to control their people."[45]

Culture and Leadership at 3M: William McKnight

William McKnight officially became president of 3M, an industrial conglomerate, in August 1929—just two months before the Wall Street crash. Over the next twenty years, he ran a company that needed to cope with a great deal of change. His achievement stands as the classic case of a leader creating the context within which his team of brilliant innovators could shine.

McKnight formulated a set of management principles that could be remarkably applicable to any innovative technology companies' culture today: delegate responsibility to stimulate individual initiative; tolerate mistakes to avoid dampening the spark of creativity; allocate free time in the working week for people to pursue their own interests; establish platforms so that great ideas can be shared across the organization.

As he prepared to step down from his role as president in the late 1940s, McKnight set down these principles in a code for the leadership team that would be assuming the day-to-day control of the company:

> As our business grows, it becomes increasingly necessary to delegate responsibility and to encourage men and women to exercise their initiative. This requires considerable tolerance. Those men and women, to whom we delegate authority and responsibility, if they are good people, are going to want to do their jobs in their own way. Mistakes will be made. But if a person is essentially right, the mistakes he or she makes are not as serious in the long run as the mistakes management will make if it undertakes to tell those in authority exactly how they must do their jobs. Management that is destructively critical when mistakes are made kills initiative. And it's essential that we have many people with initiative if we are to continue to grow.[46]

Today, these principles continue to set the context for 3M's employees. The company encourages its R&D staff members to exercise their initiative by giving them as much as 15 percent of their time for "tinkering," often on basic research topics with no obvious or immediate commercial potential.[47] In other words, "Google Time" has been around far longer than Google. These organizational and cultural elements are central to 3M's enduring success. 3M often exceeds its own goal to generate 30 percent of its sales from newly launched products.[48]

Tips and Traps

As we have seen, successful adaptive strategy hinges on continuous, disciplined execution of signal-guided, iterative experimentation rather than preset goals. To conduct such experiments effectively, you must accept the

ARE YOUR ACTIONS CONSISTENT WITH AN ADAPTIVE APPROACH?

Your approach to strategy is adaptive if:

✓ You aim to capture and decode change signals early.

✓ You create a portfolio of options and experiments.

✓ You select successful experiments.

✓ You scale up successful experiments.

✓ You reallocate resources flexibly.

✓ You iterate (vary, select, scale up) rapidly.

limits of your knowledge and your powers of prediction and prepare for the future by creating and exploiting options, rather than by deriving a single, unchanging plan through analysis and prediction.

Volatile, unpredictable environments and adaptive strategies are much discussed and are, superficially at least, familiar to most managers. Not surprisingly, then, a quarter of the companies in our survey declared that they had adaptive approaches to strategy, and more that 70 percent think that plans should evolve. Nevertheless, many companies acknowledged that they have insufficient adaptive capabilities: only 18 percent and 9 percent saw themselves as expert at reading signals or managing experimentation, respectively. Few companies, however, appeared able to identify adaptive environments accurately, and many companies tended to read such environments as more predictable or malleable than they actually are. Moreover, even when firms declare an adaptive approach, the practices the companies actually used—planning, prediction, emphasis on ends rather than means, and the like—tended to be decidedly nonadaptive. Our survey painted a clear picture of many companies recognizing the importance of adaptive approaches but having insufficient knowledge or experience of how to operationalize this understanding. Hopefully, this chapter and the tips and traps presented in table 3-1 will help remedy this gap.

TABLE 3-1

Tips and traps: key contributors to success and failure in an adaptive approach

Tips	Traps
• *Know what you know and don't know:* Look externally, beyond the obvious, to spot new opportunities in a world in constant flux. Continuously look for information that challenges long-held beliefs.	• *Overconfidence in your own beliefs:* Knowing the future in a world that is uncertain is an oxymoron. Even if your world view is spot-on, rapid change can outdate it in an instant.
• *Practice goal flexibility and means discipline:* Experiment within a broad direction, and prepare to be surprised, but manage the experimentation process with discipline.	• *Silencing dissent:* Avoid hearing only what you want to hear. Consider signals contrary to your beliefs a gift intended to help you see something new.

(Continued)

TABLE 3-1   *(Continued)*

Tips and traps: key contributors to success and failure in an adaptive approach

Tips	Traps
• *Don't bet the firm:* Use a portfolio and a series of many small, economical experiments instead of pinning your company's future on a large, single bet.	• *Planning the unplannable:* In a world that changes quickly, investing in elaborate predictions and plans is futile.
• *Choose speed over accuracy:* Force convergence quickly, toward either continuation or termination of the experiment. Detailed preemptive analysis and precise goals are a waste of time and resources when the target is unknowable and shifting.	• *Rigid directions:* If you are unwilling to change your direction as new information arises, even though the present direction will probably not survive the tides of change, then you are setting your company up for failure.
• *Iterate frequently:* Signs of success emerge organically after cycles of testing, evaluation, adjustment, and further testing. Look often to learn faster.	• *Move slowly:* Your success will depend on how much faster you can introduce new products or business models than your competitors can. So inertia and complexity can be fatal, even if sought in the name of perfection.
• *Select with discipline:* Set clear rules up front for selecting and scaling up promising experiments to support speedy self-direction and limit both gut-feel decisions and inertia.	• *Bet the company:* Large experiments that fail can drag down the firm. Experimentation is only a viable alternative to planning when the risk and cost have been reduced through an effective approach.
• *Learn from failure:* Recognize that failure is inherent to experimentation under uncertainty and yields valuable information to inform future experimentation.	• *Punish failure:* Condemning or shaming failed efforts can kill individual appetite to generate the new ideas that fuel your future success. An open-minded culture is key to success with an adaptive approach.
• *Be organizationally flexible:* With frequent experimentation comes frequent success *and* failure, both of which drive change. Organize so that resources can be reallocated quickly and smoothly.	• *Faddish application:* An adaptive approach is more necessary in today's unpredictable business environments, but following the crowd is a poor logic for selecting it. Instead, look at the specifics of your particular environment.
• *Understand the practicalities:* An understanding of and intent to graft an adaptive strategy onto a classical organization will not be effective. Learn the very different operational disciplines of an experimentation-driven approach.	

CHAPTER 4

VISIONARY

Be First

Quintiles: Building a Vision

Dennis Gillings was a thirty-year-old professor of biostatistics at the University of North Carolina when he first started helping pharmaceutical companies analyze data from their clinical trials. "Back then," he recalled, "I felt there was an opportunity to build a business that ... would complement my activities as a professor and enable a small consulting income." But the more consulting he did, the more he realized that there was an opportunity to build something bigger. "What I noticed as I was consulting was that things were a bit inefficient. I remember going inside a pharma company and thinking, 'Wow, it doesn't need to cost all this money.'"[1]

In 1982, he cofounded Quintiles Transnational as a first step toward what was, even then, a truly global vision. In doing so, he pioneered what has become known as the CRO—or clinical research organization—industry, in which companies like Quintiles don't just analyze data, but actively manage clinical trials and other activities. "I realized that I could grow the business globally and expand to drug development," he said.

Gillings's clarity of vision and urgency to achieve it guided the company throughout this period. Gillings said, "That plan never really changed." To bring it to life, he drew up a few high-level milestones, which didn't resemble the meticulously detailed planning documents characteristic of the classical approach at all. "I always laugh about strategic plans," he said. For instance, when the plan to form a single European market was announced in the late 1980s, Gillings anticipated the impact of regulatory convergence across Europe and realized that he needed to lay the groundwork to support a bet on the pan-European union. "In 1989," he explained, "all I did was to draw a little map with years along the x-axis, and then I put countries on it: the US and UK we had, and then we would do Germany, Ireland, France, Italy. And I then said we have to do Asia . . . I built the whole world on an axis over a nine-year period."

Gillings saw quite early that CROs had massive potential but that, to claim it, he had to grow the business quickly. "I decided we needed to make acquisitions if we were going to grow faster than anyone else could. In the 1990s we went from $10 million in revenue in 1990 to $1 billion in 1998 . . . we could only grow a hundredfold by being fast." He recognized that although he was creating a new market, others—including players with superior resources—would likely enter the space. So Gillings moved fast to beat larger but less nimble potential competitors.

Quintiles succeeded because Gillings had the courage not only to move quickly but also to persist in the face of skepticism. "I had to not listen to almost all the advice I got. I may look pig-headed, but I tend to be a bit logical and I thought, 'I don't know how that advice can be correct.' For instance, I got criticized for going global so early because it was expensive and I got used to the fact that other people disagreed with me, and I decided I was right. Every cultural group takes the same drugs, for the most part, so ultimately, drugs will be developed much more globally, and if you're there first, you'll gain an advantage!"

In retrospect, he needn't have worried. "I overestimated what our potential competitors could do," he said. But at the time, it was difficult to gauge where they stood. Therefore, the only thing to do was to grow quickly, to race against oneself instead of a particular competitor. "I'm glad I did—we managed to become much bigger because I was very aggressive between 1990 and 1998."

Today, Quintiles is the world's largest provider of drug development and commercial outsourcing services, with a network of more than thirty thousand employees in more than sixty countries. Over the past decade, it has conducted forty-seven hundred trials with 2.7 million patients. It has helped develop or commercialize all of the top fifty best-selling drugs on the market.[2]

Gillings attributes much of the firm's success to good timing. "There was a zeitgeist and we tapped into it," he explained. "If I had been born fifty years earlier, it wouldn't have been good timing." Partly, though, it was his realization "that it could be a multibillion dollar industry and . . . to accomplish that, we had to grow quite quickly."

But Gillings's single-mindedness, a distinctively visionary characteristic, also drove the successful development of Quintiles. He achieved the ultimate visionary payoff: "If you pick a big idea and do it well, the company gets to a leadership position in the whole space in which you operate."

The Visionary Approach to Strategy: Core Idea

In some environments, a single firm can create or re-create an industry and, as a result of that power, create the future with some degree of predictability. Under those circumstances, a firm is in a position to employ a visionary approach. As Gillings's story illustrates, you must be capable of single-handedly developing new markets or disrupting existing ones. Alan Kay, a pioneering American computer scientist, summed up the visionary perspective well: "The best way to predict the future is to invent it."[3] Your brand name may even come to define the product category for years to come, as with Xerox or Hoover.

A visionary approach involves three steps (figure 4-1). First, you need to *envisage* an opportunity by tapping into a megatrend early, applying a new technology, or addressing customer dissatisfaction or a latent need. Second, you need to be the first to *build* the company and the product that realize this vision. Finally, you must *persist* in pursuing a fixed goal, while being flexible about the means to overcome unforeseen obstacles. In terms of our art analogy, the visionary painters of the surrealist school imagine rather than observe a vivid image of what they wish to represent and which they then strive tirelessly to bring to life on canvas.

Timing is critical. By being first, you have the advantages of superior size that come with being ahead of your rivals: you can set the industry standards, you can influence customer preferences, you can develop a superior cost position, and you can take the market in a direction that suits your company.

Even though visionary approaches are most frequently associated with entrepreneurial start-ups, large, more-established firms increasingly need to familiarize themselves with the approach too. As the large corporation finds itself disrupted by small outsiders more and more frequently, at a minimum, it needs to know how its small, visionary competitors think so that it can react to or, even better, preempt them when the circumstances are right. As Gary Hamel, a business writer, noted: "Out there in some garage is an entrepreneur who's forging a bullet with your company's name on it."[4] A deep understanding and appreciation of the visionary approach can serve as a first line of defense for market incumbents.

FIGURE 4-1

The visionary approach to strategy

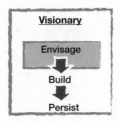

Why Timing Matters: 23andMe

In 2006, Anne Wojcicki cofounded 23andMe, a personal genomics company that provides analysis of individuals' DNA. Her firm is a clear example of a company employing the visionary approach. In the mid-2000s, Wojcicki was working as a health-care investment analyst when she came up with her vision for transforming the space she covered: "I was at a dinner with a scientist . . . and we got talking about health care and about data. Theoretically, if you had all the genotypic and phenotypic data in the world, could you solve health care? The answer is yes."[5]

From this guiding insight, she developed 23andMe with two colleagues in 2006, formulating its mission "to accelerate the development of new treatments, gain a better understanding of wellness and disease prevention, and provide greater access to those who want to understand and use their genetic data in order to manage their health and well-being."[6]

Her timing couldn't have been better. Wojcicki connected the dots between exciting developments in biotechnology, information technology, and e-commerce. At the turn of the millennium, Craig Venter, an American biologist, became the first person to map the human genome, at a cost of $100 million.[7] In the following years, the cost of sequencing the human genome fell exponentially while, simultaneously, IT opened up new frontiers to combine, analyze, and share increasingly large volumes of data.[8] For Wojcicki, these developments heralded a new opportunity: to offer consumers the chance to test their own genome, combine it with phenotypic data from questionnaires they fill in, and play the results back to them in a user-friendly, personally relevant, and intelligible way while aggregating a large and statistically powerful database of genetic information to drive new research. When 23andMe introduced its core product, an individual genomic analysis of a consumer's saliva, it was named the invention of the year by *Time* magazine in 2008.[9]

Though that product was initially introduced at $999, 23andMe quickly lowered its price to $99 in order to attain the fast growth that would give it critical mass and leadership.[10] The drive for scale is baked into every aspect of the vision. So far, 23andMe has administered seven hundred thousand tests.[11] Wojcicki's goal is twenty-five million. "Once you get to twenty-five million people, there's just a huge power because of the types of discoveries you can make. Big data is going to make us all healthier." Scale reinforces its leading position by making the proposition attractive to an even wider audience, she said: "Suddenly [our] data becomes incredibly valuable to pharmaceuticals, hospitals, and other large organizations."

As with most firsts, there have been challenges, but Wojcicki has persisted. Some states, for instance, tried to block 23andMe's tests on the basis that they are not ordered through physicians. More recently, in November 2013, the US Food and Drug Administration (FDA) ordered 23andMe to stop marketing its health reports because the agency determined that the service is technically a medical device and therefore requires FDA clearance as such.[12] In response to such setbacks, Wojcicki maintains deep faith in the end state but a willingness to be flexible about the means by which it is realized.

Clearly, there is a long way to go—and she knows she will have to persevere amid skepticism and opposition from vested interests in the health-care industry that may be uncomfortable with the model. But Wojcicki is unfazed by the challenge. She said that her early career working with the Wallenbergs, the Swedish billionaire family that runs one of Europe's most prominent investment businesses, taught her "the concept of putting capital at risk, dreaming big, and thinking about how society would or could change." She continued: "Some investors want to invest in radical change—only one out of fifty might be successful, but it will be radically successful. I want to take big bets. I'm in this for the radical change."

When to Apply a Visionary Approach

You should deploy a visionary approach to strategy when you have an opportunity to create or re-create an industry single-handedly by applying a bold vision at the right moment. That is, a visionary approach is appropriate when your company faces an environment that is malleable and, because of your firm's timely action and power to shape it, is predictable to you. Visionary circumstances can arise when you spot an emerging megatrend before another firm spots or acts on it, when technological change opens up the possibility to reshape an industry, or when unaddressed customer dissatisfaction with the dominant offering creates the possibility of a new market.

Since there is only a short moment between the opportunity opening up and the first reaction by other players, timing is critical. Successful visionary firms capitalize on this gap between the emergence of the opportunity, the recognition and acceptance of the idea, and the reaction by established players. Fortunately for visionary entrepreneurs, other firms' reaction is often delayed by initial skepticism and organizational inertia. On the demand side, timing is also critical: too early, and your potential customers may not be ready to accept your vision; too late, and you are seen as an imitator or a follower.

In our analysis, we found that many business leaders claim to employ a visionary approach, whereas fewer environments can objectively be categorized as sufficiently predictable and malleable. This conflict between perception and reality suggests that leaders may overestimate the extent to which markets are malleable and a visionary approach is applicable.

Therefore, let's take a closer look at the three signals that help identify the pivotal moment in an industry when a visionary strategy can be applied. One signal is emerging megatrends, large structural shifts that can reshape the market and that go beyond industry-specific supply and demand conditions. Examples are the aging of the world's population and the rise of the middle classes in China, India, and other rapidly developing economies. Other megatrends include urbanization, nanotechnology, obesity and dieting, wealth disparities, and the loss of trust in institutions.[13] Another signal

WHAT YOU MIGHT KNOW IT AS

Many leaders will instinctively associate entrepreneurial start-ups with visionary strategy: young, small, agile firms are often the players that create new markets or disrupt existing ones. However, entrepreneurialism has not always been treated as a fully valid form of strategy, because it is rarely accompanied by sophisticated planning techniques. In the early 1990s, however, academics began to seriously observe and appreciate the relevance of an entrepreneurial approach to strategy as more firms rode the wave of accelerating technological change to rapid success.

W. Chan Kim and Renée Mauborgne's *blue ocean strategy* deals with strategies for creating uncontested market spaces. Gary Hamel and C. K. Prahalad, in their book *Competing for the Future*, suggested that leaders should develop their firm's ability to mold the future. Clayton Christensen's *disruptive-innovation* concept explained how some companies can disrupt mature industries by simplifying their products and services, creating a base from which to assault entrenched mainstream competitors, and driving them into margin retreat. And BCG has pioneered the technique of *learning from mavericks*, a practice that enables large companies to recognize and tap into potentially disruptive entrepreneurial activity on the fringes of their industry.[14]

is the emergence of a new technology, like the automobile or mobile phone, which may provide entirely novel or disruptive opportunities in existing markets. A third is consumer dissatisfaction or unmet needs with the status quo offering. This can be explicit in the minds of consumers, but more often it is latent—consumers may not have a clear idea of what they are missing.

As turbulence has increased over the past two decades, the risk that large firms will suffer a disruption to their business model has also increased significantly. Because of more rapid technological change, especially with respect to computing power, connectivity, and mobility, we now see more frequently than ever the small firms—the Davids—conspicuously unseating incumbent Goliaths. As discussed in chapter 3, leading firms in an industry are three times more likely to lose their position in a given year than they were in the early 1960s (figure 3-4). Low-cost carriers challenge the long-haul airlines, car rental giants compete against car-sharing companies with entirely new business models, and cloud storage firms may render hard-drive manufacturers obsolete. Large, established companies are particularly vulnerable, finding it more difficult to mobilize at exactly the right moment, for several reasons: their commitment to the status quo, the inertia that often accompanies size, and their natural tendency to filter change signals through their own dominant logic. If they don't act, however, the chances are increasingly high that others will act, to the big players' detriment.

But at the same time, large companies have a few potential advantages in capitalizing on a visionary opportunity, if they can overcome their own inertia: the move may require sizable investment to reach scale quickly and considerable persistence and resources in the face of potential setbacks. In fact, well-resourced large firms can develop into formidable visionary players, as long as they do so at the right time, with the right degree of boldness.

Betting on the e-Commerce Vision at UPS

One big company that anticipated a major shift in its industry with a visionary approach is UPS. Founded in 1907 as the American Messenger Company, the United Parcel Service became one of the biggest parcel delivery firms in the country.[15] As such, it succeeded by taking a classical approach, capitalizing on its scale and market dominance (see chapter 2). But in 1994, even before Amazon.com was born, UPS saw that the trends of increased connectivity and digitization presaged a major industry shift toward e-commerce and spotted an opportunity to become "the enablers of global e-commerce."[16]

To realize this vision, it invested heavily, resolving to spend $1 billion per year on the required IT systems.[17] This boldness attracted the business of some of the biggest e-commerce companies, which typically increased their shipping volumes by up to 20 percent per year for about a decade. At the same time, UPS bolstered its brand image as the preferred online delivery service by making it easy for corporate customers to embed its leading-edge shipping and tracking functionality in their websites. In one high-profile pact, UPS gave eBay users direct access to UPS shipping options, making it simpler for them to ship packages—which had been a hurdle in completing consumer-to-consumer auctions.[18] By the year 2000, the results of this far-sighted strategy were clear: UPS owned more than 60 percent of the U.S. e-commerce shipping market.[19]

ARE YOU IN A VISIONARY BUSINESS ENVIRONMENT?

You are facing a visionary business opportunity if the following observations hold true:

✓ Your industry provides a white-space (uncontested) opportunity or is ripe for disruption.

✓ Your industry can be (re)shaped by an individual firm.

✓ Your industry is marked by sleepy incumbents.

✓ Your industry is suffering from unsatisfied consumers and unmet needs.

✓ Your industry displays high growth potential.

✓ Innovation in your industry is subject to few regulatory barriers.

The Visionary Approach in Practice: Strategizing

So how do firms put the envisage, build, and persist triad into action? Getting it right is hard. The fact that eight out of ten entrepreneurs fail underlines this difficulty.[20]

Visionary strategizing is all about envisaging the end point: a new opportunity and a value proposition that addresses the opportunity. But a visionary approach then requires a distinctive and coherent approach to implementation: a charismatic leader and an inspiring vision statement are necessary but insufficient. Implementation of the visionary approach corresponds to the building and persisting steps in the triad and requires appropriate information, innovation, organization, culture, and leadership to support building the end state fast without being preempted, and a flexibility to overcome unforeseen roadblocks along the way.

Navigating the tension between a fixed goal and flexible means is difficult and something few companies are able to realize in practice. In our survey, we found that 95 percent of the companies intending to employ a visionary approach still use detailed forecasts and plans that outline each step on the journey as if it could be preplanned, a distinctively classical practice that potentially leads to rigidity in the means of execution. Let's see how to align vision and execution.

Pull something out of midair that has never been tried before but is a sure enough bet that you can bank you career and firm on it and, in fact, can expect it to transform an industry. No small task, but that is the central aim of visionary strategizing: it's all about envisaging the end point that your firm will pursue relentlessly. The steps for success are to identify an opportunity with the right timing, to formulate a vision and a high-level plan that addresses it, and to communicate the vision broadly to gain market acceptance.

Identify an Opportunity

To start formulating a vision, you need to spot a nascent opportunity before anyone else acts upon it. There are four signals that point to the all-important industry turning point and serve as triggers for a visionary approach: the three signals mentioned earlier—megatrends, individual breakthrough technologies, and customer dissatisfaction—and, in addition, the activity of players at the fringes of your industry, the so-called mavericks. It's key to spot each of those signals before others do so and to go beyond taking them at face value but rather to see the possibilities inherent in them to uncover what could be, rather than just seeing what is.

You need to deeply understand emerging trends to steer into them at the right moment or to connect the dots between converging trends to identify a singular window of opportunity. This is the case at 23andMe, where the vision derived from seeing how new developments in both genetics and digital technology could permit the emergence of a consumer-driven genetics opportunity. The key to such trend mapping is to envisage the reality that could be, as 23andMe did when it priced its products ahead of the experience curve to bring the price to below $100.[21]

Going beyond the face value of information is also important in uncovering an opportunity in consumer dissatisfaction or unmet needs. To detect dissatisfaction signals, you often need to look beyond mainstream demand or satisfaction scores for existing products or services and focus on pioneering users, dissatisfied users, lapsed users, and nonusers. For instance, you can identify and focus on small, poorly served groups of customers at the fringes of your market or on an opportunity to serve existing demand more simply, cheaply, or effectively. Importantly, you should not just solicit the views of your current customers and employees, since the first glimpse of the next big thing often lies with nonusers. As Steve Jobs, founder of Apple, once observed: "You can't just ask customers what they want and then try to give that to them. By the time you get it built, they'll want something new."[22]

We have often seen how companies exploiting the white space between the mainstream products and services offered by incumbents can enjoy success. Take, for example, Intuitive Surgical, a surgical-robot manufacturer founded in 1995.[23] The company saw an unexploited opportunity to provide surgeons with sophisticated tools to help them perform minimally invasive surgeries, thereby improving patient safety and reducing costs. By identifying such opportunities and serving needs that had been previously unaddressed, Intuitive Surgical has seen stellar growth and realized annual revenues exceeding $2 billion.[24]

Finally, for large companies, it is always important to monitor the small companies at the fringes of your industry. These smaller players may have done something you haven't considered—tapping into a new technology, a source of consumer dissatisfaction, or an emerging megatrend—because they couldn't feasibly compete with you directly. Looking at large, well-established, and better-known competitors will more than likely reinforce your existing beliefs. It's these smaller companies with new ideas that you can learn from, partner with, or, if necessary, buy to address visionary opportunities. GE routinely buys or invests in ten to twenty smaller companies every year to gain access to their innovations.[25] We will explore how to identify and leverage these mavericks later in the chapter.

Formulate Your Vision

Once you have detected an opportunity, you need to create the vision that addresses that opportunity—to articulate a vivid, bold picture of what you will build. The vision will often comprise not only a new product or service offering but also a new business model to fully exploit it. A business model innovation is one that changes multiple elements of the way you service customers and create value. It can perhaps best be defined as the reorchestration of all assets and capabilities of a company to realize a disruptive value proposition. Hence, a business model innovation requires a quantum leap, rather than incremental and individual changes in services, products, or operations (figure 4-2). It might include changing the distribution or revenue model or your value chain footprint to fully harness the power of a new technology, or the reconceptualization of the product or service. For this reason, the new vision differs fundamentally from typical vision statements of large companies; these tend to be nebulously broad affirmations of the companies' current business models.

For Anne Wojcicki, the opportunity for a new type of company was clear. "No one had done what we'd done," she said. "We started saying, 'We're not a health-care company—we are totally outside the established order.'" This attitude allowed her to think about the possibilities of combining a

FIGURE 4-2

Business model innovation framework

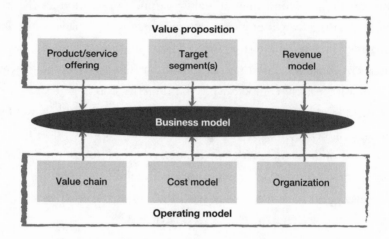

Source: Zhenya Lindgardt, Martin Reeves, George Stalk, and Mike Deimler, "Business Model Innovation: When the Going Gets Tough," *BCG Perspectives*, December 2009.

product based on genetic testing and ancestry, with a new operating model that leveraged the power of big data, e-commerce, and a consumer-centric revenue approach.

Sketching the Plan

Given that a visionary approach involves a fixed goal but flexible means to overcome hurdles to achieve it, the approach is more like a long-distance road map that allows for flexibility along the way. Because you are, by definition, charting unknown territory, you can be sure that some unexpected obstacles will force you to adjust course. Therefore, a visionary approach does not rely on the kind of elaborate documentation of detailed financial and operational milestones that you would prepare for a classical approach, even if some investors may require them. Instead, it defines high-level milestones to keep you pointing in the right direction and moving speedily toward your end vision.

As Wojcicki told us: "My dream has always been the end goal: changing the landscape of how the individual gets health care—but I never had a strong marriage to a particular path of how to get there." Although she said the company "need[s] a 'plan' to execute on the vision," the one she has devised allows for many amendments and has served 23andMe well. "The one thing that we're very good at is changing the plan as we hit multiple roadblocks or unexpected opportunities—like when we got additional funding and dropped the price [of our DNA test] to $99," said Wojcicki. "We changed the strategy from going for profitability to going for growth." What hasn't changed is the vision.

Communicate Your Vision Broadly

Finally, your vision will not be realized until it has been accepted by a critical mass of customers and investors. The visionary approach may naturally be met with skepticism since it presents something new that not only may be unfamiliar but also may even contradict more familiar ways of doing and thinking about the business. Therefore, as you develop your strategy, you need to communicate—or rather, overcommunicate—to convince customers to buy and investors to invest. In particular, you should overcommunicate the vision to your employees and customers since both groups will become your advocates and brand evangelists. Finally, you should celebrate and broadcast early wins that demonstrate that your vision has traction and is credible.

Since you are creating a new market, you are preaching to the unconverted. So you need to dedicate time and effort to inspiring and educating consumers and investors, including tailoring your message to the level of the uninitiated. "The average individual just didn't know why they should get their genome," said Ms. Wojcicki. "So educating the individual and getting them excited about it was our first challenge."

Speed Is Key: Strategizing at Mobiquity

Another company taking the visionary approach to strategy is Mobiquity, a US-based professional services firm that helps companies harness the power of mobile technology—sometimes dubbed "the fifth wave of computing" (after the mainframe, the minicomputer, the personal computer, and the internet PC).[26] Bill Seibel and Scott Snyder founded Mobiquity in 2011 after they detected an opportunity: while many companies were building mobile apps for large corporations, few companies yet seemed to provide a full-service offering to build data structures, business processes, and support platforms to ensure that mobile technologies were fully integrated into the customer's business model.

Mobiquity recognized early on the emergence of the mobile technology megatrend. "We realized that there was this train coming down the track that was more transformational and innovative than executives were giving it credit for," says Snyder, Mobiquity's president and chief strategy officer. In fact, Mobiquity expects mobile to account for 35 percent of IT budgets in 2015.[27]

Snyder resists the temptation to construct formal strategic plans, since "it would be too reactive and constraining for what's actually happening day-to-day." Instead, Mobiquity focused on the vision and a general plan to realize it, and this approach has stood the test of time: "The strategy we put together is still 90 percent intact and is still the one we anchor against," Snyder said. Snyder and Seibel also took care to communicate their vision, starting with the formation of a Wireless Innovation Council, which enlisted major companies like GE, Marriott, and Fidelity and research institutions like Babson College to create awareness and credibility. The council creates an environment where strategic decision makers from different industries collaborate to uncover new innovation opportunities.

Speed has been key to Mobiquity's success. The pace of mobile technology is fast, and so, as Snyder says, "we had to architect a firm that could run the whole relay race, quickly." The firm did this by "blend[ing] the best of design agencies like IDEO with the skills of integrators like IBM and scal[ing] it fast." The concept is to combine the best of strategy, design, and technology with development skills to execute across the full vision. The prize, of course, is first-mover advantage. "Because we're one or two years ahead of competition, we can anticipate what the future needs are going to be, design products for that, and then partner with our clients to test and roll them out." To stay ahead of the curve, Mobiquity also created Mobiquity Labs, a unique environment for rapid experimentation and co-innovation with its clients.

Within two years, Mobiquity had opened twelve offices around the world and developed a client list featuring a major share of *Fortune* 1,000 companies. Its revenue has gone from $5 million to $24 million with a book of outstanding work totaling $40 million.[28]

SIMULATING STRATEGY IN A MALLEABLE, PREDICTABLE ENVIRONMENT

In our classical and adaptive simulation of strategic options in stable or unpredictable environments, we assumed that the environment existed independently of any particular strategy or player. However, sometimes companies shape the environment by creating new strategic options, for instance, through white-space innovation or by increasing the value of existing options.

To reflect such an environment, we simulated malleable options that increase in value when a company invests in them for a certain amount of time. The resource investment is high, but so is the potential payoff.

The resulting optimal strategy in a malleable environment is to analyze, or envisage, which option would have the highest reward for a sufficient investment. Once the option with the highest potential is identified, one needs to stick with the option and invest in it to reap returns (figure 4-3). This mirrors what visionary leaders do when they anchor on a vision after a period of lengthy or deep exploration and zealously pursue it.

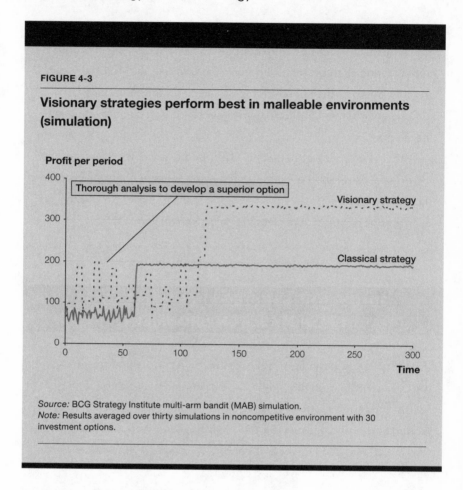

FIGURE 4-3

Visionary strategies perform best in malleable environments (simulation)

Profit per period

Thorough analysis to develop a superior option

Visionary strategy

Classical strategy

Time

Source: BCG Strategy Institute multi-arm bandit (MAB) simulation.
Note: Results averaged over thirty simulations in noncompetitive environment with 30 investment options.

The Visionary Approach in Practice: Implementation

The organization is the vehicle for realizing the vision, persisting flexibly in the face of unexpected obstacles, and executing fast to stay ahead of others. Therefore, the organization's guiding principles are goal clarity, speed, and flexibility of means, all the way from information management to organizational structure to leadership.

Information

As we've seen, detecting new opportunities early and acting on them more quickly and decisively than others is one of the critical success factors for a visionary approach. To use information successfully, aspiring visionary firms leverage it by scanning for and identifying opportunities to create a new market reality, by looking beyond the face value of signals to uncover the possibility of what could be. As Henry Ford, father of the automotive industry, reputedly remarked: "If I had asked my customers what they wanted, they would have said a faster horse."[29] For this reason, the information challenge for visionary companies is one of imagination, but is informed by real-world signals on trends, technologies, and customers.

Taking this view of what could be requires you as a leader to step back and challenge your own established view on your industry and your firm and to overcome blind spots in your current perspectives. You also need to look at information beyond the confines of your own comfort zone— beyond your company, your country, your commercial sector, your customers, and the prevailing wisdom—to see new possibilities. Sometimes, this may require putting some mental, if not physical, distance between yourself and the day-to-day business. At the height of Microsoft's dizzying rise in the mid-1990s, Bill Gates was known for taking two "think weeks" a year. He retreated from family and friends so that he could consider new and creative ideas.[30]

Established companies may find it particularly hard to create such distance or to look at their industry in a new way. Large firms can employ a *maverick scan*, an exercise that allows you to see hints of your industry's future by observing mavericks—often small players at the fringes of your industry— that may be betting against your business model. Then, you identify what their big idea is and the bet that they are making. Next, you consider what the implications for your firm *would be* if their idea proves correct. From there, you can determine what your response to those ideas is: wait to gain more information, ignore, replicate, neutralize, or buy. Facebook, for instance, continuously scans for potential disrupters at the fringes of its industry and asks what the impact on its own business model would be if these mavericks were to succeed. Sometimes, this tactic leads to new products and services or, sometimes, to large-scale acquisitions of businesses, as with Instagram and WhatsApp.[31] Scanning mavericks successfully helps large firms "stay big by acting small."

While digital technology creates many opportunities for new vision-ary strategies, expensive IT systems in themselves are not required to detect a visionary opportunity. Dennis Gillings made his observations while consulting big pharma companies, Amazon.com's Jeff Bezos sup-posedly read a report on the rise of e-commerce, and Steve Jobs had a picture in his mind of the unique product created by the combination of an MP3 player and phone in a touch-screen device. Other approaches—notably adaptive strategy—often do need powerful computing to sift for patterns in small changes in the environment. While a visionary firm may utilize such data-crunching, more important is looking beyond the obvious for new, disruptive insights. Rather, it's the search for what could be versus what is that pervades the initial phases of a visionary approach.

Innovation

Since the visionary approach creates an entirely new market reality, innova-tion naturally plays a critical role in defining and realizing the vision. This innovation is fast and bold, revolutionary but not evolutionary. To ensure speed and the concentration of resources, innovation efforts generally focus on a big one-off bet rather than a scattered portfolio of options, especially for smaller companies with limited resources. When Bezos was asked how much he was prepared to spend on the Kindle project, he replied: "How much do we have?"[32]

There are three main ways to achieve such innovation: the application of a new technology, the innovation of a business model, and the application of existing capabilities from one industry to another.

You can invent, or be the first to apply, a new technology. Across busi-ness history, many successful companies were the first to make main-stream use of great inventions: AT&T and the telephone, IBM and the personal computer, Remington and the QWERTY typewriter. More recently, in 1999 the American firm TiVo introduced the first consumer digital video recorder (DVR), allowing viewers to skip commercials or to record specific shows.[33] Because of its first-mover position, the word

"TiVo" became practically synonymous with time-shifted digital video recording and viewing.

A second way to innovate is to develop a new business model—a different way of delivering value to customers. A good example is Zipcar, the car-sharing service founded by Antje Danielson and Robin Chase in 2000. They saw that car ownership rates were declining and, in light of greater urbanization and the growing emphasis on environmentally friendly activities, Danielson and Chase saw an opportunity to launch a new way of renting cars.[34]

A third way to innovate is to transfer your capabilities from one industry to another, as Louis Dreyfus Group has done. Founded in 1851, its core business is agricultural commodities. But, in 1998, it entered the telecommunications infrastructure business, competing with the established leader, France Telecom. Despite having no prior experience in that industry, Louis Dreyfus's knowledge of volatile commodities businesses gave it an advantage in navigating the boom-bust cycle of the recently deregulated telecom market. The firm leveraged its ability to choose the right moment to invest in financing infrastructure and then again to profitably dispose of those assets.[35]

Organization

The visionary organization must deliver the vision quickly, with fidelity to the goal, but also with flexibility to overcome unforeseen obstacles. And as the vision matures, the organization needs to eventually anticipate the requirements of the next approach to strategy. To ensure focus on the goal while avoiding rigidity, visionary organizations combine top-down direction setting with a flexible, informal organization that minimizes cumbersome rules and processes. To achieve scale and professionalization as the vision matures, the organization eventually switches to the organizational requirements of a new approach to strategy.

Explicit guiding principles and a clear direction, set from the top, help to focus the visionary organization. Mobiquity learned that lesson quickly when, initially, the firm did not communicate its direction or individuals' roles and responsibilities clearly enough and too many people tried to take the firm's direction into their own hands. "After a year," recalled Snyder, "we realized that we'd hired the best guys, but that we had seventeen former CEOs in the company. We were like the US Olympic basketball team that lost the gold medal in 2008: great athletes, wrong team, too many leadership genes. We needed employees who put the firm above themselves." He reformed the leadership team, and as Mobiquity expanded, he developed a more focused approach so that clients would receive a uniform service whether they were based in Atlanta, Amsterdam, or Ahmedabad. "We had to get the formula right and then scale it as little geographical business units that run identically." In other words, visionary organizations do not need the same level or kind of organizational diversity we saw in adaptive companies, because the direction is preset.

While clarity of direction is crucial, only the long-term goal is fixed. Consequently, firms need short-term flexibility for rapidly spotting and overcoming unexpected roadblocks. As Bezos said: "We don't focus on the optics of the next quarter, we focus on what's going to be good for customers."[36] To maintain short-term flexibility, visionary firms are usually informal, allocate resources with flexibility, and limit their detailed operating procedures or specialization. They maintain cross-functional teams and encourage direct communication between top management and the shop floor to help facilitate rapid decision making and execution. That means that visionary firms do not require the kind of detailed operating procedures that classical firms employ to increase efficiency or to make execution consistent.

This mind-set shift is particularly difficult but important for large corporations attempting to adopt a visionary approach. For these organizations, entrenched processes do not easily convert into the informal and flexible ones that support a visionary approach. As we will discuss later in the book, large firms might therefore need to separate their visionary units from the core business.

As we saw with Quintiles, which eventually made the transition to a more classical approach, the visionary approach is more frequently the beginning than the end of a strategic journey. Hence, successful visionary leaders anticipate and gradually introduce features of the next required strategic approach into the organization, usually moving toward a more classical approach to strategy and execution. An eventual switch toward another approach is usually necessary because the informality and top-down focus on a single purpose that make visionary firms great can sometimes self-limit them as they scale and mature. "As a function of size and age, there will be change," Wojcicki explained. "We're 140 people, our budgets are much bigger [than when we started], and we [now] have people who know how to manage! In the early days, it's great as a start-up without much management. But after a while, people want to mature and have more structure."

Culture

Consistent with the implications for organization, a visionary culture combines a clear sense of direction to ensure speed with a certain degree of flexibility to overcome hurdles along the way. Most importantly, the culture encourages employees to chase something that others might not yet see, with a hint of "us against the world." Such a culture focuses energy on the vision's realization and sparks the individual's passion and creativity to accelerate that process. Visionary cultures are anchored on their vision, which provides a cultural pole star. Wojcicki said: "I love the potential of the company. This may sound trite, but it applies to us and many other start-ups: if we are successful, 23andMe will truly change the world." By anchoring on the mission, employees not only internalize it but also serve as brand or product ambassadors: ideally, a visionary firm's employees are its biggest groupies. The culture also needs to encourage boundless opportunity for individual initiative that accelerates the vision's actualization, and such an aspirational culture can be a powerful recruiting tool. As Wojcicki said: "I need to create a culture that will bring in . . . the great people to make hard decisions about supertechnical areas."

Finally, as the vision matures, the firm shifts its cultural mind-set to begin moving to another approach. For instance, the firm could become more externally oriented or systematic in an adaptive or classical spirit.

Leadership

The successful leader of a company taking a visionary approach fully embodies the *envisage, build, and persist* dynamic from end to end: you have the eureka moment, and you set a clear direction. You are the chief evangelist and keeper of the flame; you build the organization to deliver the vision, communicate the end state, and celebrate early wins. And you visibly commit—and recommit and recommit—to seeing the vision to fruition. "I'm convinced that about half of what separates the successful entrepreneurs from the non-successful ones is pure perseverance," said Steve Jobs.[37] Finally, you need to guide the firm through the difficult, but necessary transition to other approaches after the visionary one comes to a natural end.

Fortunately, charisma and enthusiasm are rarely challenges for the visionary leader: he or she is often a pragmatic dreamer. "I see myself as the visionary strategist that's trying to pioneer in an area that doesn't exist," said Wojcicki. "I've always been the kind of person who's not afraid of being unemployed or about doing something and not having it work. I accept the fact that there's risk—but to me, the worst thing in life is just to accept the status quo. To sit there and say, 'This is just the way the health-care system works.' I would much, much rather put my time and effort into changing it . . . The downside is to say, 'I just accept a broken system.'"

Finally, the leader must recognize when to shift strategic approaches. As discussed earlier, business environments conducive to the successful application of a visionary approach rarely persist for very long. As we have seen with Quintiles, the company has already moved from a visionary to a classical approach. Gillings, its founder, reflected on this transition and said that visionary firms need to systematize as the firm matures: "As our industry developed, you saw what I would call a systematization of the visionary strategy."

Few people can combine these divergent characteristics. But those who can do so are equipped to transform their business and their industry.

**ARE YOUR ACTIONS CONSISTENT WITH A
VISIONARY APPROACH?**

You are embodying a visionary approach if you observe the following
actions:

✓ You observe gaps in the status quo offering of the industry.

✓ You create a vision of what could be.

✓ You build a high-level plan toward the end state.

✓ You persist in realizing your vision.

✓ You adapt flexibly to obstacles along the way.

Tips and Traps

As we've seen throughout this chapter, the keys to a successful visionary
approach are being the first to spot and act on a new opportunity before
others do, building a business model to address it, and persisting flexibly in
the face of inevitable roadblocks. But as we also discussed, nearly 80 percent
of entrepreneurs fail—and not just because of bad business ideas.

In our survey, we found that business environments are most commonly
perceived as visionary, despite the actual measured conditions. The survey
betrays a bias toward overestimating how malleable and predictable environments actually are. Furthermore, judging from the reported practices of companies, the visionary approach is also the most commonly practiced approach
to strategy, again despite the actual declared strategy and environmental
conditions. This conflict between perception and reality probably reflects the
same biases as well as a high degree of familiarity with visionary techniques.

Table 4-1 lays out some of the tips and traps you might encounter when
selecting and applying the visionary approach.

TABLE 4-1

Tips and traps: key contributors to success and failure in a visionary approach

Tips	Traps
• *Understand that timing is everything:* Take advantage of a turning point in your industry's or market's development. Act neither too early nor too late, by spotting and acting on an opportunity before others do.	• *Confusing detailed planning with clear direction:* A detailed plan is not the same as a clear direction. You should expect to adjust your plan as you go. The only thing you should keep fixed is the vision.
• *Create a bold vision:* Be revolutionary (not evolutionary) by looking beyond your company's or customers' current world view to envisage a fundamentally new and better way of doing business.	• *Pursuing a delusional vision:* Firms or founders embrace a fleeting fad or become obsessed with an idea, not a legitimate opportunity. You'll be making a big bet, so be as certain as you can that the odds are in your favor.
• *Be first and stay first:* There is no prize for being second in a winner-takes-all game, especially in businesses with network effects and stakeholder lock-in.	• *Incrementalism:* No visionary leader ever changed the world by taking baby steps. Companies that take this bold approach must have a compelling vision.
• *Have a clear vision and flexible means:* Be flexible in the short-term tactics to pursue the long-term end to navigate unexpected obstacles.	• *Being slow to act:* Every company needs process—but avoid overly bureaucratic procedures that prevent you from being first and staying first. Look for investors who value growth over profitability in the near term.
• *Communicate, communicate, communicate:* Your vision is radical: you need to tell people about it—and inspire them. Only then will your workers work their hardest for you, your investors invest in you, and your consumers buy what you have to offer.	• *Failing to convince:* It's one thing to have a vision, quite another to persuade people of its power. Companies that fail to develop a tight value proposition to educate colleagues, customers, and investors won't get traction.
• *Set up the next game:* If you are successful, you will become the market leader, and that will eventually require a different approach to strategy. Make sure you're prepared for this strategic transition.	• *Staying visionary forever:* The visionary approach is only appropriate for so long in the company life cycle. Once the business is established, companies may need to adopt other approaches to sustain competitive advantage.
• *Aim for the sky, but kiss the ground:* It is hard but necessary to balance idealism and realism. Dream big *and* attend to the details.	• *Perception bias:* Be careful not to overestimate the malleability and predictability of the environment. Apply a visionary approach only where it is justified by careful observation.
	• *Visionary rhetoric:* Leaders are prone to use the word *visionary* lightly. Be careful not to confuse *vision* as a rhetorical flourish with the selection of the appropriate approach to strategy.

CHAPTER 5

SHAPING

Be the Orchestrator

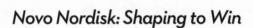

Novo Nordisk: Shaping to Win

When August Krogh cofounded Novo Nordisk in 1923 in Denmark, he couldn't have predicted that his firm would play a critical role in the development of China's sizable and booming insulin market. The company now controls about 60 percent of the market.[1]

Novo began building its Chinese insulin operation in the 1990s, well before the coming diabetes threat was widely appreciated or the market for diabetes care was fully developed. Early entry was critical, said CEO Lars Sørensen: "We came into China very early; we were one of the first international pharmaceutical companies that established a fully owned enterprise [there]."[2] When Novo came to China, diabetes awareness was low. There were no established treatment protocols, and Novo had no educated physician base that it could work with to fight the disease. Then, diabetes was thought to affect 2.5 percent of the Chinese population, but the disease was underdiagnosed; today, approximately one in ten Chinese people are known to suffer from the chronic condition—some ninety-nine million patients.[3]

Initially, Novo tried to collaborate with local pharmaceutical companies to enter the Chinese market, said Sørensen, but found that those firms had little in the way of financial resources or technologies. Instead, Novo turned to other stakeholders to create a concerted effort to educate doctors, patients, and regulators to raise awareness and pioneer treatments.

Novo invested heavily in physician education to teach the medical community—potential customers and evangelists—about the diabetes threat and potential treatments. Sørensen established partnerships with the Chinese Ministry of Health and the World Diabetes Foundation, and Novo toured the countryside with its Changing Diabetes Bus program to reach remote rural physicians.[4] In total, Novo has facilitated more than two hundred thousand training sessions and congresses to improve screening, treatment, and patient education.[5]

Sørensen said that partnering with doctors and regulators was critical: "What we did initially, which is what we do everywhere in the world, is to start building a relationship with the government, explaining to them about diabetes, the problems they have and starting to educate the whole public health sector. To date, we have educated maybe 50,000 to 60,000 physicians in China about diabetes. So you could say our marketing in China has been education."[6]

Additionally, Novo reached out to patients to improve grassroots understanding. Its innovative support group, NovoCare Club, has more than nine hundred thousand members and redefines the drug company's role. More than just a provider of insulin, the company has become a partner in care, offering dietary and lifestyle support and mechanisms to help manage the medication regimen.[7]

Finally, Novo invested in local communities to get a seat at the table with policy makers. In 1995, the firm opened its first production site, and in 2002, Novo became the first pharmaceutical multinational to open an R&D center in China.[8] Sørensen says that these investments gave Novo the opportunity to help drive the development of nationwide clinical treatment guidelines through close work with the government and the China Diabetes Society.

As a result of these interconnected efforts, Novo has grown awareness and codeveloped treatment standards to support diabetes care, earning a leading market position along the way. By 2010, the company's share of the country's diabetes care market was twice that of its nearest competitor—in a market where the number of diabetes patients is expected to double by 2025.[9]

Sørensen explained how this shaping approach is a blueprint for his company's strategy in other emerging markets: "The strategy we employ is exactly the same in emerging economies . . . Basically, we start by building a relationship with the ministry of health, with the medical association for diabetes and with the patient associations, and then start to educate doctors about diabetes. That means that after they start diagnosing people with diabetes, they can start treating them. We teach them how to treat the patients and they eventually end up buying our products. It's a very simple model."[10]

The Shaping Approach to Strategy: Core Idea

Like Novo, you sometimes get the extraordinary opportunity to shape or reshape an industry at an early point in its development, when rules have not yet been written and there is an opportunity for the industry to become large, attractive, and favorable to you, the shaper. Such an opportunity both permits and requires you to collaborate with others because you cannot shape the industry alone—you need others to share the risk, supply complementary capabilities and resources, and build the market quickly. A shaping firm operates under a high degree of unpredictability, given the nascent stage of industry evolution it faces and the participation of multiple stakeholders that it must influence but cannot control.

In these highly malleable and unpredictable circumstances, in order to succeed, firms *engage* other stakeholders to create a shared vision at the right point in time, building a platform through which they can exercise influence and *orchestrate* the collaboration, and finally they *evolve* the platform and ecosystem by scaling it and keeping it flexible (figure 5-1).

FIGURE 5-1

The shaping approach to strategy

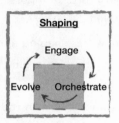

To return to our art metaphor, shaping is like creating a large mural with the help of many artists. You have to engage them with a compelling shared vision and, to avoid chaos, deploy your influence to orchestrate the efforts of the painters. You leverage their creativity by iterating on the emerging design as you proceed.

When applied successfully, a shaping approach can be extremely rewarding: a group of firms or stakeholders together creates a new market with the shaping firm as orchestrator, often with a disproportionate capture of rewards relative to latecomers. The parallel efforts of diverse ecosystem participants allow for faster innovation at lower costs and risks for any single participant, which allows the system to grow rapidly and to adapt quickly to change. Moreover, business ecosystems can be extraordinarily powerful because they can benefit from strong lock-in and network effects. What's more, there is often only room for a single orchestrator and ecosystem to serve an entire market.

Since shaping firms operate in unpredictable environments, the approach shares some features with the adaptive approach: the dynamics of the new industry cannot be fully anticipated and will emerge evolutionarily via multiple iterations. But, like visionary organizations, shaping firms presume that the environment is malleable and seek to exploit a window of opportunity to define or redefine an industry to address a new problem or solve an existing one in a much better way. However, because the scope of the endeavor is greater and more unpredictable, instead of making a singular bet and going it alone, the shaping firm builds a new market collaboratively with other players. Even though many firms aspire to a shaping role, they rarely have the power and opportunity to play a central role in the evolution of an industry and to reap its disproportionate benefits.

WHAT YOU MIGHT KNOW IT AS

The notion that businesses can be successful by both collaborating and competing with external parties has its origins in *ecological thinking*, where concepts like symbiosis, or mutually beneficial relationships between organisms, originated. In the 1960s, Bruce Henderson already drew elaborate comparisons between competition in the natural and business spheres. More recently, *complex adaptive systems theory* has explored how such dynamic collaborative systems behave and evolve.[11]

Stakeholder management theory, or the notion that external stakeholders should be considered in designing business strategy, emerged in the 1980s. Initially this concept emphasized the wider implications of firm actions but did not focus on the codevelopment of markets.[12]

The early 1990s saw an increase in high-tech businesses using "deconstructed" business models, with one company orchestrating the activities of many others. Greater connectivity and lower transaction costs fueled the trend. Business theorists like James Moore and, later, Marco Iansiti and Simon Levin formalized the concept of a *business ecosystem*: a set of firms that could benefit from mutually beneficial coevolution. Around the same time, Adam Brandenburger and Barry Nalebuff published the idea of *co-opetition*, which held that firms sometimes needed to cooperate with potential competitors, rather than just with external stakeholders not directly involved in the value chain.[13]

In 1999, BCG's Philip Evans and Tom Wurster, in their book *Blown to Bits*, explored how the *new economics of information* redefined the link between businesses and their customers, suppliers, and employees. The authors suggested new models for competition in digitally disrupted industries, including the "orchestrator" model, which is central to shaping strategies. Later, BCG elaborated the ideas of *system advantage* and *shaping strategies* as an alternative to classical scale and position-based strategies under certain circumstances.[14]

Henry Chesbrough codified the idea of *open innovation*, which advocates for the incorporation of external ideas and players in the innovation process to share resources and risks. In 2004, C. K. Prahalad and Venkat Ramaswamy introduced the concept of *cocreation* of products between firms and their customers, arguing that value creation was increasingly shifting beyond the traditional boundaries of the firm.[15]

When to Apply a Shaping Approach

Firms need to deploy a shaping strategy when there is an opportunity to write or rewrite the rules of an industry at a nascent stage of its evolution. These circumstances can apply in highly fragmented, young, dynamic industries; freshly disrupted industries; and emerging markets. In these cases, a shaping strategy can stimulate demand, build the economic infrastructure to address it, and minimize regulatory or other barriers as the market develops. Accelerating technological change and globalization make these opportunities evermore common.

Young or recently disrupted, dynamic industries, like software and internet services, offer significant upside to companies brave enough to try to shape them. The opportunities are intrinsically unpredictable: no one could have forecast with confidence the size, growth rate, and profitability of the markets created by Facebook or the pioneers of fracking. And such industries are malleable, too: barriers to entry are often low, products are new to regulators, and it is not obvious which firms or business models will come out on top. Disruptive innovation can have a similar effect too, thrusting a previously stable, nonmalleable industry into a new phase of unpredictability and malleability.

Emerging markets, like China and India, are characterized by similarly unpredictable and malleable circumstances: industries are at an early stage of their development, with underdeveloped regulation, few dominant players, and rapid growth. Our analysis suggests that emerging markets are fully twice as unpredictable and malleable as mature ones. Emerging markets greatly depend on exports and foreign direct investment and face vulnerability to fluctuations in commodity prices and exchange rates, shifting demographics and patterns of demand, evolving regulation, changing patterns of competition, and high growth rates (figure 5-2).

In these young industries and economies there is usually no dominant player with the resources or the risk tolerance to own the market single-handedly. Furthermore, product requirements in new markets are often unclear or change too quickly to be easily managed by a single player. Finally, firms may need to interact with a broad set of stakeholders, because the development of the market depends on shaping regulation or educating

FIGURE 5-2

Emerging markets are more malleable and unpredictable than developed ones

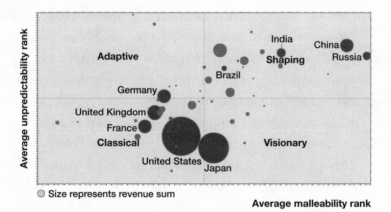

○ Size represents revenue sum

Source: Compustat, World Bank economic data, BCG analysis.

Note: Nonweighted average of industry environments within the country; uncertainty is measured as market-capitalization volatility and malleability using a composite index of growth, returns to scale, and industry fragmentation.

consumers. Therefore, the way to win is through codevelopment of the market and industry by multiple players.

Consider mobile phone ecosystems. The Android and iOS operating systems are much more attractive to customers because Google and Apple ceded control of app creation to outsiders during the infancy of the smartphone industry, inviting external developers onto their platforms in a mutually beneficial arrangement. At the same time, incumbent players like Nokia were challenged by legacy software architectures. The Symbian platform, used by most of the leading mobile phone companies before Android and iOS emerged, lacked the architectural flexibility and proper app store infrastructure to create a wide variety of apps quickly.[16] Conversely, Apple's App Store became the thriving nexus for apps du jour developed by many players—apps from Angry Birds to Candy Crush.[17] Stephen Elop, the former Nokia CEO, reflected on the competitive dynamic: "Our competitors aren't taking market share with devices; they are taking market share with an entire ecosystem."[18] Nokia has since reinvented itself: it has exited the mobile devices business to refocus on network equipment, technology licensing, and location intelligence.[19]

So what are some of the metrics that may suggest an unpredictable but malleable environment? Limited forecast accuracy and volatility in market cap, earnings, or competitive positions can signal unpredictability. Limited or diminishing returns to scale, high growth rates, lack of dominant incumbents, and embryonic and changing regulation suggest malleability.

Shaping conditions are on the rise because of accelerating technological change, increased global connectivity, the liberalization of trade, and demographic shifts that create new customer needs. However, external environmental conditions are not the only factor in considering whether you should adopt a shaping approach. Two other factors are critical: timing and your ability to orchestrate. Shaping strategists must seize an inflection point in the early development of a market or in the disruption of an existing one. And a firm must also have enough influence to attract other powerful stakeholders to its ecosystem. Most firms have insufficient influence to take a leading role, which partly explains why successful shaping strategies are rarer than the other approaches to strategy.

A firm may gain sufficient influence if, for instance, it innovates disruptively to put itself at the center of an ecosystem, as Apple did with its creation of the iTunes platform. Alternatively, a firm may secure influence through knowledge or scale advantage, like Novo in China; through the control of a dominant platform for interaction, like Facebook; or by serving as an access point to a fragmented customer or supplier base, like the supply chain orchestrator Li & Fung.

Lack of influence disqualifies firms from leading the shaping approach, but not from playing a role in an ecosystem: many firms build attractive businesses by participating in other firms' ecosystems, utilizing an adaptive or a classical approach. Zynga, Playfish, and Playdom, for example, have all developed multi-million-dollar businesses by participating on Facebook's platform as app developers.[20]

Why the Ecosystem Matters: Red Hat

Software provider Red Hat has built a $1 billion business by orchestrating the development of open-source software based upon the Linux language.[21] The company supports software development by outside developers, engages with enterprise communities, and monetizes its investments by selling subscriptions for professional-grade versions of free software.

How did Red Hat build such a successful business based on open-source software, which is essentially available free of charge, using resources the firm doesn't directly control? To start with, Red Hat has developed a clear, collaborative vision: "To be the catalyst in communities of customers, contributors, and partners creating better technology the open source way."[22]

The firm constantly and deeply engages its external collaborators. Red Hat never acts without considering the implications for its stakeholders, especially software developers. Jim Whitehurst, Red Hat's president and CEO, explained the importance of developing and evolving a win-win proposition: "When there are changes to make . . . we interact and consult carefully with all players in the system." And serving as system orchestrator can require selfless contribution to earn the trust and goodwill of other stakeholders: "We add a massive amount to Linux that isn't directly relevant to us—we are the largest contributor to virtually all open-source communities in which we participate. We choose to do it because it's what our ecosystem contributors use and value."

By being a responsible contributor to and orchestrator of its ecosystems, Red Hat accrues influence and license to monetize its services. Whitehurst, again: "Our strategy revolves around ecosystems: Scale is in our DNA for upstream credibility. We then work to build our own downstream commercial ecosystem around versions of open-source technologies that are unique to us." For instance, Red Hat's software certification program ensures that major applications from companies like SAP, Oracle, and IBM are guaranteed to work on Red Hat's open-source products, effectively establishing Red Hat as the industry standard for Linux in enterprise data centers. Through its large contributions to open-source projects, Red Hat can influence the direction of the open-source industry. Simultaneously, the firm creates a path to monetization via industrial-grade versions, certification services, customer service, and software maintenance, since the open-source community and its customers trust and value the Red Hat seal of approval.

On the flip side, Red Hat doesn't try to play in markets where it lacks sufficient influence. In other words, the firm carefully chooses where to employ a shaping strategy. Whitehurst explained: "Our key question is, can we construct the world of competition in a way that we can win? It's not about execution or playing by the rules. It's about defining the rules." Without the power to influence, a shaping strategy will fail. "If the rules are unfolding in a way that isn't playing to our strength," Whitehurst told us, "we will abandon the sector or change technologies: pedaling harder doesn't work."

The benefits for Red Hat as the orchestrator are significant. The company believes it can develop, launch, and adjust software much more quickly than traditional closed-source competitors, like Oracle or SAP. As a result of its successful shaping approach, Red Hat has seen its stock go from a low of $8 to over $50 between 2009 and 2014 and is the first open-source software company with annual revenues over $1 billion.[23]

The Shaping Approach in Practice: Strategizing

Applying a shaping approach effectively is easier said than done. In part because shaping is the least familiar approach to strategy for most firms, companies tend to use the concept very loosely, to overestimate the malleability of business environments, and to employ practices inconsistent with a true shaping approach. For instance, we found that roughly two-thirds of companies intending to use a shaping approach still create detailed long-term forecasts for their business, a typically classical practice. What's more,

ARE YOU IN A SHAPING BUSINESS ENVIRONMENT?

You are facing a shaping business situation if the following observations hold true:

✓ Your industry holds unexploited potential.

✓ Your industry is shapable through collaboration.

✓ Your industry's regulations are shapable.

✓ Your industry does not have a dominant player or platform.

less than half of firms think that their success depends on collaboration with others, and only a third actively try to change the external environment by influencing regulation. Clearly, there is a need to develop a deeper understanding of the challenging but powerful shaping approach.

As with the adaptive approach, the shaping strategy eventually emerges from continuous iteration of three elements—engagement, orchestration, and evolution of the ecosystem. Therefore, there is no clear separation between a strategizing phase and an execution phase, unlike a classical strategy. All three elements should therefore be deeply embedded in the intra- and inter-company structures and mechanisms.

Strategy setting for the shaping approach begins with engaging external stakeholders to develop a collaborative vision of the industry's development. Then, the orchestrator builds and operates a platform that brings together stakeholders and allows the orchestrator to exercise its influence to create and extract value from the ecosystem. Finally, the orchestrator evolves the platform and the ecosystem by scaling and extending it and keeping it flexible in the face of external change.

Engage Stakeholders

The benefit of a shaping strategy comes largely from harnessing the resources and capabilities of other powerful stakeholders, so the orchestrator must engage others in the setting of strategy. The orchestrator needs to develop a collaborative shared vision, identifying the best stakeholders to enlist to that vision, understanding and incorporating those stakeholders' interests, and launching the ecosystem at the right time.

Develop a Shaping Vision

A shaping vision outlines how the intended collaborators in the ecosystem can solve a problem dramatically better than any individual company could and how they can stimulate demand, build the economic infrastructure to address it, and remove potential constraints, like regulatory barriers, as the market develops. The vision needs to be mutualistic, emerging either through iteration with stakeholders or from within the orchestrator's firm.

The shaping vision needs to be win-win to enlist other stakeholders and should anticipate that the orchestrator needs to share resources without the expectation of an immediate return. These collaborative qualities build trust, goodwill, and influence—advantages that pay dividends down the road. Ideally, resources shared come at a limited cost, as in the case of Novo: Sørensen's firm shared its preexisting knowledge of diabetes care with Chinese doctors and regulators to secure them as future partners and, eventually, prescribers.

The shaping vision can emerge singularly or collaboratively. For instance, Novo single-handedly created its vision and then brought stakeholders on board, whereas Red Hat's vision emerged through iterative interactions with developer communities. Regardless, a shaper should think of vision setting as an ongoing conversation with its ecosystem coparticipants especially since it may sometimes be difficult to understand external parties' interests a priori and because those interests will evolve. Facebook, for example, changed the rules of its external development platform multiple times since its founding in 2007 to accommodate changing developer interests.[24] Classical strategy is often called competitive strategy: winning classical firms concentrate primarily on exceeding their competitors. In contrast, shaping strategy is essentially collaborative. In fact, if a shaping strategy is successful, competition may be a limited concern because of the strong network effects inherent in an ecosystem structure: the greater the number of participants, the greater the value of the system to those participants.

The shaping vision does not imagine a precise end state or a final product spec. Rather, it details the ecosystem's mutual value proposition: how value is created and shared by different players (figure 5-3). This is different from the vision in a visionary approach, which essentially imagines a specific outcome. It didn't matter to Apple that the most popular app in 2014 was Goblin Sword, and no longer Koi Pond, as it was in 2008, the year in which the App Store—the realization of the ecosystem vision—was launched.[25] What matters to Apple is that the system itself, rather than any specific app, stays attractive for developers and users and profitable for itself, the orchestrator. Several companies successfully deploying shaping strategies emphasized to us that tending an ecosystem was more about the catalysis of effective market mechanisms than "managing" toward specific outcomes.

FIGURE 5-3

Facebook's extensive app and web ecosystem

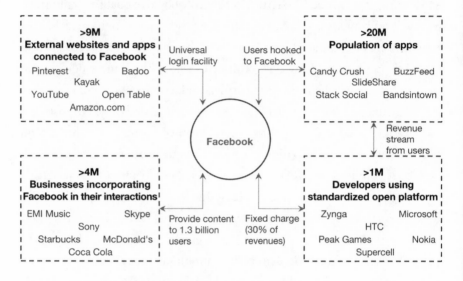

Source: Facebook annual reports; "Floating Facebook: The Value of Friendship," *The Economist*, February 4, 2012; Appdata.com; BCG analysis.

Identify Stakeholders and Understand Their Interests

To this point, we've stressed the importance of collaborating with multiple stakeholders. But this begs the question—which stakeholders? Whose resources or talents do you need? In some cases, like the Novo case study, the set of stakeholders can be easily identified in advance, but sometimes that is not possible or desirable. If the attractiveness of your platform depends on the variety and dynamism of its offering, then you need to cast the net widely. If you are developing a new market, you need key opinion leaders, firms that build complementary products, customers, and sometimes even competitors (Google Maps is one of the most popular apps in the Apple store).

The interests of the stakeholders in the ecosystem should be aligned with those of the ecosystem as a whole. Hence, the orchestrating firm should map how the interests of stakeholders fit with a potential ecosystem, how they contribute, and how they might influence other players. Are the stakeholders interested in obtaining access to your customer base, brand, or IP? Do they want to leverage your firm's scale or resources?

Launch Collaboration at the Right Moment

Finally, timing is key. Act too early, and market conditions may not be favorable enough yet to compel others to join; act too late, and an alternative platform with a different orchestrator may have already gained prominence, with potential network effects and lock-in making it impossible to catch up.

Orchestrate

Orchestrating the collaboration between many different, often-changing players requires building and operating a platform that facilitates interaction and monetization, locks in stakeholders, and provides a focal point for the shaper to deploy its influence. Let's look at these steps in detail.

Building a Platform

The goal of a platform is primarily to facilitate the direct interaction between ecosystem participants or between participants and customers. Therefore, the ideal platform reduces transaction costs for the stakeholders and management costs for the orchestrator. These would otherwise be prohibitive for large ecosystems, given their complexity. Successful platforms often provide feedback to participants so that they can adjust their contributions without direct, explicit mandates from the orchestrator. Finally, good platforms lock in value by inducing network effects that make it unattractive for stakeholders to leave or for rivals to build competing ecosystems. How many of us would wish to desert our app and data collections to move to a rival smartphone ecosystem?

For those reasons, platforms are often (digital) marketplaces that facilitate interaction at low cost and provide instant, market-based feedback. To return to the familiar example of Apple's App Store, developers make apps in genres where customer demand is visibly the highest; users rate the apps up or down, depending on the apps' perceived quality, and "vote with their fingers." Developers get feedback and accrue rewards accordingly, but they cannot easily move their app to another platform, since the app is designed for the iOS operating system.

But platforms can take different forms, too, including either non-digital or non-marketplace formats, like the conferences Novo organized for regulators and doctors, or digital distribution channels like Red Hat's Fedora. They can also, for instance, constitute a set of contractual standards that lay out the rules for collaborator engagement, like Li & Fung's supplier terms.

Operating a Platform

Building a platform is a start, but it's like a football stadium: there's no game until the players are out on the field. Like a good referee (albeit one who also owns the stadium), shaping firms need to actively manage the platform through selective control of few key variables. Since it would be impossible and undesirable to control everything, the focus is on locking in stakeholders, monetizing value created, and adjusting the system to maintain win-win outcomes.

Successful ecosystem orchestrators often control the rules and mechanisms of interaction. Doing so allows them to catalyze, rather than directly manage in detail, the evolution of the ecosystem. Consider the platform operation of supply chain orchestrator Li & Fung: the company owns no looms, sewing machines, or textile factories, yet it is one of the largest consumer products trading companies in the world, providing time-sensitive, high-volume production and distribution services. How? All the work is done by an extensive network of third-party suppliers that connect with one another via Li & Fung's platform, which matches independent production facilities and retailer needs. Li & Fung specifies the rules that its network members must follow to remain part of its ecosystem, and it manages its supplier system according to several principles, like constantly refreshing the ecosystem and monitoring, benchmarking, and providing feedback to its stakeholders. In other words, Li & Fung controls how companies participate and interact and therefore how the ecosystem performs and evolves. The outcome is unmatched speed, flexibility, and efficiency, with delivery lead times half the industry average. Finally, Li & Fung captures value by monetizing services like quality assurance via agency fees charged to customers. As of 2013, its revenue exceeded $20 billion.[26]

Effective platform management keeps value within the ecosystem by making participation in the ecosystem attractive, by maximizing network effects that discourage potential rival shapers from building a competing base, and by limiting value portability beyond the collaborating partners. Successful shapers do this by sharing their resources "with strings attached"—offering things that only have value inside the ecosystem, like platform-specific tools for app developers.

Evolve the Ecosystem

The power of a shaping strategy lies in the depth and breadth of stakeholder contributions, which support the ecosystem's fast growth and quick adaptation in response to external change. Diversity in and of itself can drive end-user uptake: as mentioned above, Apple's App Store trumped Nokia's in part because of the former's breadth. Diversity should therefore be maintained, even at the expense of efficiency. Shaping firms should also persistently invest in opportunities to maximize network effects by extending or scaling the platform. For instance, Alibaba, the Chinese e-commerce giant whose strategy we will explore in more detail below, invested so heavily in getting more sellers onto TaoBao, its eBay-like consumer-to-consumer marketplace, that it was unprofitable for eight years.[27] But as of 2014, it's the eleventh-most-visited website in the world.[28]

SIMULATING STRATEGY IN AN UNPREDICTABLE, MALLEABLE ENVIRONMENT

In highly unpredictable and malleable environments, companies need to both explore multiple options over time and invest deeply in shaping selected options to ensure success. To model such an environment, we simulated malleable options whose value increases with investment. In addition, we changed their rewards over time to reflect unpredictability. The resulting landscape is challenging for most strategies: classical ones lose out because they bet on an option whose relative value declines over time. More explorative, adaptive strategies fail to capture the value from deep and prolonged investment into shaping a limited number of options. Finally, a visionary strategy that displays a one-off phase of analysis and subsequent investment into a single option risks obsolescence in the face of changing circumstances.

Rather, our simulation showed that a strategy that invests periodically in exploring and investing in a select set of options and shifting this focus over time will trump others (figure 5-4). Such a strategy resembles the shaping approach, which requires investment in a family of options through an ecosystem. In such an ecosystem, you do not have to know exactly which option will turn out best, but leadership of the ecosystem will put the firm in a prime position to benefit once options crystallize.

FIGURE 5-4

Shaping strategies perform well in unpredictable and malleable environments (simulation)

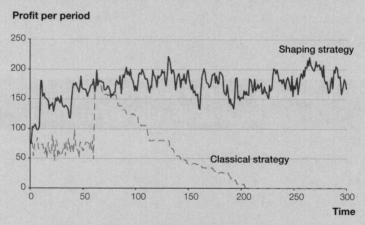

Profit per period

Time

Source: BCG Strategy Institute multi-armed bandit (MAB) simulation.

Notes: Results averaged over thirty simulations in noncompetitive environments with thirty investment options.

Once the system has gained critical mass, the orchestrator must keep the ecosystem flexible—shaping environments change, and the ecosystem must, too. As the platform grows, the orchestrator should allow the stakeholder mix to change to maintain alignment. We see ecosystems fail when they become rigid. Sometimes, the orchestrator falls prey to the temptation to overextend its control, alienating stakeholders. Sometimes, it's the lure of efficiency and specialization, for instance, when the shaping firm reduces the number of ecosystem players or the redundancy between them to lower management costs. Ultimately, these classical tendencies damage the ecosystem's long-term appeal and adaptiveness by reducing its diversity and dynamism. And if only one player can produce a certain offering, the ecosystem risks becoming locked into that player's demands.

Strategizing at Alibaba

The Alibaba Group is the unsung giant of global e-commerce—though that may change after its initial public offering on the US markets on September 19, 2014.[29] The company, founded by Jack Ma in 1999, began with the business-to-business portal Alibaba .com, which connects Chinese manufacturers with foreign purchasers. Four years later, it launched its consumer variant, Taobao .com. By 2013, the group handled a larger transaction volume than Amazon.com and eBay combined, accounting for more than half of all Chinese parcel mail.[30] In the meantime, Alibaba extended its platform into other complementary businesses, with associated portals, like AliPay for payment services and Aliyun for cloud computing. The firm has managed to grow at a remarkable 60 percent annually since 2008 by setting an expansive vision, engaging a broad set of stakeholders on its platforms, investing in platform expansion, and constantly evolving its ecosystems.

Chief Strategy Officer Ming Zeng explained to us how Alibaba's vision recognized the unpredictability of the digital world but committed to shaping the market: "The original vision was that the internet would change everything, and we wanted to be there. But we did not know payments or B2C or anything—it was, 'Can we add something to society by leveraging internet technology?' So first, we started with international trading, then on to SME [small or medium-sized enterprise] growth, then retailing then payments then cloud computing." Alibaba screens carefully whether to enter any platform business according to the opportunity to stimulate the development of a sizable market. "Don't be in a business that only offers services to a limited number of customers," Zeng said. "If a business targets only a specific segment, leave it to a third party." He told us that Alibaba only wants to be the orchestrator where there are significant network effects. "Our business is a platform business, so everything is a platform. The most important thing is the number of clicks—people using it—whether you have enough critical mass on the platform."

Alibaba's orchestration philosophy is market-based rather than managerial. "We try to . . . intervene as little as possible," said Zeng. Instead, Alibaba pursues win-win relationships by creating incentives at the platform level. "We have a unique competency in the market-place. You need sellers so there's something to buy, then you shift emphasis to buyers so that more sellers will come. [We can influence] the development of a positive feedback loop to reach scale." He added wryly, "We don't put MBAs near marketplaces, because they have been taught to 'manage' things."

Alibaba constantly coevolves its platforms. For instance, it added instant messaging and seller credibility ratings to its Taobao platform to improve trust building between participants, an aspect traditionally important in Chinese commerce and a criti-cal potential hurdle that can keep people from entering into online transactions.

Perhaps most importantly, Zeng realizes that Alibaba's strategy is collaborative and part of a multiround game: "We are managing dis-ruptive innovation," he told us. "We disrupt existing paradigms by leveraging technology so we need to have a clear vision but to be extremely patient to work with partners who may also be newcomers."

The Shaping Approach in Practice: Implementation

Since the direction of a shaping strategy emerges from the frequent engagement and orchestration of an evolving set of collaborators, the approach needs to be embedded in every aspect of the "organization" to be effective. A shaping strategy must however reach beyond firm boundaries, from fostering external innovation to developing an open organizational structure to leading with an eye toward inspiring and influencing other ecosystem participants.

Information

An ecosystem orchestrator must facilitate and monitor the relations between multiple parties and catalyze these interactions to create mutually favorable outcomes. This can be challenging given the enormous transactional complexity of interactions between all the parties in a large ecosystem. Li & Fung's network has over 15,000 suppliers; there are more than 275,000 iOS developers in the United States alone.[31] Information is the lubricant that smooths the interaction between orchestrator and stakeholders, facilitates coordination, and, as the vehicle for constant feedback, stimulates collective learning, thereby increasing the perceived value of the platform. Therefore, information needs to be easily sharable, accessible, and current, facilitating a market-based adjustment mechanism not requiring the constant intervention of the orchestrator.

Most naturally, the (digital) platforms described earlier function as the information-sharing mechanism, though sometimes orchestrators need to take a more active physical role, as Novo does with its conferences for the

Chinese health-care community. Ideally, platforms are designed to auto-matically generate information on customer satisfaction, demand patterns, and the overall health of the ecosystem and do not need ad hoc orchestrator intervention to collect and share the information. Successful virtual mar-ketplaces both collect data from and share it with participants in an easily digestible and valuable manner.

Alibaba leverages the information it collects to identify new opportuni-ties to extend its platforms. With its huge data firepower, the firm is driving an economic transformation in Chinese retailing, delivering more products faster and to more people via more, new, and different business models. Feedback can enhance the vitality of Alibaba's platform and its participants' offerings. Alibaba sales data gives merchants insights to new opportuni-ties, and its user feedback lets participating retailers improve their offerings, while giving Alibaba clues on how to adjust standards as end-user demand evolves. Zeng confirmed the critical importance of such information for Alibaba's shaping strategy: "It's trial by error. Economists can't guess this, so we just keep trying. We get feedback from the market and we make some adjustments."

Finally, select quantitative measurements can tell orchestrators whether the coevolution process is working. Measurements could include capturing a new-product vitality index, ecosystem growth, and combined profitability or the market share of an ecosystem as a whole. For Apple, measurements could include, for instance, the profitability and concentration of its app developers and the market share of end users who have iOS devices versus other devices, like Android.

Innovation

The very point of an ecosystem is to harness outside resources to support rapid, parallel innovation. Therefore, innovation mostly happens externally, drawing on the diversity of participants in the ecosystem but catalyzed by the shaping firm. Innovating with a shaping approach doesn't mean directly managing every innovation; nor should it—a managed as opposed to a mar-ket-based approach would be infeasible at scale and would curtail the speed and variety of the ecosystem's innovations. The orchestrator catalyzes innovation by putting in place incentives and providing feedback to stakeholders to allow them to innovate in ways aligned with the interests of the ecosystem.

Of course, not all innovation happens externally. The orchestrator's innovations are mostly second order—designing and improving the business model and interaction platform, which reinforces the shaper's right to orchestrate the ecosystem. Facebook innovates internally to continuously improve its platform's value proposition for outside collaborators by selectively investing in two areas that help to legitimate its role as an ecosystem orchestrator. First, it prioritizes improvements to its development applications and platform infrastructure so that other parties can easily collaborate. Second, and perhaps more importantly, it continues to adapt its user interface, adding features like PhotoStream, Timeline, and other hooks to maintain interest and engagement from the critical mass of users that determine the platform's attractiveness for advertisers and app developers.

Organization

Unlike the other approaches to strategy we've explored, the key unit of analysis in a shaping context is the business ecosystem, not just the firm itself. This larger view has implications for organizational structure, culture, and leadership. Shaping organizations need to be open to, and intertwined with, the external environment, in order to extend their reach beyond the boundaries of the firm and build a covenant of trust. Structurally, this means that orchestrators have few organizational boundaries; they leverage and share resources and knowledge externally and give up a certain degree of control by leveraging the same market-based mechanisms as the ecosystem itself.

For instance, the orchestrating firm might integrate itself with other stakeholders by rotating staff, investing in upstream and downstream ecosystem players, or by sharing IP when it serves the interest of the wider ecosystem. Google, for instance, regularly holds developer conferences, where it invests in collaborators by giving them training, offers one-on-one feedback sessions, or lets collaborators codevelop apps with Google engineers.[32] Inevitably, this open organizational approach can require a mind-set shift—especially for leaders or employees who are used to a clear division between "them" and "us." It requires comfort with letting go. Instead of giving strict, detailed operational rules, leaders set broad guidelines to foster external collaboration.

Culture

The same tenets of going beyond the boundaries of the firm hold true for culture. The culture of a shaping firm should look outward, have an inclusive attitude toward external parties, and encourage both catalysis rather than control in stakeholder interactions and collaboration rather than competition.

The firm should stimulate and reward employees for reaching beyond the boundaries of the company to build relationships. Openness and humility help to generate the trust necessary to build long-term, successful interaction with ecosystem participants. As Novo CEO Lars Sørensen said: "Then we have an open culture in the company; we hopefully have been able to create a culture whereby people feel they can be critical of the decisions that are being made, all of course with the intention to do a better job." And, above all, shaping cultures encourage employees to respect other players in the ecosystem. Shaping firms often promote a nonmanagerial culture in which building relationships, rather than directly managing or controlling them, is most prized.

Leadership

It's more of the same with leadership, where, counterintuitively, shaping leaders gain clout and respect through willingness to cede a degree of control. Shaping leadership extends beyond the boundaries of the firm. The shaping leader sets the ecosystem vision—often collaboratively—communicates the vision, builds external relationships rooted in mutual interest, resolves conflict, and influences rather than commands. In this way, the leader is more of catalyst than a manager who strictly enforces his or her will.

Organization, Culture, and Leadership at Red Hat: Jim Whitehurst

Red Hat CEO Jim Whitehurst underlined a number of the organizational and cultural imperatives for a shaping approach. For instance, Red Hat's organization is strongly focused on building external relationships, which requires hiring very selectively: "Red Hat has been able to influence communities to get things done—to influence creative communities and accomplished techies with big egos where you don't have control—because we respect the ecosystem. Organizationally, that means that we are surgical in who we hire. We understand the people with the most influence and get them to work for us."

Red Hat's decision-making culture reflects a willingness to selectively cede some control since, in a shaping organization, engaging internal and external stakeholders in a fair process can be as important as the outcome of that process. Most energy therefore goes into creating a culture that supports open, transparent dialogue:

> Our associates have always expected this: tell me why we're doing what we're doing, and allow me at least a voice in the decision process. Now, a voice doesn't mean decision rights. It doesn't mean you have any say in the answer. But at least you have a vehicle for an opinion to be heard . . . Engaging people in how decisions are getting made means it can take forever to get decisions made. But once you make a decision, you get flawless execution because everybody's engaged. They know what you're doing and they know why you're doing it.[33]

Whitehurst sees the requirements of a leader in a shaping organization as quite distinct from those in a more classical organization, like the one he experienced as a chief operating officer at Delta Air Lines. "Red Hat is fundamentally different culturally," he told us. "I came in thinking I was adult supervision, but recognized that . . . openness generates openness. We have six thousand–plus people in eighty offices around the world who are working in a bottom-up management system."

Nor does Whitehurst see the CEO's role as one of command and control. "Leadership at Red Hat isn't about internally focused control measures," he said. "We are the catalysts in communities." That external view helps him understand his role: "The leader is the 'catalyst,' not the leader—I don't rule by fiat and that's not how I want to position myself in an open-source community. We don't lead anything, because leadership implies that you have control. So, in a way, I'm the chief catalyst for Red Hat. I catalyze, I help direct, but I don't formally lead. And so that was a key word we spent a lot of time on: [being a catalyst means] credibility; consultation not control; contribution."

ARE YOUR ACTIONS CONSISTENT WITH A SHAPING APPROACH?

You are embracing a shaping approach if you observe the following actions:

✓ You select and engage stakeholders.

✓ You create a shared vision for a better way of doing things.

✓ You build a platform to orchestrate collaboration.

✓ You coevolve the ecosystem and the collaboration platform.

Tips and Traps

As we've seen, the essential elements of a successful shaping strategy are engaging stakeholders with an attractive vision at the right time, orchestrating the ecosystem to push toward outcomes that are mutually beneficial for all stakeholders, and evolving the ecosystem to keep up with external changes.

In spite of the rising popularity of the word *ecosystem* in business, the shaping approach to strategy is clearly the least widely understood. Indeed, even leading practitioners whom we interviewed talked freely about how they are still figuring out how to create and shape advantaged positions within advantaged ecosystems. No surprise then that unlike the overrepresentation of the highly familiar classical and visionary approaches, the shaping approach was the least frequently encountered approach. It is both the least declared and also the least practiced approach to strategy. We also observed much inconsistency between the actual measured environment, the perceived environment, the declared strategy, and the practiced strategy for the shaping approach. For example, when companies perceive their environment to be malleable and unpredictable, they are more likely to adopt the practices of an adaptive rather than a shaping approach.

Table 5-1 presents a few tips and traps that firms should heed to sharpen their game in selecting and applying the shaping approach.

TABLE 5-1

Tips and traps: key contributors to success and failure in a shaping approach

Tips	Traps
• *Employ selectively:* Only pursue markets that are at an early enough stage of development or have sufficient growth potential and that your firm can conceivably orchestrate.	• *Bad timing:* Starting a shaping approach when the opportunity is already far developed or a rival orchestrator already has a head start can lead to wasted effort.

(Continued)

TABLE 5-1   *(Continued)*

Tips and traps: key contributors to success and failure in a shaping approach

Tips	Traps
• *Understand your role:* Few firms have the combination of influence and capability to deploy the shaping approach, but many others can benefit from participating in the ecosystem.	• *Value leaks:* Don't let value leak from your ecosystem. Ensure that collaborators have high switching costs or cannot easily export the capabilities or IP you helped them develop beyond the ecosystem.
• *Give generously . . . with strings attached:* Develop a win-win proposition that creates and monetizes value in your ecosystem. Network effects reinforce the value of your platform and make it more robust. But limit the portability of intellectual property beyond the ecosystem.	• *Overextending control:* Avoid dominating and overmanaging the ecosystem. Vertical or horizontal integration will reduce ecosystem variety and dynamism.
• *Build your influence:* Develop relationships to harness the energies of other stakeholders. Create a focal point, a platform, from which you can deploy your influence.	• *Allowing rival orchestrators onto the platform:* The flip side of too much control is losing control to rival orchestrators with detrimental effects on your firm's value creation.
• *Control selectively:* Carefully select where you deploy your influence, and control the mechanisms of interaction and adaptation, not operational activities or outcomes.	• *Efficiency at all costs:* Prioritizing efficiency and specialization over long-term ecosystem health can hurt a shaping approach. Redundancy and variation keep an ecosystem robust.
• *Maintain platform health and attractiveness:* Encourage diversity and dynamism in the ecosystem, and avoid hoarding all the gains or prioritizing efficiency at the expense of diversity.	

CHAPTER 6

RENEWAL

Be Viable

American Express: Renewing Advantage

When the financial crisis hit world markets in 2008, American Express, currently the world's biggest card issuer, with $950 billion in billed business, faced very difficult circumstances.[1] Defaults on credit card payments rose sharply, consumer spending plummeted, and the funding markets dried up. In previous recessions, Amex's wealthy clientele had kept spending—but not this time.[2]

The circumstances called for a drastic response, and Ken Chenault, Amex's CEO, took swift action. He launched an aggressive cost-cutting and restructuring program to focus the organization and to impart a sense of urgency. Chenault explained to us: "First we had to deal with the cost issue. The environment is such that we couldn't act the way we did precrisis. We had to act immediately—but we had to be thoughtful about it and be governed by both short- and long-term considerations."

He reduced personnel costs, shedding approximately 10 percent of the workforce and temporarily reducing senior management salaries.[3] He lowered marketing expenses and the fees paid for professional services, but maintained the budgets for customer service.[4]

Finally, to raise new sources of funding, Amex entered into the deposit-gathering business, and, Chenault said, "in a period of only several months, we raised over $8 billion."

Organizationally, Chenault focused on role clarity and tight plans with clear success metrics: "Personal accountability was driven down through the organization." But amid the gloom, he was careful to project a sense of optimism. "The company had been around for 160-plus years. We had faced crises before," he said, "and we knew it was critical to maintain confidence in prospects for the longer term. Our mantra was 'Stay liquid, stay profitable, and invest selectively to grow the business.'"

Chenault's swift actions saved the day. By the end of 2009, Amex's stock had recovered to $40 per share, from a low of $10 in March.[5] American Express was one of the few financial companies to maintain its shareholder dividend and remain profitable throughout the crisis. Five years later, Amex trades at more than $90, an accomplishment attributable to the second phase of Chenault's mantra: the plan for future growth.[6] We reminded Chenault what he had told investors in 2009: "At the start of the year, the economy appeared to be in a free-fall, the drop in card member spending was accelerating and loan loss rates were rising rapidly. But throughout this time our short-term challenges did not stop us from investing in our future."[7] Chenault acknowledged that there were skeptics: "People said to me: 'You know, Ken, how can you even think about growth at a time when the company is being hit and the economy is in a shambles?'" But, he said, "I'll make the obvious point: don't waste a crisis. Despite all the craziness that was going on, [Amex was] going to selectively invest in growth."

Chenault had led Amex through crises before. He took the helm at Amex a few months before 9/11. He knew how the company should react. "While pressure on the bottom line intensifies during weaker times, it is short-sighted to slash and burn all growth investments," he explained. "Doing so will likely put you at the back of the competitive pack when the economy begins to recover and will end up costing you more in the long run."[8]

While many competitors were still grappling with losses, he focused on building a platform for future growth. He developed a vision of the future, with Amex as not just a card company but as a broader financial services company supported by a strong digital platform, and he invested in technological innovation.[9] Chenault looked for ways to drive profits by offering customers more ways to spend their money, like increasing the number of merchants connected to Amex's iconic membership rewards program.[10] He explained: "This is why, even as we've cut operating expenses, we have continued to fund major growth initiatives."[11]

Amex's success would not have been possible if Chenault had not ensured that his strategy—to survive and to grow—cascaded through the whole company. Culturally, he encouraged the organization not to "hunker in the bunker." Chenault was inspired by a saying from his lead director, Bob Walter: "Bob says, 'Keep your nose to the grindstone and your eyes on the horizon.' It might be physically impossible, but it's a great metaphor . . . It emphasizes the need to focus on the day-to-day, but with a view of, 'What's the transformation you'll bring about?'" Thanks to the efforts of Chenault and his team, Amex is well positioned for future growth, with its stock now up around ninefold from recession lows.

The Renewal Approach to Strategy: Core Idea

A renewal strategy, like the one employed at Amex, renews the vitality and competitiveness of a firm when it is operating in a harsh environment. Such a challenge can be caused by a protracted mismatch between the firm's approach to strategy and its environment or by an external or internal shock.

When the external circumstances are so difficult that your current way of doing business cannot be sustained, changing course to preserve and free

FIGURE 6-1

The renewal approach to strategy

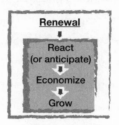

up resources, and then later redirect toward growth, is the only way to not merely survive, but to eventually thrive again. A company must first notice and *react* to the deteriorating environment as early as possible. Then, the firm needs to *economize* to decisively address its immediate impediments to financial viability or even its very survival. To do so, it focuses the business, cuts costs, and preserves capital while also freeing up resources to fund the next part of the renewal journey. Finally, the firm needs to pivot to one of the four other approaches to strategy to ensure long-term *growth* and competitiveness, by resetting the strategic direction of the company in line with its environment and innovating strategically (figure 6-1).

The renewal approach is unique both because it is temporary and because it is actually a combination of two approaches to strategy, each with its own distinct logic. The combination is challenging because the two approaches' requirements are in some ways diametrically opposed. We will extend this idea of combinations of approaches in chapter 7.

In terms of our art metaphor, renewal strategy is perhaps like a cubist painting. Cubism breaks with the complexity of previous schools of art; objects are analyzed, broken up, stripped of nonessential forms and shapes, and then reassembled to create a new perspective.

When to Apply a Renewal Approach

You should deploy a renewal approach when your firm faces harsh circumstances, because of either a protracted mismatch between your firm's strategy and its environment, or because of internal or external shocks. Such a mismatch can come about, either because a firm chose the wrong strategy or, more often, because the environment has changed and the strategy didn't, leading to chronic underperformance. Many computer hardware firms found themselves in this bind as mature technologies were replaced by emerging ones and as value shifted from hardware to software, services, and connectivity. Their historically successful business models were outdated in the face of environmental change.

A renewal strategy is also appropriate when external circumstances make the environment suddenly harsh. Economic or political shocks or instability may constrain the capital markets, or consumer spending or demand in your sector may drop off unexpectedly. Sometimes these situations can take place at the same time with devastating consequences. The financial crisis that erupted in 2008—and which caused Amex to take a renewal approach—was an especially severe instance of reduced liquidity and declining demand.

WHAT YOU MIGHT KNOW IT AS

Renewal strategy is a well-known concept and reality, albeit under different names, like *transformation, turnaround,* or *streamlining.* In the 1980s, the practices of restructuring and turnaround were progressively codified and popularized, in part because of the lucrative returns generated by successful turnaround firms. Private-equity firms and banks popularized the *leveraged buyout* and similar financial engineering techniques, like working-capital factoring and novel debt structures that helped companies free up cash in harsh circumstances. The private-equity industry has made a science of the techniques that support the first phase of transformation, maximizing the cash flow of businesses by cutting costs, shedding excess activities, and optimizing capital structures.

Around the same time, companies themselves captured and codified some of the efficiency driving techniques of the "economizing" phase of the renewal approach. In the 1980s, US manufacturing companies developed *activity-based costing*, which helped them to link activities to profitability and to streamline selectively without harming performance. In the early 1990s, Michael Hammer and James Champy introduced the concept of *business process reengineering*, building on BCG's idea of *time-based competition*: activities that are not part of main processes that ultimately serve the customer should be minimized. Only a few years later, over 60 percent of *Fortune* 500 companies had engaged in some form of reengineering.[12]

BCG later developed *delayering*. The concept suggests that the number of organizational layers a company has is a surrogate for its complexity and inefficiency and that reducing excess layers and increasing spans of control improves the competitiveness of a firm.[13]

Finally, in the mid-1990s, academics and practitioners alike gave increased attention to the softer side of change. Authors like John Kotter argued that without considering human factors and building large-scale *change management* capabilities, transformations are bound to fail.[14]

Finally, large, existential challenges can arise closer to home, such as an internal cataclysmic event like supply-chain contamination, the breakdown of important production infrastructure, or a high-profile crisis of trust. When BP's *Deepwater Horizon* drilling rig, owned and operated by Transocean and on contract to BP, spilled oil into the Gulf of Mexico, the accident threatened the company's survival not only because of the mishap and its financial consequences but also because of its impact on trust and stakeholder relations.[15]

Though you may not notice immediately that your firm is entering a distressed state, once the pain is sharp enough, it's hard not to recognize that you need a renewal approach. Protracted competitive underperformance in terms of margins or sales growth, sharp drops in free cash flows, or reductions in available capital are all signs that the long-term survival of the firm may be at risk. The need for strategic renewal is increasing. Abbott, Bank of America, Conoco Phillips, Daimler, Ericsson, FMC, GlaxoSmithKline—this is just the start of an alphabet of firms that have publicly announced transformation efforts over the past few years. Why the rise? There are two primary reasons: first, the accelerating pace of change and, second, the expanding reach of economic crises because of the increasing interconnectedness of economies.

Today's businesses face more and faster change, raising the likelihood that a company's approach to strategy will become mismatched to the changing environment. Our analysis reveals that businesses now progress more quickly through the different stages in their life cycles—from question mark to star to cash cow to dog—and overall life cycles are therefore also increasingly compressed: in 75 percent of industries, the average time a firm spends at any stage of its life cycle has halved (figures 6-2 and 6-3).[16]

Therefore, leaders must be ever vigilant for change and must ensure that their strategies don't get out of step with their environment. In addition, economic crises seem to be deeper and to go beyond the sectors in which the crises started, because of the increasing interconnectedness of the global

FIGURE 6-2

Decreasing lifetime of companies

Average span of public listing for companies active in a given year

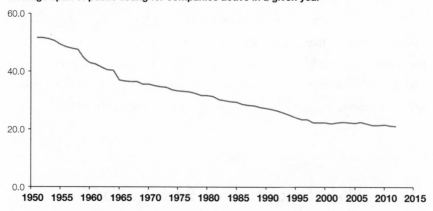

Source: BCG Strategy Institute analysis (September 24, 2014), Compustat.

Note: Cross-industry analysis based on thirty-four thousand companies in seventy industries (unweighted average), excluding companies with unknown start or end of public listing (listed and reporting sales in 1950 and/or still listed and reporting sales in 2013) and companies never reaching peak sales of greater than $2 billion.

FIGURE 6-3

Competitive positions change two times faster today than in 1992

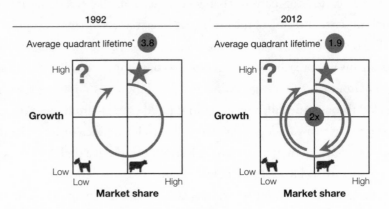

Source: Compustat data on publicly listed companies from 1980–2012.

Note: Excludes industries in which circulation decreases.

*Average time any single firm spends in a specific growth-share matrix quadrant.

economy. Formerly, crises were often confined to their industry or geography of origin. For instance, the South American debt crisis in the 1990s stayed largely in that region, and the oil crash in the United States in the 1980s primarily affected only the energy sector.

The environmental factors that trigger the need for an adaptive approach— turbulence, faster change, and more fundamental change—are the same as those that trigger the need for renewal. Adaptation, as we discussed, is not always easy, but when a firm misses the baby steps of adaptation, then a large, riskier, one-shot change in the form of a corporate transformation becomes necessary.

Why Focus Matters: Bausch & Lomb

The story of Bausch & Lomb, an eye care products manufacturer, exemplifies when and how to use a renewal approach. In 2010,

Brent Saunders was appointed to lead the turnaround of the company, which had fallen out of step with its competitive environment over a sustained period. "There were telling signs," he said. "Three CEOs in three years; no growth in thirty years; moving from being the market leader in most categories in which it competed to being the market laggard in those same categories; and enormous complexity."[17]

First, he needed to persuade people that the company should take a renewal approach, and so, as he told us, he looked for "some of the indisputable facts . . . to show that we need to do something different." On nearly every key metric for the company—sales per employee, growth rate over the past thirty years, innovation record—Bausch & Lomb was last in its peer group. Saunders showed others the case for change: "Probably the most compelling statistic was our willingness to recommend B&L as a place to work and a customer survey of doctors' willingness to recommend B&L products. It was awful."

Recognizing that Bausch & Lomb was woefully out of sync with its environment, Saunders responded with a three-part plan (stabilize, grow, and break out) that focused on stabilizing the entity, creating small wins, and investing in growth via targeted product development. Saunders explained: "Winning is contagious, so if you can start off by having small, quick wins, in a company like this that hadn't won for so long, it brings back that muscle memory."

Indeed, over two years, Bausch & Lomb's equity value increased by about 2.5-fold; sales grew by 9 percent a year, and EBITDA rose by 17 percent per year, driven by "right-sizing" the organization, targeted growth-focused acquisition, and an incredible string of thirty-four new product introductions.[18] In 2013, Valeant purchased B&L for $8.7 billion.[19]

ARE YOU IN A RENEWAL BUSINESS ENVIRONMENT?

You are facing a business situation that calls for renewal if the following observations hold true:

✓ Your industry or company displays low or negative growth.

✓ Your industry or company is losing money.

✓ Your industry or company suffered from an internal shock.

✓ Your industry or company suffered from an external shock.

✓ Your situation poses a viability risk for you.

✓ Your industry or company is subject to restricted access to capital.

The Renewal Approach in Practice: Strategizing

Strategic renewal is increasingly important: it's a high-stakes game that sometimes affects the very survival of the company. Most leaders are familiar with the approach under the guises of "transformation," "turnaround," or just plain cost cutting. However, executing a successful renewal approach to strategy is harder than you might think: our analysis demonstrates that 75 percent of transformations fail to create both short- and long-term impact (figure 6-4).[20] To understand why and to define what sets apart successful and unsuccessful renewals, we undertook a quantitative and qualitative comparison of the long-term performance of two dozen transformation programs.

The resulting pattern was striking. All of the firms we studied underwent what we call a "first phase" of economizing. But while essential, economizing alone is not sufficient: unsurprisingly, you really cannot cut your way to greatness. Painful cost cutting and other defensive measures are familiar approaches for staying afloat, but while they are quick and obvious and deliver tangible results, they are not by themselves a recipe for long-term

FIGURE 6-4

Few companies succeed in transformation efforts

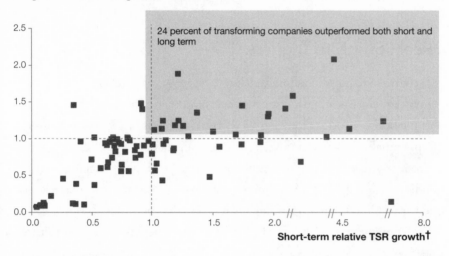

Long-term relative TSR growth*

24 percent of transforming companies outperformed both short and long term

Short-term relative TSR growth†

Source: BCG analysis.

Note: Total shareholder returns (TSR) adjusted by S&P 500 or relevant global industry index growth; 1 = same growth rate as the industry; N = 88 firms undergoing transformation, from 2001 to 2013.

*Five years from start of effort, or until today.

†One year from start of transformation effort.

success. Just economizing will likely restore total shareholder return to sector parity at best, but will not stem a decline in long-term competitiveness.

For successful renewing firms, the transformation story doesn't end there. No single firm we studied managed to thrive in the long term without embarking on a "second phase" of transformation by pivoting to a new approach to strategy focused on innovation and growth. We ascribe a high proportion of transformation failures to firms that never went beyond the first phase of cost cutting. Hence, for a renewal strategy to be successful in the long term, a firm must initiate both the first phase of economizing and the second of growth—in other words, the firm must pivot to one of the other four approaches to strategy.

Strategizing for renewal begins with a swift reaction to early indications of a harsh environment; the firm must move into the first phase of economizing—the identification of opportunities for cost savings and capital preservation and strict planning to achieve those benefits. Then, the firm will be ready for the second phase, a new strategic approach focused on growth and strategic innovation (figure 6-5).[21]

React Swiftly to Triggers

Recognizing and responding quickly to signals that your firm is in a harsh environment is the most critical step to improving the odds of survival: as in medical situations requiring CPR, the timeliness of the first response in a potentially life-threatening situation often dictates the outcome. Firms frequently react too late to a situation of distress. Hubris, lagging financial indicators, or the lack of an immediate burning platform can make it easy to turn a blind eye to impending distress. Furthermore, a maturing business model might throw off lots of cash and appear healthy when, in fact, the seeds of obsolescence have already been sown. By the time financial pressure hits, challenges may have already multiplied and progressed significantly.

Some firms can anticipate a harsh environment by recognizing leading indicators like technology shifts, the emergence of maverick competitors, shifts in how and where smart money is being invested, customer

FIGURE 6-5

Transformation trajectories

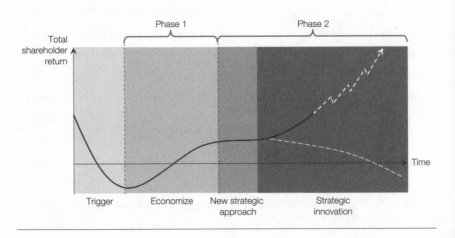

dissatisfaction or defection, or declining growth rates. However, such pre-emptive cases of renewal are surprisingly rare.[22] Here, we will focus only on the more common instances of reactive transformation.

Phase 1: Plan to Economize

Once a firm recognizes the harshness of its environment, it needs to embark on a first phase of renewal, with two goals in mind: first, the firm must restore the financial viability of the company and, second, it must then fund the journey back to growth. To that end, firms draw up a plan to focus their business by shedding noncore activities, reducing costs, and preserving capital.

Good Intentions Aren't Enough: Kodak

The story of Kodak exemplifies not only the speed and ferocity of technological disruption but also the incredible sensitivity of the transformation process to making the right decisions.[23] Even the most sincere attempts at transformation can get it wrong. In 1975 Kodak owned 90 percent of the US film market and 85 percent of its camera sales. Few brands were as synonymous with their industry. So it was a sad day when the company filed for bankruptcy in 2012.

While it would be easy to see the Kodak story as an example of executive incompetence, the firm, in fact, did many things to adjust to the demise of film and the rise of digital photography. Kodak developed and patented the first digital camera in 1975. It wasn't until 1981 that Sony announced the first commercial product, the Mavica, but the camera's quality was low and its price inaccessible to the mass market. Meanwhile, Kodak made continued side investments in new technology throughout the 1980s and 1990s, for instance, switching some of its hiring and M&A from a chemical focus to electronics and engineering.

In an unprecedentedly short period—about four years—the industry was fundamentally upended. The year 1999 was the peak year ever for film sales, but by 2003 Kodak had announced publicly that the film business was in secular decline. What went wrong?

Although Kodak made a genuine effort to transform, it just didn't do so thoroughly or nimbly enough. Kodak's phase 1 was characterized by multiple, but insufficient rounds of cuts and layoffs, steps that degraded morale and failed to attract talent to fuel innovation. At the same time, even though Kodak had clearly identified the inevitability and necessity of shifting to digital technology, the company ran into the "proportionality trap." That is, Kodak did not allocate sufficient resources to develop and expand this new strategy, nor did it anticipate the incredible rate of technological change. Falling into the "persistency trap," Kodak stifled new projects that did not meet the benchmark economics of its existing film business. And, in the "legacy trap," the company continued to make heavy investments in its core business, not wanting to cannibalize film sales.

To some extent, Kodak's mistakes are understandable. For instance, it made major capital expenditures in film manufacturing facilities in China in the late 1990s, anticipating that that country would become the world's last and largest market for film photography. Instead, China leapfrogged film photography altogether. As a source in the company told us: "We wanted to put money into the new technology, but we'd gotten some false security because the speed of technology substitution had been historically slow. When, in the early 2000s, quality, cost, and usability aligned, we were unprepared."

In early 2013 the firm emerged from bankruptcy, but as a much smaller operation.

Firms in renewal mode identify opportunities to refocus on their core activities. They restructure their portfolios by revisiting the industries and business units they want to maintain and determining which products and customer segments do or do not contribute to overall profitability and cash generation. At least in the short term, as Per Gyllenhammar, the CEO of Swedish automaker Volvo, reputedly observed after the stock market crash in 1987: "Cash is king."[24]

Reducing the cost associated with remaining assets can help to restore short-term profitability and to close performance gaps. Many firms optimize profits and reduce bloat by cutting into their personnel costs, restructuring their organizations, or making processes more efficient through lean management, six sigma, or related approaches. Potential savings lurk in many corners: the cost of goods sold can be lowered by rationalizing your supplier portfolio, reducing intermediaries, shifting the geographic sourcing mix, or initiating more collaborative efforts like reductions in supply chain waste and lead times. Indirect costs are often an easy source for savings that do not immediately affect the customer experience: marketing budgets, discretionary R&D, and indirect personnel expenses are all candidates for phase 1 cuts to stem the bleeding.

Apart from rationalizing their portfolios or cutting costs, firms can also free up resources on their balance sheets. For instance, they can reduce asset redundancy, adjust their debt structure, or optimize working capital by improving inventories, changing supplier terms, and eliminating bad payment practices. More radically, they can sell and lease back core assets where feasible.

The opportunities that the company identifies then get rolled into a detailed, milestone-rich plan. Disciplined management of the firm's phase 1 strategy allows it to "live to die another day." The firm focuses on high-level savings targets that cascade down into granular month-by-month plans or individual targets, reflecting required progress toward the short-term goal of financial viability.

The guiding principle for the first phase of renewal should be to maximize immediate performance while preserving optionality for long-term growth. It's a tough balance between "no sacred cows" and "don't just slash and burn." When reducing costs, decisions of what to cut or sell should hinge on future growth prospects. Firms that "burn the furniture"—selling off units with high potential—risk cannibalizing their long-term prospects. Rationalization is necessary, but assets with high future strategic value should be sold only as a last resort to generate cash. A good approach is to de-average cuts and investments, cutting deeply in some areas while selectively reinvesting for long-term growth in others.

Even though the first and second phases play out sequentially, they are also intertwined. First, firms must not cut elements that will be essential for phase 2. Second, phase 1 funds phase 2 growth, and cost-cutting targets must therefore reflect this. And, finally, while most of the firm's attention in phase 1 will be fully dedicated to saving the firm, leaders need to have their eyes on the horizon, too, to anticipate and set up the strategizing process for a successful second phase.

Phase 2: Pivot to Growth

Strategizing in the second phase is about doing two things well: defining a new strategic approach—and investing in the strategic innovation to support it—and communicating the new strategy.

To set the direction for the second phase of transformation, successful firms assess their environment to inform their long-term vision. Regardless of which strategic approach the firm pursues in the second phase, the firm needs to adjust the focus from a short-term, internal perspective that centers on efficiency to a long-term, external one that focuses on growth. To pivot to the new approach, firms need to innovate strategically, often making multiple fundamental changes to their business model. The appropriate approach and accompanying innovation required should be based on the firm's assessment of the postcrisis environment.

Earlier in the book, we detailed the various strategic approaches that might be adopted in the second phase. Here, let's briefly explore something unique to the second phase: the need to persuasively communicate the new vision to overcome inevitable skepticism and restore confidence. Given the pressure to focus on short-term survival and the possible damage to the firm's credibility during its crisis period, leaders must reset the firm's internal compass steadfastly and invest in communication of the strategy, both externally and internally. This helps to bring along outsiders like financial stakeholders by giving them a new logic to anchor against and to improve morale with insiders by giving employees a new frame and vision.

Strategizing at AIG

Like Amex, American International Group (AIG), one of the world's big-gest insurers, was engulfed by the global economic crisis that struck in 2008.[25] It is perhaps the poster child for a corporate existential cri-sis. That year, it received a record $85 billion bailout from the Federal Reserve and by March 2009 had grown to $182 billion. Its brand was seen as toxic, and its long-term viability was insecure. In the summer of 2009, the federal government recruited Bob Benmosche, a seasoned insurance executive, to embark on a spectacular example of strategic renewal.[26]

Benmosche and his team prioritized and acted decisively to create value, preserve and simplify the core insurance business, and ultimately pay back the US government. They shifted from an AIG "fire sale" to a thoughtful and methodical plan to divest some businesses, invest in others, and unwind certain portfolios. These actions focused on the remaining, most profitable, parts of the property casualty, life and retirement, and mortgage insurance busi-nesses. "Everything else was for sale," said Peter Hancock, AIG's current president and CEO, who was AIG's executive vice presi-dent for finance, risk, and investments at the time. "The organization needed clarity as to what would be sold and what would be kept. So we decided to preserve the core." In the remaining assets, the AIG team tackled operational efficiencies. "Looking at big, mature parts of the business and thinking about how to optimize can be powerful," he said. "We pay $100 million in claims per day; so if you can optimize it by just a little, it pays for a lot." Finally, Benmosche oversaw a significant streamlining of the organization. Hancock explained: "We're executing a significant simplification exercise to reduce organizational complexity and to improve decision-making."

This focus on simplification and solvency fueled the first phase enough to relieve AIG of its creditor burdens and to get back to the public markets, where it could grow again. By the end of 2012, AIG had paid back the government, including a profit of $22.7 billion, retained its A investment rating, attracted more than $3 billion of credit from private-sector banks, and returned to the stock market.[27] But, as Hancock explained: "That wasn't the turnaround point. That was the starting point!" Hancock was appointed to a new role: as the CEO of the property casualty (PC) business, he had to pivot the unit back to long-term growth. The second phase had begun.

In this new role, Hancock looked toward a classical approach, capitalizing on his business unit's scale benefits and globalizing the management structure to create synergies and avoid cannibalization. Additionally, he refocused investments to position the firm better in higher-growth areas, like emerging markets: "Importantly, we have created a new source of growth, by giving AIG entities around the globe a sense of common belonging and access to common infrastructure and by creating a limited number of strategic business expansion countries, where we are willing to invest considerable sums with a longer payback horizon."

From 2011 to 2013, AIG more than tripled its profits, in no small part because of the contribution from PC, in which operating income increased from $1.1 billion to almost $5 billion during this period.[28]

SIMULATING STRATEGY IN A HARSH ENVIRONMENT

In harsh environments, firms win by preserving resources and not expending unnecessary effort on exploration. Our simulation bears this out: when the environment is harsh, exploration carries a high opportunity cost and eats into the limited resources necessary for survival. To model this, we introduced a budget of resources that any single strategy is allowed to use.

If resources are scarce, the budget is stricter or the opportunity costs get higher, and strategies that overinvest in exploration quickly run out of resources and cease to be viable (figure 6-6).

FIGURE 6-6

Renewal strategies win by conserving resources (simulation)

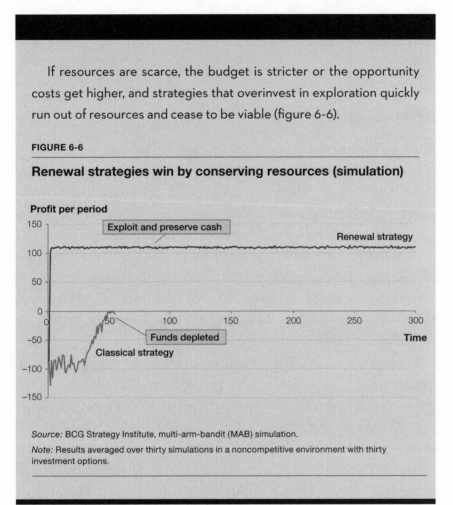

Source: BCG Strategy Institute, multi-arm-bandit (MAB) simulation.

Note: Results averaged over thirty simulations in a noncompetitive environment with thirty investment options.

The Renewal Approach in Practice: Implementation

Strategic renewal is a high-stakes game that demands the full dedication of the entire organization initially to economize and eventually to grow again. As Henry Ford said: "Failure is simply the opportunity to begin again, this time more intelligently."[29] Both phases of renewal, from information management through structure, culture, and leadership, need to be embedded in the organization. And that is exactly the challenge: successful renewal requires firms to balance the potentially contradictory requirements of a short-term focus on restoring the firm's viability with a long-term focus on growth.

Information

A successful renewal strategy executes the plan to focus and economize and then pivots to a new strategy for long-term prosperity. Information management supports those ends in three critical ways: detecting warning signals, informing the development of savings plans, and tracking progress against those plans. The focusing and economizing steps require the disciplined execution of financial improvement projects. Detailed action plans, cascaded into every level of the organization to ensure accountability and frequently iterated to track progress, support that goal. The information requirements for the second phase of transformation vary according to the needs of the specific strategic approach deployed.

In phase 1, firms should use a suite of analytical and measurement tools to plan and track performance improvement. Every dollar matters, so companies undertake detailed activity-based cost assignments to correctly identify cash-positive and cash-negative products. Then, they leverage analytical tools like benchmarking and delayering analysis to identify potential cost savings. To assess the likely success of each project, successful firms use methods like DICE, which estimates success based on duration, integrity, commitment, and effort, highlighting those areas where intervention is required.[30] Finally, once firms are aligned on a restructuring plan, they track progress against it with tools ranging from simple Gantt charts to more complex project-management software.

We've seen some of these information management tools in the classical approach. Here, as there, the tools must be deployed in an insightful rather than mechanical manner, to bring out new, if uncomfortable, truths about the current state and progress of the improvement program. Using tools to facilitate conversations rather than replace them helps avoid the ritualization of the process.

Information Management at Bausch & Lomb

At Bausch & Lomb, Brent Saunders used the company's information capability to diagnose the problem it was facing, create a restructuring plan, and track progress from stabilization to growth. Once he had developed his plan, he monitored progress in minute detail. "Everything was measurable and everything had a plan that we tracked and measured," he said. "In fact, I changed the metrics from bottom line and cash flow and, while those remained important, we put a heavier weight than anything on the top line. You can't cut costs to win with the margins we have."

As he turned to the future, Saunders developed a vision that was founded on revenue growth and, in particular, on getting products to market. He realized that development was the company's stumbling block. So, to reflect this, he told us, "I changed R&D to D&R," and ensured that the right information was collected to capture this change of emphasis. For instance, he changed incentives to reward the number of products that made it to market instead of the number of projects residing in research.

Innovation

As we've seen, innovation is not a major part in the first aspect of renewal, but it is essential in the second one. For this reason, renewal firms need to balance two opposing priorities: reducing discretionary costs in phase 1 but then innovating strategically in phase 2 to renew the business model.

In fact, in the first phase, innovation may be unavoidably reduced to safeguard the financial viability of the company, with two exceptions. First, firms should support innovation that leads to short- and medium-term cost or profit improvements, if the improvements directly fund the renewal journey. Second, firms should encourage innovation if it could support the business model changes necessary in the second phase of transformation. The renewal firm needs to de-average its innovation dollars to make sure that spending is focused on those two ends.

At the start of the second phase, if not before, once the imminent threat to viability has been averted, successful renewal companies embark on limited strategic innovation to test new approaches to drive growth. Often, since phase 2 may involve uncertainty and exploration, this step can resemble the adaptive approach: small, low-cost bets with short iteration cycles to limit cash outlay and get directional answers quickly. Later the firm may invest in larger-scale innovations appropriate for the specific approach to strategy it has chosen for the longer term.

Ken Chenault was adamant that Amex should continue to make targeted strategic investments in innovation to support the business in the short term and to prepare it for growth in the long term. As we have seen, even during the crisis, Amex developed a digital platform, an enhanced membership rewards program, and cobranded partnerships with firms like Delta and British Airways.

Organization

First, the renewal organization needs to pursue the phase 1 job—a temporary, life-critical project—with focus and discipline. The project requires rigorous cost cutting, which may include the restructuring of the entire firm and, often, the use of a temporary overlay organization to design and oversee the process. On the other hand, the firm needs then to pivot to a growth-focused approach to successfully execute the second phase. Given that the two phases overlap, renewing firms need to consider separating the seeds of growth from the phase 1 restructuring efforts to ensure the seeds' protection.

In the first phase, firms streamline to reduce costs and ensure disciplined execution, often overlaying a temporary program management layer on the organization to design and keep plans on track. Leaders "right-size" their company by reducing noncore parts of the organization. On the personnel side, delayering, a proven method for reducing organizational

layers and increasing spans of control, lowers costs and enhances vertical communication and accountability. Operationally, tools like process
reengineering help firms to reduce complexity in processes by removing
steps that do not directly add value to the end product. Often, companies
in renewal mode use strict hierarchy to ensure the diligent execution of
their savings program, with accountability even in the smallest subunits
of the organization.

Because firms in a renewal approach are operating in a sort of temporary state, they may superimpose a program management office, or PMO,
a dedicated temporary organizational overlay that ensures discipline, can
provide greater objectivity, and drives the tough decisions required to avoid
vested interests impeding progress. The PMO can design restructuring projects and track and roll up frequent, standardized project reports and metrics for regular C-level updates. In addition to providing discipline, a PMO
allows line managers to focus entirely on the ongoing business, while providing transparency about progress and potential obstacles throughout the
organization.[31]

For the sake of the second phase, firms need to cut with sufficient
audacity without damaging prospects for growth. It can be difficult to
combine competing short-term and long-term metrics and incentives for
the same teams, especially when team members may be fearful for their
own job security. There are multiple ways to navigate this challenge. For
instance, renewing firms can de-average their organization when handing
out restructuring targets to protect targeted innovation from widespread
cost-cutting efforts. Alternatively, firms can try to directly implement the
steps necessary for the second phase of their transformation, even when
they are still in the first. For instance, Amex intentionally built digital
transformation into the whole organization, rather than create a separate digital unit, to position the entire business to meet the future trend.
Sometimes simultaneous attention to phases 1 and 2 is not possible, because
the legacy organization is too far removed from the targeted one. In those
cases, firms can create separate organizational units that nurture and protect growth while allowing full-fledged restructuring in their existing core
business (see chapter 7).

Culture

A firm in renewal needs to pivot between two very different cultural empha-ses. First, the firm must be internally focused and approach tasks from the top down, with an emphasis on execution. Then, it must flip to a completely different, often polar opposite, mind-set that is externally focused and in line with the strategic approach to be pursued in the second phase. Don't be fooled into thinking this cultural pivot is easy—it is hard but necessary. As Andy Grove, former CEO of Intel, stressed: "A corporation is a living organism; it has to continue to shed its skin. Methods have to change. Focus has to change. Values have to change. The sum total of those changes is transformation."[32]

First, firms in crisis need a heads-down mentality to support disci-plined, action-oriented execution of the survival plan. Adherence to a plan should be publicly rewarded, and risk taking discouraged. Where possible, the company should be very transparent to reduce fear and fric-tion over cost savings and to help protect lay-off survivors from guilt or resentment. Firms in phase 1 often unintentionally breed a culture of pessimism, fueled by job insecurity or low morale over missed targets or historic lagging performance. To soothe these concerns as much as possi-ble, celebrate small wins to help maintain focus on the bigger long-term picture.

Then, leadership needs to catalyze a cultural change timed to coincide with the pivot to an alternative strategic approach. This change requires firms to create a new cultural identity and to build the confidence in this identity so that the firm can pivot toward a more outward-looking, growth-focused, and risk-taking culture after a period of anxiety and short-term focus. Like any cultural transformation, this is a difficult task that requires leaders to truly inspire their employees with a new vision for long-term success. Additionally, leaders need to heavily endorse the cultural elements that the next approach to strategy requires, be it the need to foster constructive dis-sent for an adaptive approach or the commitment to a clear, common goal in a visionary approach.

Organization and Culture at AIG

As described earlier, prior to the arrival of then-president and CEO Bob Benmosche, AIG initially focused solely on solving for constraints by cutting costs and restructuring its organization. After Benmosche, AIG focused on creating value. One way was by reducing or spinning off more than thirty companies with operations in more than fifty countries. "We had to cut some branches off the tree," said Hancock, "but the tree is still there and it has a big trunk." Leadership brought closer the three remaining core businesses—property casualty, life and retirement, and mortgage guaranty—through streamlining and centralization, changing the organization, in effect, from a federation to a union. In PC, Hancock radically changed the structure to drive synergies: "I changed the PC business from being a federation of rival insurance businesses—we had five different entities that could compete with one another and undermine our own pricing power— and reorganized on global product dimensions. Those leaders were empowered to optimize risk around the world and to create a critical mass of expertise to underwrite better."

To position itself for a successful second phase, AIG also renewed its identity to inspire a return to confidence. Benmosche developed a One AIG identity and got rid of the separate brand name Chartis, the temporary name for AIG's PC business put in place by a former CEO who believed, perhaps correctly at the time, that the AIG brand was radioactive.[33] As Hancock said: "We dropped the Chartis brand and went back to 'AIG,' and we rebranded the subbrands as 'AIG,' too, to create a more cohesive company in terms of incentives and information sharing under a 'One AIG' umbrella." AIG also worked to restore confidence internally, Hancock said: "The core had to be a credible going concern, but we had [tens of thousands of] employees with five CEOs in five years. The only way to hold on to our customers and to

continue to grow and prosper to the point where we could raise public equity is if these employees believed this company would survive
and thrive. That's where Bob Benmosche's personality came in. Town
hall after town hall, he showed in his eyes that he believed and that he
cared about them."

Leadership

The key challenge that leaders using a renewal approach face is managing phases of renewal effectively in spite of their almost-opposing charac-
ters. This balancing act demands ambidextrous leadership that resolves the
apparent contradictions between phase 1 and phase 2 and navigates the company successfully through both phases of renewal. Leaders on the cusp of a
transformation, therefore, need to embrace some inconvenient and contradictory truths. Renewal requires attention to both the short term and the
long term, to efficiency as well as innovation and growth, to discipline and
flexible adaptation, and to clarity of direction and empowerment.

This means that initially, leaders need to make the hard decisions with
attention to detail, clarity, and speed to support a rapid first phase rollout.
They stay close to performance analysis and tracking efforts and are open
about the state of affairs, even in a prevailing climate of fear. Simultaneously,
they maintain more optimistic, high-level messaging to keep spirits up and
to focus employees and other stakeholders on the longer-term renewal story.
This approach may be easier for a leader brought in expressly for a turnaround, but the leader who was in place as environmental conditions turned
harsh may be starting from a position of fear, personal disappointment, or
insecurity that he or she needs to overcome to lead successfully.

Renewal leaders need to be at the forefront of thinking about and setting
the broad vision for the second phase. While everyone else is busy "saving"
the company, they need to picture the targeted end state and the foundational
innovation that will support new growth. Then, once the firm's survival is

reasonably secure, they need to communicate the change of gear between the first and second phases and force the pivot toward a new, external, growth-directed approach. An effective renewal leader may need considerable powers of persuasion and communication, as transformational posttraumatic stress may produce organizational inertia. Leaders can facilitate this shift by communicating early wins on the journey toward the new strategic approach, by selectively backing critical strategic innovations with additional resources or organizational visibility, and by communicating patience and persistence. The leap from the familiar comfort of short-term cost cutting to exploratory, unfamiliar innovation may feel foreign to the organization, so top leadership must visibly and confidently take the first steps.

Leadership at Bausch & Lomb: Brent Saunders

Bausch & Lomb's Brent Saunders explained his role in focusing the company and reacting as early and swiftly as possible to harsh circumstances: "The day I started, I went to Rochester [where B&L is based] for a town hall with all the employees. I did one-on-ones with key executives, and then I left. For four weeks. I spent virtually the entire four weeks with customers or people who make or sell our products. I did that to have a deep understanding of how customers viewed our company. And I did that around the world and across the business."

Most importantly, Saunders explained, you have to lead in a top-down manner, focusing on setting, communicating, and tracking the plan: "The plan came from me, very much so. And the plan stayed the plan. Some items changed, but more or less the plan stayed constant." Additionally, discipline and speed are critical, as is displaying great attention to detail. Saunders said: "You have to make tough calls and move quickly. If you're not willing to make the tough call and drive operational excellence and put the right people in the right seats, it's probably not for you."

At the same time, you must prepare the long-term vision and generate employee and market enthusiasm. "The CEO sets the strategy," said Saunders. In doing so, you need to convey a sense of optimism. "When you're new, you get a lot of wonderful opportunities to change course more radically, people will hear you out, people are nervous so you can take advantage of that to get them bought in."

ARE YOUR ACTIONS CONSISTENT WITH A RENEWAL APPROACH?

You are embracing a renewal approach if you observe the following actions:

✓ You reduce your cash burn rate.

✓ You limit the use of capital.

✓ You focus your activities.

✓ You create a restructuring plan.

✓ You execute through an overlay structure.

✓ You later pivot toward growth by selectively innovating and investing in new approaches.

Tips and Traps

As we've seen throughout this chapter, an increasing number of firms face renewal challenges, either as a result of external shocks or because they have failed to adapt to shifts in the basis of competition. We have also seen that as widespread and familiar as renewal or transformation programs are, they are rarely successful in spite of very high stakes. Our analysis of paired comparisons of successful and unsuccessful renewal strategies suggests that the value at stake, calculated as the present value of the difference in total shareholder return and its duration, is of the order of the value of the enterprise itself. Nevertheless, three-quarters of such efforts fail to restore short- and long-term returns to short- and long-term industry averages. The key to a successful strategic renewal is the ability to manage, reconcile, and pivot between the contradictions of two seemingly diametrically opposed phases—one focused on solving constraints and the other on growth. Table 6-1 presents some tips to follow and traps to avoid if companies are to improve their odds of success.

TABLE 6-1

Tips and traps: key contributors to success and failure in a renewal approach

Tips	Traps
• *Immediately cut, with courage:* Cut deeply enough in the first round: multiple rounds of cost cutting can be demoralizing to the organization and draw out the period before the company can fund and return to growth.	• *Early wins:* Companies declare premature victory after phase 1 and fail to declare or develop a second phase focused on innovation and growth.
• *Turning the page:* Make a conscious decision to go beyond the efficiency moves of phase 1 and create a vision for renewal focused on growth and innovation.	• *Burning the furniture:* Firms continue with multiple rounds of cost-cutting and efficiency-improvement measures instead of looking to the future.
• *Envisage the future:* See (and communicate) what the future looks like, determine which approach to strategy is required in the second phase.	• *Legacy thinking:* Companies fail to shed core assumptions and practices of the legacy model even when these habits are self-limiting or no longer relevant. They thereby undermine the second-phase approach by keeping it too close to the core business.
• *Support foundational innovation:* Innovate across multiple dimensions of the business model to pivot to another approach to strategy. A new product within the current business model frame may not be sufficient.	• *Lack of proportionality:* Firms make promising moves—such as a series of new business pilots—that are insufficiently bold to address the scale of the challenge.
• *Inspire hope:* Hardship inevitably breeds a culture of pessimism or insecurity. Paint the long-term vision vividly for employees to show them there is more than short-term survival focus. Reinforce this with quick wins.	• *False certainty:* Companies believe that the course of action for phase 2 can be rigorously planned, and they overemphasize disciplined implementation of a fixed plan instead of recognizing that there is usually high uncertainty in finding a new growth strategy.
• *Encourage commitment and patience:* Persist in the face of inevitable setbacks and internal opposition to unproven shifts in strategy. Often a vision for renewal requires persistence over a multiyear period.	• *Lack of persistency:* Companies often underestimate the time needed to see results (often, inconveniently, up to a decade), and, consequently, they let up too soon.

TURNING AROUND THE *SUCCESSFUL* COMPANY

Most companies adopt a renewal style reactively, rather than preemptively rematching their style to their environment. Our analysis suggests that prior to embarking on transformation efforts, less than a quarter of companies had outperformed the market and nearly half were systemic underperformers. The difficulty and rarity of preemptive turnarounds for successful companies is, however, no argument against the necessity and possibility of such a turnaround.

Some companies, in fact, manage change preemptively, without the need for risky, step-change transformation initiatives. We studied several disruption-prone industries—industrial goods, consumer discretionary goods, IT, health care, telecommunications, and financial services—over a thirty-plus-year period (from 1980 to 2013). We identified a number of companies that, challenges notwithstanding, managed to generate relatively stable, attractive long-term returns by preemptively evolving their business models, when others in their industries faltered. What was the successful companies' secret sauce? We identified four categories of preemptive transformers (figure 6-7).

Continuous adapters constantly evolve their business and operating model by making many small changes. McDonald's, for example, successfully rode the baby boom of the 1960s and the swelling ranks of teenagers and women in the labor force by providing convenience and an inexpensive, selection-rich menu. In the 1970s and 1980s, the company harnessed the globalization megatrend to expand its footprint internationally. Today, McDonald's continues to evolve. It adjusts its product portfolio to reflect new consumer preferences, creates new restaurant formats, and accelerates adaptation by franchising locally to businesspeople with direct market knowledge.

Ambidextrous players maintain a balance between leveraging existing assets and exploring new possibilities, even after the company has found a successful model. Qualcomm Incorporated, for instance, has

FIGURE 6-7

Models for preemptive transformation

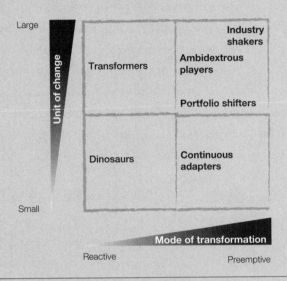

thrived despite massive shifts in the telecommunications industry. The firm has consistently delivered on its mission—"to continue to deliver the world's most innovative wireless solutions"—through a business model that uses returns from its core businesses to fuel future ones. Its early innovations in its cellular service standard (code division multiple access, or CDMA) enabled a global licensing business, whose profits Qualcomm reinvested into a mobile chip-set business that has also become a global success. Today both these businesses support continued internal R&D, as well as fund external partnerships through Qualcomm Ventures, the company's venture-capital business unit.

Portfolio shifters run a portfolio of businesses that the shifters actively rebalance over time. Industrial conglomerate 3M, for example, has more than thirty-five business units divided among five reporting

segments. While the sales contribution by segment naturally fluctu-
ates in response to market conditions, the mix of underlying business
lines reflects very active portfolio management. 3M's approach to
strategic acquisitions and divestments reflects the evolving demand
landscape. For example, 3M spun off its print film division in 1996 in
advance of the rise of digital imaging, and the conglomerate makes
acquisitions in anticipation of future growth trends, such as its 2010
purchase of Cogent Systems, a manufacturer of automated finger-
print identification systems. This shifting mix, combined with tight
financial management, has allowed the firm, remarkably, to increase
dividend payouts to shareholders on an annual basis for the last fif-
ty-five years and keep operating margins well above 20 percent for
more than a decade.

Industry shakers seek to drive and shape industry change rather
than be victims of it. Amazon.com consistently delivers breakthrough
innovation, even as it generates only razor-thin profits. Why? Precisely
because it continually reinvests in its future—in refrigerated ware-
houses for groceries, in same-day delivery in urban centers, and in
data servers and analytics, for example. Though the company built an
unassailable lead in book distribution, it did not rest on its laurels. It
self-disrupted its book business with the launch of its e-reader, the
Kindle, in 2007; by 2010, the company was selling more e-books than
print copies. What's next? Amazon.com continues to succeed by combining its ability to recognize and position itself optimally to leverage
nascent long-term trends with its ability to create and set standards
for new markets. And investors reward it—in 2014, Amazon.com's
price-to-earnings ratio was above 200, versus a market average of
between 10 and 20.

CHAPTER 7

AMBIDEXTERITY

Be Polychromatic

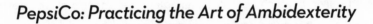

PepsiCo: Practicing the Art of Ambidexterity

When you think of PepsiCo, the first thing that comes to mind is likely its iconic carbonated drink, one of the most famous brands in the world. But PepsiCo is a much more diverse company. In all, it has twenty-two food and beverage brands worth more than $1 billion, and more than forty others worth between $250 million and $1 billion. Lay's, Walkers, Lipton, Quaker Oats, and Mountain Dew are just some of the household names that PepsiCo manages. The company is geographically diverse too. Today, PepsiCo operates all around the world—only 50 percent of its sales come from the United States and Canada.[1]

As a result of this breadth, PepsiCo needs to employ multiple approaches to strategy at the same time. In particular, it needs to take both a classical approach (to capitalize on scale advantage in its core brands) while simultaneously deploying an adaptive approach (to build its business in fast-developing and unpredictable markets, categories, and products to match changing competitive conditions or tastes).

In many food and beverage categories, PepsiCo is the global leader, pursuing a scale- and positioning-based classical approach: it's number one for salty snacks, hot cereals, and sports drinks; number two for carbonated sodas and juice or juice drinks. And in many countries, it is the market-leading food and beverage company—notably in the United States, Russia, and India. In several others, like the United Kingdom and Mexico, PepsiCo is the number two company.[2] There are enormous economies of scale to be obtained in each step in the value chain for the core business, from spreading marketing budgets over larger volumes, to negotiation power with large customers, to manufacturing scale in bottling.

PepsiCo also requires more adaptive capabilities. It needs to respond to shifts in consumer behavior, such as a greater focus on healthy living, which requires managing the uncertainty of developing new products and marketing approaches and facing unfamiliar competitors beyond traditional rivals like Coca-Cola. At the same time, PepsiCo needs to react to rapidly evolving conditions in emerging markets to capitalize on a major source of growth. As a result, PepsiCo is experimenting with a rapid and economical "lift and adapt" approach to innovation, where the company tests new products and services in one country before rolling them out globally. For instance, Lay's "Do Us A Flavor" competition, which crowdsourced a new flavor of potato crisps by capturing the tastes and enthusiasm of consumers and offering a $1 million prize, started in the United Kingdom and migrated to Australia before going to the United States.[3]

To combine these seemingly contradictory requirements, PepsiCo has become a deliberate exponent of the art of ambidexterity. "Different businesses at different times go through different stages of strategy," Indra Nooyi, PepsiCo's chief executive, told us. "In particular, business leaders have to negotiate the central contradiction that lies at the heart of the company." As she explains: "PepsiCo (and any large MNC) must both run and reinvent the business, in each business. It's a hard thing to do."

Running the company and, at the same time, reinventing it—that's the challenge. Nooyi told us that there's a balance to strike between delivering the quarterly numbers and upending current business models to prepare for the future. To resolve this dichotomy, she has pursued what we call the *separation* model of ambidexterity. "In each business," Nooyi said, "we have two strands [running in parallel]: the day-to-day group, and the future group thinking, 'How do I disrupt myself?'" She went on: "The team that runs the core business should keep doing what they're doing efficiently: worrying about the cost per pound to the decimal, as though their life depended on it." The other team should not be "motivated by the current model and [should] focus totally on disrupting [it]."

"Look at our company's soft drinks business," she added. "We need to push Mountain Dew and PepsiCo to get the last dollar of growth, but we're also designing in-home carbonation machines that will totally disrupt the business."

Of course, the idea of disruption is deeply uncomfortable. But Nooyi is adamant that it has to be addressed because "if someone else does it, we'd be disrupted anyways." The thing that has changed is that such contradictions need to be addressed simultaneously—and not sequentially—because "what we used to think about as long-term disruption is now happening on that same timeline." This means "we have to run and transform on parallel tracks."

Ambidexterity: Core Idea

Like PepsiCo, most large businesses operate in multiple business environments that change quickly over time, spanning many increasingly diverse geographies and product categories and supported by a wide range of enabling functions. This diversity requires firms to be ambidextrous, which we define as the ability to apply multiple approaches to strategy at any given time or successively. Ambidexterity is not another color on the strategy palette; it's a technique for using the five basic colors in combination with one another.

Referring back to our art analogy, ambidexterity might be epitomized by Pablo Picasso, who not only mastered classical technique but also shifted his style markedly on multiple occasions throughout his life: the Blue Period (1901–1904), the Rose Period (1904–1906), the African-influenced Period (1907–1909), Analytic Cubism (1909–1912), and Synthetic Cubism (1912–1919).

WHAT YOU MIGHT KNOW IT AS

The notion that companies need to combine different, potentially opposed strategic approaches to thrive in the long run is not new.

In the early 1990s, businesses redoubled their efforts to break the efficiency-innovation trade-off, as increasing technological change made business models and products obsolete more quickly. At the time, *separation* of established and emerging businesses was the dominant approach.

Around the same time, scholars like James March studied the organizational trade-offs between *exploration and exploitation*. In the late 1990s, Michael Tushman and Charles O'Reilly outlined how companies could build *ambidextrous organizations* capable of both exploiting existing opportunities and exploring new ones.[4]

By the early 2000s, Julian Birkinshaw suggested that companies solve this challenge by introducing the concept of *contextual ambidexterity*. It calls for individual employees to choose between exploring and exploiting on an ongoing basis, thus avoiding some of the pitfalls of the separation approach.[5]

More recently, BCG identified *four approaches to ambidexterity*, together with a choice framework that outlined how to select the most appropriate means of achieving ambidexterity depending on underlying business characteristics.[6]

Ambidexterity is hard. Only a small minority of firms consistently out-performed their industry in both turbulent and stable periods, one measure of ambidexterity, because ambidexterity requires combining ways of think-ing and acting that can be diametrically opposed (figure 7-1). But ambidex-terity is valuable, too: the most ambidextrous companies outperformed the market by 10 to 15 percent of total shareholder return on average between 2006 and 2011.[7] In earlier chapters, we have seen the importance of ambi-dexterity for firms like Telenor in combining classical established units with newer, more adaptive businesses and for Amex and Quintiles in switching from one approach to another over time.

Although many managers will be familiar with one well-tried approach to solving the challenge, namely, separation into different units, we have identified four potential and distinct approaches to ambidexterity. These approaches depend on the degree of diversity (how many different environ-ments you face) and dynamism (how often they change) in your business environment (figure 7-2):

- **Separation:** Like PepsiCo, many firms deliberately manage which approach to strategy belongs in each subunit (be it a division, geography, or function) and run those approaches independently of one another.

FIGURE 7-1

Few firms are successfully ambidextrous

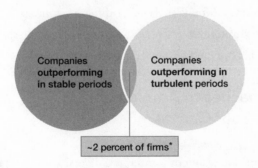

Companies outperforming in stable periods

Companies outperforming in turbulent periods

~2 percent of firms*

Source: Compustat, BCG analysis.

Note: Analysis of US public companies, 1960–2011; outperformance based on market-cap growth, calculated relative to industry-average growth.

*Outperforming in 75 percent of both turbulent and stable periods; 30 percent of all observed quarters defined as turbulent.

FIGURE 7-2

Four approaches to ambidexterity, as a function of the environment's diversity and dynamism

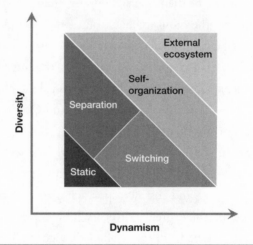

- **Switching:** Firms manage a common pool of resources, and the pool switches between approaches over time or mixes them appropriately at a given moment.

- **Self-organization:** The firm's units self-organize, and each unit chooses the best approach to strategy when matters become too complex to manage these choices in a top-down manner.

- **External ecosystem:** Firms source different approaches to strategy externally through an ecosystem of players that self-select the appropriate approach.[8]

Four Approaches to Ambidexterity: Which Fits Your Canvas?

So how can firms navigate environmental diversity and dynamism in practice? We will explore how some major firms, like Towers Watson, Corning, Haier, and Apple, deploy multiple colors of the strategy palette to achieve balance and success under diverse conditions.

Separation

In the most straightforward situations, both the diversity and the dynamism in a firm's environment are very low. The firm doesn't need an ambidextrous strategy, since a single approach will suffice. When the environment gets more diverse, the first-line approach to ambidexterity is *separation*, in which firms select from the top down which approach to strategy belongs in each subunit (often at the level of a division, geography, or function) and run those approaches independently of one another.

Separation has been the dominant historical approach: Lockheed Martin used a separation technique as far back as 1943. The company was tasked with creating an advanced fighter while it was mass-producing its established bombers. Lockheed created two fully separate units (marking the birth of what would become known as the Skunk Works), each with its own physical location, resources, and culture.[9] More recently, companies like IBM and Toyota have successfully used similar approaches too.[10]

Separation is the simplest and most common approach to achieving ambidexterity and is appropriate for companies facing environments that are moderately diverse but relatively stable over time. Although separation involves structurally separating units that deploy different approaches to strategy, this approach is different from just creating separate business units deploying similar approaches. Each unit requires its own resources, metrics, incentives, and culture to support fundamentally different approaches to strategy.

Traditional and New Revenue Sources: Separation at Towers Watson

Towers Watson, one of the world's biggest pension benefits companies, faces a testing challenge: ensuring its main revenue driver—the traditional defined-benefit pension business—continues to perform while finding new sources of revenue.[11] CEO John Haley said: "We've seen the long-predicted demise of the defined-benefit pension plan market, and while it will still be a key part of our business in ten years from now because it's so big, we can't rely on it for growth going forward." For the first part of the challenge, Towers Watson, as the market leader in benefits consulting, pursues a fundamentally classical approach to strategy.[12] For the second part, however, the company has started to take a more adaptive approach. Like PepsiCo, it is employing the separation model of ambidexterity. Haley explained: "We have to take care of our core business in order to keep investing in innovation. We didn't want fourteen thousand people going away and spending 20 percent of the time tinkering."

Haley described his firm's approach to strategy in terms of three pillars: the first focuses on executing and growing the core business, the second focuses on growth through M&A, and the third on developing innovation as a core competency and deploying it to drive growth.[13] As he explained: "The whole existence of the third pillar is something that we simply didn't have before. People tinkered with things, but our innovation was incremental." Haley realized that to accelerate growth, the firm would have to take "some slightly risky and unpredictable bets." As part of the effort to "look beyond existing spaces to drive growth," Towers Watson would have to try things "even when there are no statistics to help us know if it's a good idea." That is, the firm would have to experiment, rather than plan and therefore adopt an adaptive approach.

Towers Watson deliberately pursued a separation approach to prevent the exploratory, adaptive side of the business from getting in the way of the efficiency of the existing one, and vice versa. "Most of the organization should be focused on making sure the trains run on time," Haley noted. Another reason is that it is not easy to bridge the large cultural gaps between the two approaches, Haley said: "It's hard to shift into a risk-taking mentality."

The approach includes giving the new, adaptive "innovation engine" its own supporting infrastructure and ability to allocate resources. For instance, Haley has launched a special investment committee for vetting every proposed innovation project (i.e., the third pillar of company strategy). "We make sure that people have to get funding to proceed: if we decide not to fund something, you can't work on it." Also, he has created a cadre of so-called Chairman's Fellows. These distinguished employees are given the freedom to spend between 25 and 75 percent of their time on creative solutions to boost the company's commercial prospects through innovation. In 2014, the Fellows were focused on potential models for health-care exchanges.

It is three years since Towers Watson launched its three-pillar strategy, and the signs of progress are encouraging. "We've had some ideas that are just banging around a little bit," Haley said, "but there are some that we're ready to roll out to the marketplace—and even one that could be [worth] several hundred million [dollars] in a few years."

Separation is the most common approach to ambidexterity, in part because it's the simplest. But separation may not always work, since a company's structure tends to be semipermanent, while its environment may not be so. Separation also creates barriers that prevent the flow of information and resources among units, potentially impeding the units' ability to coordinate, collaborate, or cross-fertilize and to change emphasis or style when required. This leads us to when alternative approaches, like switching, are appropriate.

Switching

Dynamic environments, where the company faces only a limited number of environments that are fast changing, require instead a switching approach. When the environment or interfaces are too complex or dynamic to separate out the different approaches, the artificially imposed boundaries of a separation approach would unacceptably reduce organizational effectiveness. In switching, a company manages a common pool of resources to fluidly mix approaches or to change between them over time as its environment changes, similar to how new companies naturally evolve.

Markets that may require switching are those that witness a high rate of change or a lot of product turnover, like fashion or technology. Switching is often used by companies in the early stages of their life cycle, where evolution is rapid. Start-ups, for instance, tend to switch approaches once their breakout product has been established. Initially, start-ups deploy an exploratory style when looking for a breakout product, service, or technology. Then over time, they make the transition to a more exploitative style to scale up and secure a profitable market position.

One company that has switched from one approach to strategy to another in this way is Quintiles. As we saw earlier, Dennis Gillings, the cofounder of the company, took a canonically visionary approach to strategy. But as his firm grew to become the world's largest clinical research organization, the approach evolved to a more classical one under the current CEO Tom Pike. As Gillings put it, the current classical approach is really "the systematization of the visionary strategy." And as we also saw, Pike's emphasis on "one foot in the future" is increasingly requiring a more adaptive or shaping emphasis as change pressures escalate in the healthcare industry.

Several tactics help a firm manage switching, either in the context of the transition between approaches to strategy or in the coexistence of multiple approaches to strategy within a single unit. First, leadership must reduce barriers that prevent resources and information from flowing freely, since boundaries are antithetical to the fluidity needed for switching. Breaking down silo boundaries helps units to share resources and avoid conflicts. Similarly, the firm creates incentives geared to fostering flexibility and collaboration, for instance, rewarding both efficiency and innovation, rather than focusing on only one of these.

Switching is a more difficult approach to manage because it requires both flexibility and effective oversight: when leaders decide to change styles, resource conflicts may erupt between units, staff may resist the change to an unfamiliar approach, and the organization might not make the transition promptly. These culture clashes can be real and frustrating, and leaders can support conflict resolution by providing flexible central functions, like IT and HR, that can cater to different needs over time and help ease complexity during the switchover. That is, partial separation (of support functions) can ironically facilitate switching for other units.

Successful Oscillation: Switching at Corning

Corning, the US-based manufacturer of glass, ceramics, and other related materials, is a consistently successful practitioner of switching—typically oscillating between classical and adaptive or visionary approaches. Perhaps its biggest transition took place in the mid-2000s. In 2006, prices for one of its core sources of revenue—glass for LCD screens—plummeted.[14] In response, Corning looked to develop another profit driver. As CEO Wendell Weeks explained in 2014: "When we experience inevitable challenges, we innovate our way out."[15]

Corning's scientists got to work, turning to Chemcor, a "muscled" glass that their predecessors had developed in the early 1960s.[16] With further refinements, Corning launched a new, supertough, scratch-resistant glass called Gorilla Glass, which was first brought to market on Apple's iPhone, and the material was an immediate success.[17] But then, as detailed earlier, Corning had to switch from innovation mode to implementation mode so that it could produce as much glass as profitably as possible to meet the extraordinary demand for smartphones. It could do so quickly because of a very flexible organizational structure, a lack of silos, and a set of common incentives that ensured that everyone was pulling in the same direction. For instance, Corning kept its R&D and commercial departments tightly linked, often bringing members of those teams together in ad hoc task forces to solve new innovation and marketing challenges. By the early 2010s, Corning's Gorilla Glass was found on more than 2.7 billion devices.[18]

The company is now on a new innovation cycle, having developed an entirely different and new, highly flexible glass application called Corning Willow, which is designed for slim displays and smart surfaces of the future.[19]

Self-Organization

Highly dynamic and diverse environments may not wait for a firm to manage a switch. When a company needs to deploy multiple styles simultaneously—and those styles are changing over time—a self-organizing approach is called for, since managing the switching or separation process in a top-down manner becomes too complex and infeasible. Here, individuals or small teams are empowered to choose for themselves which style to employ at any given time.

Companies can achieve self-organizational capabilities by breaking the organization down into small units and creating individualized performance contracts for each. Each unit negotiates with its peers according to some rules of interaction established by the center and deploys whatever approach—classical, visionary, adaptive, or shaping—it thinks will maximize its performance contribution. In other words, each unit independently determines the approach that fits the nature of its challenge and role. In effect, the company employs a market-based model rather than a managerial paradigm to the selection of strategy approaches. This requires setting high-level, long-term metrics and incentives and clear "rules of engagement." The center needs to define the level at which units self-organize; it should also set the rules for interaction (e.g., transfer pricing between internal units), provide resource pools for which individual units can compete, facilitate self-organization, and manage conflict.

Self-organization is a very challenging "ask" of the organization, with obvious drawbacks. The firm potentially incurs significant costs from duplication, from lack of scale of the individual units, and from enforcing the local rules of interaction and keeping score. Further, management must trust its employees to choose the correct strategic approach. Because the cost of coordination is high, only environments that are highly dynamic and diverse are good candidates for a self-organizing approach.

Room to Maneuver: Self-Organization at Haier

Haier, the world's biggest manufacturer of refrigerators, washing machines, and other white goods, is one of the pioneers of the self-organization approach to ambidexterity.[20] The model was the brainchild of Ruimin Zhang, the company's inspirational chairman and CEO, in answer to a set of diverse challenges: Haier produces a vast array of products—as of 2002, some thirteen thousand in eighty-five categories.[21] It competes in fast-changing markets, with fierce competition from local and international rivals, and it needs to adopt the right approach in each category, innovate quickly, and yet, at the same time, specialize and gain experience to improve quality to stay ahead.

Zhang took control of the company in 1984, when it was on the brink of bankruptcy. He set about finding a way to manage such a diverse business. His guiding light was the Chinese philosopher Lao-Tzu, who said: "In the highest antiquity, the people did not know that there were rulers."[22] Zhang took this to mean that "a leader whose existence is unknown to his subordinates is really the most brilliant one."[23]

His goal became to create an organization where units have room to make their own decisions. "The enterprise will become great when it is able to operate by itself," said Zhang, "with employees acting as their own leaders, understanding what to do to satisfy market and customer demand."[24] The global conglomerate flattened its organization structure and developed two thousand self-governing units. Each unit functions like an autonomous company, with its own profit-and-loss statement, operations, innovation program, and motivation. To support this arrangement, Zhang devised high-level targets to steer performance as well as rules of engagement to regulate interaction between the units—including transfer pricing and compensation for interunit delays.

In the twelve years up to 2013, Haier has seen its revenues grow from $9 billion to more than $30 billion.[25]

OVERCOMING THE AMBIDEXTERITY CHALLENGE: SELF-TUNING ALGORITHMS AND EVOLVABLE ORGANIZATIONS

At first sight, ambidexterity is a paradox, requiring firms to combine seemingly contradictory imperatives without muddling their intentions. This is the exploration-versus-exploitation trade-off.

But is ambidexterity really about breaking a contradiction? In our strategy and environment simulations, we discovered algorithms that not only perform well in specific environments, but also automatically find the optimal balance between exploration and exploitation, outperforming simple algorithms that emphasize one or the other in mixed or changing environments. Furthermore, the algorithms can automatically adjust or self-tune to changing conditions (figure 7-3). In other words, apart from algorithms that represent the primary colors of the strategy palette, we have identified ambidextrous, self-tuning algorithms that break the apparent trade-off between exploration and exploitation by mixing and remixing primary colors as appropriate.

We believe that organizations can replicate the essential features and functions of these self-tuning algorithms to constantly retune their strategies by embracing the following practices:

✓ Defining a very broad option space to explore

✓ Modeling expected payoffs from options by leveraging all available information

✓ Testing promising options quickly and cheaply

✓ Rapidly updating option assessments in light of new information, and reallocating resources by scaling up, stopping, or repurposing investments

✓ Quickly iterating the above steps, assisted by appropriate analytics, thereby overcoming the information complexity and speed constraints of explicit managerial decision making

✓ Measuring outcomes and optimizing the algorithm itself in response to changing circumstances

Perhaps not surprisingly, firms that build business around such algorithms, such as Netflix, Amazon.com, and Google, appear to do these things well, applying the same principles to their organization and strategy, albeit informally, so that their entire business supports rapid adaptive learning. These firms are able to build what we call *evolvable organizations*, which embody self-tuning ambidexterity organizationally. We predict that the creation of evolvable organizations and strategies will become increasingly important to all enterprises as techniques like these become more widely understood and codified.

FIGURE 7-3

Ambidextrous strategies adapt well to changes of environments (simulation)

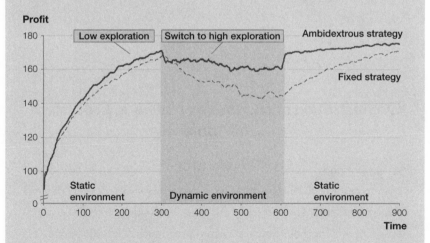

Source: BCG Strategy Institute multi-armed bandit (MAB) simulation.

Note: Fixed strategy has a fixed exploration rate, ambidextrous strategy has a self-tuning exploration rate.

Ecosystem

In the most complex and dynamic cases, when a firm cannot create or manage the full suite of required strategy approaches internally, companies may need to orchestrate a diverse ecosystem of external parties. This approach is only appropriate in the most complex cases because of the high costs and risks involved—the company incurs expense to build ecosystem-sustaining platforms, it must give away profits to incentivize third parties to participate, and it risks potential loss of control over its business model through its dependency on the actions of others. A diverse ecosystem is, in essence, an externalized version of the self-organizing approach. In many respects, the trade-offs and requirements for success are also similar to those of the shaping approach to strategy.

As with shaping, when building an ecosystem, the company first defines which capabilities it can provide and which it will source externally. It needs to ensure that it develops win-win relationships with outside players. Incentives and processes in the ecosystem should be structured such that they ensure the long-term vitality and diversity of the ecosystem. Internally, company culture should be focused on relationship building, diversity, and an external orientation.

Orchestration of a Complex Network: Ecosystem at Apple

We have already seen how Apple shaped an ecosystem of app developers to cater to the range and diversity necessary to make its devices valuable for users. The same logic applies for the diverse set of components it needs for the physical devices it produces. Without a manufacturing ecosystem, Apple could never have created the iPhone in 2007. From a consumer point of view, Apple's signature product is defined by its elegant simplicity: an easy-to-use interface, a sleek design, and a fast and effective operating system. Yet its creation relies on a complex network of companies, put together and orchestrated by Apple.

To build the iPhone, Apple needed several approaches: a visionary approach to develop both the overall concept and new chip technologies, an adaptive one to adjust software and hardware components to rapidly changing customer needs and technological possibilities, and a classical approach for achieving assembly scale and efficiency. Furthermore, the requirements shift with and within each product generation. Apple could not realistically have accommodated all of the required diversity and dynamism in-house—it had, after all, never built or sold a mobile phone, let alone a smartphone, before.

Hence, Apple skillfully created an ecosystem of companies—rather than own the full iPhone supply chain. China's Foxconn assembles the components, Corning makes the glass cover (as discussed earlier in this chapter), Broadcom makes the Wi-Fi chips, Infineon makes the baseband processor, and ARM Holdings designs the iPhone's brain—the mobile processor—to name just a few key players in the iPhone ecosystem.[26]

Strategy Operating on Two Levels

At first sight, the requirements of the different approaches to ambidexterity around organization, incentives, and resource allocation may seem confusing. Each of the strategic approaches discussed in earlier chapters also had a distinct set of requirements for structure, resources, and metrics. Do the requirements of ambidexterity replace those?

They don't. The practical imperatives for ambidexterity affect the firm at a higher level than those of each specific approach to strategy. To give an example: the *classical* and *adaptive* approaches manage for scale and economics of experimentation, respectively. In order to ambidextrously combine the two in a *separation* approach, a firm would need to set up separate units that are each individually managed for either scale or experimentation. For this reason, ambidexterity does not give you more detail about each of the basic strategy colors, but rather tells you how to combine those basic colors in such a way that they maintain their integrity.

Beyond Ambidexterity? Tinting and Shading with the Strategy Palette

In the five preceding chapters, we explained the five archetypal approaches to strategy—each comprising distinct ways of thinking and acting to win in different types of environments. And this chapter has explored how to mix or use multiple approaches, at the same time or sequentially, to respond to the range of environments that large businesses face in practice.

So far, though, we've highlighted only the far ends of the spectra of predictability or unpredictability, malleability or nonmalleability, and attractiveness or harshness. In reality, though, firms' strategic approaches will occupy intermediate and changing points on those continuums. So while the basic colors of the approaches to strategy and their combinations are the building blocks for a business, in practice, a firm will also use the shades and tints of the colors in the strategy palette.

In other words, each approach needs to be calibrated. For instance, adaptive and classical firms exist on opposing ends of a continuum of strategic clock speed. But in practice, even the most adaptive firms do not experiment as much and as fast as theoretically possible, and classical firms still have some elements of experimentation. Instead, the pace and extent of experimentation is determined by the cycle-time of change in the environment, the adaptiveness of competitors, and the costs of experimentation. The same is true for shaping. While classical firms rarely create entirely new markets, they may still try to shape demand through tactics like branding, category building, and promoting new usage occasions.

When considered as part of this broader spectrum, the thinking behind each of the canonical approaches becomes less polar and absolute. Rather, it provides a language and logic for making choices within the context of a specific strategic challenge, empowering leaders to ask the right questions and to develop the right set of capabilities in light of where the environment and company fit on the continuum. Familiarity with the thinking legitimates and facilitates the need to think in different ways depending on the environmental circumstances and helps leaders recognize signals that may require adjustments to the approach.

Ultimately, it is the leader who serves as the animator of the firm's collection of strategic approaches, a topic we will turn to in chapter 8.

CHAPTER 8

LESSONS FOR LEADERS

Be the Animator

Pfizer: Embracing Complexity

Pfizer is a large and complex organization by any measure: with about seventy-eight thousand people and over $50 billion in revenues, it is the largest research-based pharmaceutical company in the world. When Ian Read assumed the CEO role in 2010, Pfizer faced significant challenges: the completion of the integration of Wyeth; the patent expiry of Lipitor, the world's best-selling drug; declining R&D productivity; and a sharp drop in market capitalization from historical heights in the early 2000s.[1]

Under Read, Pfizer has succeeded in addressing these challenges and the stock value has appreciated accordingly. How? For one reason, Read understands that a company as large and complex as Pfizer needed a de-averaged approach to strategy and execution, between units like consumer products, vaccines, and innovative drugs and between mature and emerging markets: "A big, diverse company plays in several boxes [of the strategy palette] at the same time." Read stressed that each unit requires its own approach to strategy: "These units are distinct and global, and they have their own culture and their own focus."

Early during his incumbency, Read led a strategic reassessment that showed that Pfizer needed to rethink how it managed its varied portfolio of businesses. As a result, he refined the organizational structure, creating separate, global business units for innovative pharma and for established products and creating separate units for consumer, vaccines, and oncology under a single senior executive. Additionally, he led the successful divestment of Pfizer's infant nutrition and animal health units in 2012 and 2013, respectively.[2]

The result is a collection of commercial operations, each of which faces a very different strategic environment. The Global Innovative Pharma (GIP) unit is responsible for novel, high-value, new therapies, which are often prescribed by specialist doctors. Global Established Pharma (GEP), on the other hand, focuses on long-established products that have or will soon lose their exclusivity and will compete in highly contested, dynamic markets. Read compared the two units: "The culture we need in GIP isn't the same as that in GEP. The question is, Can we have them coexist if we create enough degrees of separation?"

As Read explained, Pfizer indeed faces multiple, differentiated business environments. The consumer business competes in a less regulated environment and enjoys a relatively speedy route to market. Vaccines prevent rather than treat disease, have very different economics, and involve public-health authorities. Oncology is quite different again, since products are launched in one indication and then tested in others and are dispensed by specialists, increasingly in combination with genetic diagnostic tests.

Alongside these varied environments, Read created functional units, like global supply, R&D, and finance, all with very distinct strategic approaches. For instance, R&D needs to capture and mobilize around new discoveries, which are often serendipitous. This requires an exploratory approach and flexible resource-allocation mechanisms, all hallmarks of an adaptive approach. However, Pfizer's early science work, often performed in partnership with academic medical institutions and universities, more closely resembles a visionary approach, focusing on cutting-edge science in areas of high unmet medical need—innovative science that could one day revolutionize health care.[3]

Read thus effectively differentiated the strategic approach for each part of the organization, but he recognized that the resulting apparent complexity might seem confusing to employees or investors. In response, he devised four simple themes or imperatives: (1) improve the performance of the company's innovative core, (2) allocate resources effectively, (3) earn society's respect, and (4) create an ownership culture where colleagues feel fully accountable for their decisions and results. These four themes coherently describe the common thread that runs through Pfizer's combination of strategic approaches, Read said: "I set a clear purpose and mission based on our four imperatives that help us to align across businesses. All of our conversations rest on that context."

For example, the third imperative requires demonstrating to stakeholders, including governments and private payers, that innovation in the prevention and treatment of disease is vital to the health of society. The strategy for executing on that imperative depends on the business unit. And while the strategies within Pfizer are unique to each business, the fourth imperative strives to create an ownership culture throughout the company and signals to colleagues that thoughtful risk-taking is encouraged within the context of the unique go-to-market approach for each of the businesses.

Read emphasizes the importance of culture in cascading the appropriate approach to strategy and implementation into each unit: "To be successful you need the right culture. Strategy and organization come in the same breath. I don't think the hardest part is getting the strategy right. It's implementation."

In short, Read identified the need to differentiate approaches to strategy and execution in different parts of the organization and created the right level of segmentation of the organization, deciding which approaches to apply where. He then sold his strategy internally and externally by creating unifying themes that allowed managers to see the common thread in the strategic choices he made.

In an industry that is still struggling with R&D productivity, Pfizer has brought a succession of new, branded drugs to the market, including two launched and a third getting FDA approval in 2013 alone. Simultaneously, while de-averaging the strategy, the firm has also reduced complexity, and it has shrunk its annual cost base by over $4 billion from 2011 to 2013. Finally, under Read's tenure, Pfizer's market cap has increased by almost 50 percent through 2014.[4]

Animating a Combination of Approaches: Core Idea

Pfizer illustrates a common theme that has surfaced throughout this book: large corporations need to execute multiple approaches to strategy because they inevitably operate in multiple strategic environments and, furthermore, these environments change over time. Successful firms meet the challenge of selecting, combining, and effectively implementing the appropriate combination of strategic approaches and adjusting it dynamically as circumstances change. In chapter 7, we looked at several organizational and operational solutions to this challenge.

But there is a critical, overarching role for the leader in animating the dynamic combination of strategic approaches, what we might call the *strategy collage*, across the organization. The leader must manage a state of artful disequilibrium, often against an organization's natural tendency to lock in a familiar, comfortable, or successful recipe. Leaders are uniquely positioned to read the external context to determine which approach to strategy is applied where and to put the right people in the right place to execute each approach. Moreover, leaders have a vital role in selling the strategy narrative externally and internally. Equally importantly, they keep the collage up-to-date by maintaining an external orientation and triggering self-disruption by forcing changes in strategic approach. Finally, they selectively influence the execution of the strategic approaches of individual units, by asking the right questions, preventing a dominant logic from clouding a unit's perspective, and putting their weight behind critical strategic initiatives.

Many of the CEOs we interviewed stressed that animating the strategy collage is the critical differentiator between effective and ineffective strategy-setting and implementation and a key role for the CEO. As Indra Nooyi, CEO of PepsiCo, said, "You talk of a single approach to strategy— and therein lies the problem! For a company as relatedly diverse as PepsiCo, you must apply different models of strategic thinking to different parts of the business. For instance, how we choose to play in the e-commerce world with our products has to be fully rethought, and we might break new ground there."

We also heard over and over that animating this collage of approaches to strategy is hard, since it involves reconciling apparent contradictions, but also that it is a critical dimension of leadership. Peter Hancock of AIG said: "I always hear, 'You're giving me mixed messages.' I say, 'You're a leader— you're paid to deliver mixed messages!' Grow and shrink. We're in a complex world where we have to be growing in some places and shrinking in others, and that's what we need to pay managers to do—to think!"

Key Leadership Roles in a Complex and Dynamic World

With the multiple, complex environments of today's markets, leaders need to be *the animators of a dynamic combination of multiple approaches to strategy*. Such a task requires that leaders adopt and excel at eight roles to ensure that the strategy collage delivers results and continues to do so as circumstances change. Figure 8-1 is an example of how a company's approaches to strategy vary over time and with each business unit or function.

FIGURE 8-1

The strategy collage and the eight leadership roles needed to dynamically preserve its fit with a shifting environment

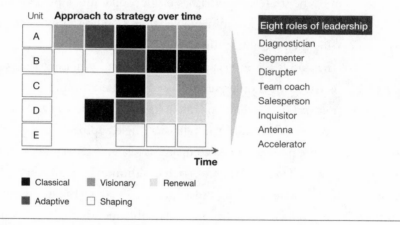

- **Diagnostician:** Continuously take an external perspective to diagnose the degree of predictability, malleability, and harshness of each business environment, and match this with the required strategic approach for each part of the firm.

- **Segmenter:** Structure the firm to match the strategic approach to the environment at the right level of granularity, balancing the trade-off between precision and complexity.

- **Disrupter:** Review the diagnosis and segmentation on an ongoing basis, in line with shifts in the environment, to protect the organization from becoming rigid and to modulate or change approaches when necessary.

- **Team coach:** Select the right people for the job of managing each cell in the collage in line with their capabilities, and help develop their understanding of the strategy palette, both intellectually and experientially.

- **Salesperson:** Advocate and communicate the strategic choices as a whole in a clear and coherent narrative to investors and employees.

- **Inquisitor:** Set and retune the correct context for each particular strategic approach by asking probing questions—not dictating answers—to help stimulate the critical thinking flow that is appropriate to and characteristic of each approach.

- **Antenna:** Look outward continuously, and selectively amplify important signals to ensure that each unit stays in tune with the changing external environment.

- **Accelerator:** Put weight behind select critical initiatives to speed up or bolster their implementation, especially when the required approach has changed, is unfamiliar, or is likely to be resisted.

We'll look in detail at these eight roles and how various CEOs embody them.

Animating the Collage: The Eight Roles of Leaders

Diagnostician

The leader's first important role is diagnosing each of the firm's environments to determine the best strategic approach. This is the leader as metastrategist. By assessing the dimensions of unpredictability, malleability, and harshness by geography, function, and industry segment, leaders can select the appropriate approach of strategy for each part of the firm.

In the role of diagnostician, leaders need to deeply understand the underlying dimensions of the environment and, in light of this information, choose the appropriate strategic approach. For instance, Ian Read explained that in Pfizer's commercial business, different approaches are appropriate: "Global Established Pharma's approach is far more customer- and service-centric, whereas Global Innovative Pharma's is far more oriented toward delivering value for innovation. They each have to answer fundamentally different questions." For GIP, that means considering, "Can I make innovation predictable? Can I produce products with enough added value?" GEP, on the other hand, needs to ask, "Can I get my cost base down? Can I get into areas that are differentiated and growing?"

Getting the diagnosis right depends on identifying which characteristics are most discriminating for where a business is positioned in the strategy palette. This is not always simple, given that many businesses often have characteristics on both sides of the spectrum, and the differences may be nuanced. For instance, Read explained that in his firm's established-products business, a classical approach is most appropriate even though there are some complex dynamics and sources of potential instability: "The Global Established Pharma's business is theoretically predictable. Prices may be volatile, but given the unmet need, we would expect volume to adjust for it."

Segmenter

Leaders need to segment their organization at the right level of granularity when determining where to apply different approaches to strategy. To do so, leaders must balance an accuracy-complexity trade-off. The more granular a leader is in assigning strategic approaches, the better matched those approaches will be. In theory, every intersection of geography, function, and industry could require a differentiated approach: a plan for a mature category in a mature market may require a very different approach from an emerging one in a fast growing market. But in practice, finely differentiated segmentation would generate too much complexity and coordination costs to justify itself (there are exceptions to this, as highlighted earlier in the book, when we discussed self-organization).

Sometimes, assigning approaches purely on a geographic or functional basis might be appropriate; other times, the CEO might decide that a more granular segmentation is necessary despite the additional cost. Regardless, the responsibility resides at the top. At PepsiCo, Indra Nooyi assigns approaches at the business-unit level but also runs "disruption" teams parallel to the day-to-day operations of most of her core business units. For instance, as mentioned earlier, she has a team developing in-home carbonation devices with an adaptive mandate at the same time that her Mountain Dew team works to maximize carbonated soft drink sales with a more classical approach: "In each business, we have two strands: the day-to-day, and the future group thinking, 'How do I disrupt myself?' The people running it can't be the same ones thinking about its disruption."

On the other hand, the leader may set a single approach across the entire organization, especially if the industry is on the cusp of a fundamental shift that will eventually affect all parts of the business. For instance, Ken Chenault wove a strategic approach aligned with building technological disruption into every part of the firm's fabric as Amex came out of the recession: "We had to make the choice," he said. "Do we form a separate unit focused on digital, or do we have the whole company embrace the digital transformation? I decided the whole company. And what we articulated was not just that the digital transformation was taking place but why we could be successful at leading it."

Disrupter

Throughout the book, we have seen how important it is not only to select the right approach to strategy initially but also to keep the match dynamic by pivoting to new approaches over time. Leaders have a key role in guiding or even forcing these transitions. As environments change and businesses develop—and do so faster and faster—leaders need to continuously reexamine their collection of strategic approaches and adjust it where necessary to keep up with shifts in unpredictability and malleability in their environment.

This continuous adjustment is neither easy nor natural. As BCG's founder, Bruce Henderson, noted: "Success in the past always becomes enshrined in the present by the overvaluation of the policies and attitudes which accompanied that success."[5] Therefore, one of the leader's key roles is to keep the organization's approach to strategy fluid. In practice, this means that leaders need to be on the lookout externally for changes in the underlying characteristics of the environment that affect the choice of approach at the segment level. Through that external assessment, the leader must serve as both a counteracting force against the unit's natural organizational inertia to stay on its established path and a catalyst for periodic self-disruption.

As Nooyi told us, the possibility of self-disruption needs to be continuously on the leader's radar: "I am always asking, 'How do I disrupt myself?' Look at the trends in the world and say, 'Gosh, if that or that or that happened in our industry, I'm dead.' Just because you don't want to look at the problem doesn't mean it will go away." Then, the leader needs to drive that change through the organization: "If the disruption doesn't happen at the top, the organization will kill it in committee since today's cash flow trumps unfamiliarity."

Team Coach

Since leaders set the strategic approaches and then turn to their teams to execute them, the task of putting in place the best people and familiarizing them with the strategy palette, both intellectually and experientially, is one of the most important jobs a leader has. Getting the right talent in the right places in their organizations was a prevailing theme from our CEO interviews.

Ideally, any manager should be able to execute any of the approaches to strategy, but often, individual managers are naturally inclined to thrive more in one of the five approaches than in the others. The forward-looking visionary manager may have intrinsically different traits from the disciplined, classical one. And since teams will perform best in environments suited to their strengths, it is critical to fit the team to the purpose: the team members' specific skills should match those required to execute their unit's approach effectively.

Nooyi said: "There are two types of people: there are the ambidextrous, and then there are those who are very good today but can't see beyond their blinders. As the CEO, we can't expect everyone to be ambidextrous. Ain't going to happen . . . [But] let them be very good at keeping the trains running on time."

At the same time, even managers who, for example, need to execute on a disciplined, classical approach may sometimes need to deploy at least some aspects of other approaches. Therefore, successful leaders also develop their people's strategy palette, both intellectually and experientially. Ken Chenault explained Amex's approach to development: "In our leadership model, I talk about situational leadership. People ask, 'What type of leader are you?' But that's the wrong question. At the end of the day, you have to lead according to the situation and the readiness of your people. You have to be willing to, in fact, go through not only multiple phases, but you have to simultaneously follow a range of styles."

Intellectually, a leader develops people's ability to reflect on how they approach strategy and on the value of and distinction between different approaches. He or she teaches others how to cultivate an awareness of their environment and the most important underlying drivers for success in different environments. A leader also encourages self-reflection.

Leaders also give their reports opportunities to directly experience different approaches to strategy. Ever since Peter Hancock joined AIG in 2010, then-CEO Bob Benmosche helped him to diversify his understanding of different strategic approaches by experiencing them firsthand. In 2011, Benmosche switched Hancock's role from manager of Finance, Risk, and Investments to CEO of the Property Casualty division. Hancock needed to familiarize himself quickly with a new approach. "When we paid back the Fed and did the share exchange in 2011, Bob asked me to take a different role, so my life changed overnight from thinking about restructuring to thinking (a) how do I learn enough about the insurance industry and (b) how do I forge a business for this firm to thrive? . . . Then we had to think about how to innovate and do new business in a sensible way." Pushing reports into new, challenging roles not only builds the metastrategic repertoire within the firm's top talent base but also helps employees to feel trusted, credible, valuable, and empowered.

Salesperson

Given that success depends on both internal stakeholder alignment and the buy-in of external parties like investors, customers, or partners, the leader needs to communicate his or her firm's strategic rationale externally and internally. However, as we saw with Ian Read at Pfizer, a dynamic and changing collection of strategic approaches could seem confusing for employees and investors alike. Therefore, one of the leader's roles is to craft a narrative to help stakeholders make sense of the strategy in total and articulate the common denominator.

Take for instance, the role of leaders in communicating with investors. When a leader cannot forecast the firm's performance with a lot of accuracy, because, for instance, the firm leverages an adaptive approach, Wall Street may still expect the firm's reporting to follow an essentially classical line. The CEO, then, needs to send a message that satisfies external stakeholders without distracting or confusing internal ones.

Nooyi explained that challenge to us. In her case, she must balance investor communication to capture both PepsiCo's traditional classical elements and its novel—but less familiar—approaches to disruption: "When investors are talking to you, it's often about giving them inputs for a row and a column [of a spreadsheet]—so whatever you do, you have to land the plane by scale, market share, cost. Only after you land the plane, while the plane is taxiing to the gate, can you say, 'I'm doing something else, too.'"

Likewise, Hancock told us the story of how Benmosche persuaded stakeholders to support his strategic approach after the financial crisis, convincing the US Treasury and Federal Reserve to back his plan to keep the company intact and return it to the public markets, in exchange for repaying the US taxpayers in full: "We had to get multiple investors to write billion-dollar tickets in the equity investment, and there was no playbook for managing that initial float. We needed to persuade an assortment of stakeholders who could veto what we wanted to do in the near term and whose support was critical to what we needed to do in the long term."

Benmosche recognized that the stakeholders were essentially failing to coordinate and that the lack of agreement on whether the company was a set of assets to be broken up or an ongoing concern was depressing AIG's enterprise value by as much as $15 billion. He convinced the stakeholders to take a step back and demonstrated that if they could bury their differences, they had, effectively, a $15 billion "peace dividend" to share.[6] His persuasion tactics worked: AIG's creditors agreed to cooperate, and in a series of six offerings during 2011 and 2012, AIG sold over $44 billion of AIG stock, netting the US government a profit of $22.7 billion and successfully concluding the period of government ownership of the company.[7]

QUESTIONS BY APPROACH

Each approach to strategy has its own characteristic thought flow and, therefore, its own specific set of questions to guide strategy formulation and execution. Let's look at some sample questions for each of the thought flows. By no means exhaustive, these questions will illustrate how to shape and sharpen a team's strategic approach through appropriate probing.

For a *classical* approach, questions follow a linear sequence, in line with the thought flow of analyze, plan, and execute. Leaders wanting to apply a classical approach may, for instance, ask their management team: "Where will we play? What is our competitive advantage? What is the goal? What are the steps required to achieve our goal? Which capabilities do we need to build to realize our goal?"

In an *adaptive* setting, leaders should repeatedly ask questions that check whether the organization is following the *vary, select, and scale up* mantra. For instance, to check whether the focus of variation is correct they might ask: "What is the pattern of external change? What is predictable? What do we not know? Which blind spots do we have? Does our clock speed match that of the environment?" They can pressure-test selection mechanisms, asking: "How do we know if a project is worth continuing? Are we failing enough? What have we learned from failed projects?" And, finally, they question the approach for scaling up successful projects: "What do we need to know to move from pilot to product? What would it take to turn this pilot into a $1 billion business?"

Leaders promoting a *visionary* approach should expect very clear answers to questions in line with the *envisage, build, and persist* thought flow. They can first ask questions like "What future do we want to realize? What is the basis of our confidence that this is plausible and valuable and hasn't been preempted? Does the organization clearly see and believe the vision, too?" Then, to verify whether the proposition is practically implementable, they ask: "What are we trying to build? How do we make it happen?" And finally, they verify whether the vision is being deployed with enough persistence: "Are we staying ahead of the pack? How do we educate the marketplace on our vision? What roadblocks could we be coming up against, or what roadblocks already exist, and how will we overcome them?"

The *shaping* organization needs to answer different questions altogether. To ensure that the strategy works to *engage, orchestrate, and coevolve* with external parties, leaders ask questions like these: "What is the win-win here? How can we influence the stakeholder ecosystem to our advantage? What specifically can we control, and what do we need to control? How do we ensure that our ecosystem stays healthy?" Rather than directly asking about the strategy, leaders check whether the mechanisms are in place to let that strategy continuously emerge by itself: "Are we evolving our platforms effectively to facilitate learning?"

To create the context for a strategic renewal, leaders check whether their management is preparing for both the survival and the renewal phases of the *react, economize, and grow* thought flow. First, they verify whether enough is done to ensure survival: "Have we cut sufficiently deeply? How do we know we cut the right things?" Thereafter, they ensure that the long-term vitality of the company is being thought about too: "How do we innovate strategically to ensure that we thrive in the long term? When do we switch from *survive* to *thrive*? Is our organization set up to support growth and innovation?"

Inquisitor

Once they have selected the appropriate approach to strategy for each unit and assigned the right people for the job, leaders set the context for effective execution by asking the right questions. Obviously, the CEO has neither the time nor the information to direct every unit or be involved in every day-to-day decision. By asking the right questions, executives help their reports to think along the lines of the appropriate approach-specific thought flow, be it *analyze, plan, and execute* for a classical part of their business or *vary, select, and scale up* for a more adaptive unit.

Many CEOs we interviewed emphasized the value of questions. Nooyi explained: "You have to ask the right questions, assuming you have the right people to give the answers. CEOs should go an inch deep and a mile wide on most areas but go a mile deep on areas where you don't believe [the organization] has the skills. The onus is on the CEO to know the lay of the land to ask the right questions."

Through inquiry and framing, CEOs empower their organizations to execute the appropriate strategic approach correctly rather than dictating its implementation through instructions. In addition to empowering his or her people, the CEO who is overseeing many approaches gains informed visibility. The readiness and quality of the answers lets the leader know how well management understands the strategy. At the same time, the questions focus management's attention on what matters most to get the strategy right.

Antenna

Well after leaders have selected the appropriate approach for each unit, they facilitate its ongoing execution by making sure the organization stays in tune with the external environment. To do so, they continuously look outward and selectively amplify important signals. They confront their organizations with reality.

The leader is in a unique position to step outside the firm's dominant mind-set and to challenge established beliefs. This can mean, for example, spotting a new visionary opportunity, identifying false knowns in an adaptive approach, or taking a fresh look at industry boundaries in a classical one.

Over time, established units tend to become inward-looking and reliant on a self-reinforcing, dominant logic—tendencies that come with increasing success at executing a particular approach. The leader can help to combat this natural tendency. As Ken Chenault stressed to us: "The danger in a large organization is that you embrace only one way of thinking and one way of doing. A very simple point I make to the organization is, if you say we live in a changing world, that means that one formula doesn't work."

The leader as antenna can actively seek external, different views—even ones apparently disconnected from the business. For instance, Nooyi looks for diverse sources of inspiration: "I go to trade shows—unrelated trade shows: snack and beverage shows are fine, but I go to shows on supply chain, digital, consumer electronics, design shows, speed-dating events in Silicon Valley."

Like Nooyi, AIG's Hancock saw that his teams were doing fine on a day-to-day basis but would benefit from more external perspectives and an expanded use of more innovative approaches. Consequently, Hancock founded a science team to bring a wholly unique perspective to staid insurance-industry practices. Hancock explained that the team, a collection of social scientists, data scientists, physicists, biologists, and economists, has one core task: to keep offering disruptive views on AIG's core business.[8] "This is essentially an R&D team that is funded centrally and has a mandate to revolutionize the way we do business," he explained.

Accelerator

Finally, the role of accelerator goes beyond spotting external changes and offering disruptive points of view, since even the most convincing stories can fall on deaf ears in large, inert organizations. Yet the leader can't possibly chase down every possible promising initiative. Instead, artful leaders selectively put their weight behind high-profile, critical initiatives that demonstrate to the organization that change is possible, beneficial, necessary, exciting, and—most importantly—supported from the top.

Nooyi selectively deploys her efforts where they have the highest chance to fundamentally influence the direction of the firm. She gave us this advice: "Lean in on themes that need a little bit of a push . . . Initially it's a push from the top, then it becomes a pull." For instance, she recognized that the fountain equipment group at PepsiCo was at risk of not succeeding in the time frame, so she formed and funded a separate group to develop more innovative equipment. "One day our incumbent team woke up and realized, 'We need completely different fountain equipment with a new user interface and new flavors,' and the other group was able to say, 'Oh, yeah, we have it for you.'" The incumbent group wouldn't have pushed for the change on its own, since the new equipment would have had to bet against the current business—a scary prospect. But from her vantage point, Nooyi could anticipate the future need and put her influence against it.

Tips and Traps

The leader has a number of critical roles in matching strategic approaches to environments, keeping the resulting strategy collage dynamic, and catalyzing the execution of those approaches. From the CEOs we interviewed for this book, we heard that the toughest and most valuable challenge of all is managing the dynamic complexity inherent in large companies that require multiple simultaneous or successive approaches to strategy.

A CEO needs to master leading the ambidextrous organization and animating the strategic collage. With all of its inherent contradictions, this is what distinguishes great leaders from good managers. Table 8-1 offers some trips and traps that we picked up in our interviews and research.

TABLE 8-1

Tips and traps: key contributors to success and failure for leaders in navigating diverse and changing strategic environments

Tips	Traps
• *Embrace contradiction:* The demands of the many approaches you lead may be diametrically opposed, and that's okay—but tailoring your messages to each environment is critical.	• *Single-color palette:* Any large organization is probably too complex for a single, unchallenged, and unchanging view of strategy. Avoid oversimplification and uniformity.

(Continued)

TABLE 8-1   *(Continued)*

Tips and traps: key contributors to success and failure for leaders in navigating diverse and changing strategic environments

Tips	Traps
• *Embrace complexity:* Introduce complexity in your organization where this will improve the match between environment and strategy without incurring excessive coordination costs.	• *Managing instead of leading:* Getting too deeply involved in managing each approach can prevent you from shaping the strategy collage at a higher level, as encapsulated in the eight roles of leaders.
• *Explain simply:* The resulting strategic collage may be confusing to workers and investors; find the common thread to communicate a clear story.	• *Planning the unplannable:* In a world that changes quickly and unpredictably, overinvesting in precise predictions and plans can backfire. An effective leader recognizes that sometimes plans are *not* the sign of good leadership.
• *Look outward:* Use your unique position to counteract the self-reinforcing tendencies of your organization to perpetuate dominant beliefs by keeping the organization externally focused and fluid.	• *Rigidity:* Some leaders select an approach but are unwilling to change as new information arises, even though the original course will likely not survive the tides of change.
• *When in doubt, disrupt:* Organizations naturally become entrenched in their established ways of doing things. In a dynamic world, an overemphasis on continuity is a larger danger than unnecessary disruption.	

PERSONALLY MASTERING THE STRATEGY PALETTE

We have seen how the diverse circumstances of business require fundamentally different approaches to developing effective strategies and implementing them. We have also seen how large corporations with businesses in multiple environments need to master the art of applying more than one approach to strategy sequentially or simultaneously. And we have seen how leaders play an essential role in animating the resulting collage of approaches. A corollary of these conclusions is that our individual success as leaders or managers will also depend on personally mastering the art of applying the right approach to strategy to the right circumstances at the right time.

But understanding is only half of the journey. How can you build and harness the necessary skills to put the strategy palette to work for you? How should you personally develop a better approach to strategy? How do you bring what you learned in this book to life?

Essentially, strategy is problem solving, and in both your professional and personal life, you have many opportunities every day to choose between alternative approaches—if only you give yourself that explicit choice. By engaging with each opportunity with the right framing and awareness, you can accelerate your own personal learning journey.

Here are a four practical ways to help build the essential skills:

1. First deepen your understanding of the strategy palette.

2. Practice applying it both to the business at hand and in nonwork situations.

3. Broaden your experience.

4. Practice the skill of setting and shaping the context for others.

Deepening Your Understanding of the Palette

Work on deepening your understanding of each of the different approaches in the strategy palette by reading some of the references in appendix B. As you do so, ask yourself how the thinking process, the critical questions to ask, the tools and frameworks, and the approach to implementation differ between styles. Ask yourself also how these differ from what you are most familiar or comfortable with. Stretch your comfort zone by asking yourself which approach is appropriate for different businesses that you read or hear about or otherwise encounter.

Applying the Palette to Business and Life

Probably the single most powerful step you can take is to ask yourself one extra question as you approach any strategic challenge: what sort of challenge or opportunity is this, and what is the best approach to solving it? That is, before embarking on any particular favorite thought flow to address the challenge, pause to consider which one is the best for the challenge at hand.

More technically, use the diagnostic tool in appendix A (or the more detailed online version) to determine the appropriate strategic approach for your business. Reread the appropriate chapter and try to apply various techniques and tools associated with that style. Note what is unfamiliar or difficult, and look around for role models that you can learn from. As you do so, you will begin to develop your own repertoire of questions, tools, and techniques.

You can also practice the different mental disciplines of each style by applying them in everyday problem solving. In mapping out your personal investment strategy, for example, you might try out different approaches. You could plot out future inflows and outflows and create a detailed end-to-end plan (classical). You could spread your investment across many types of risk and then reallocate rapidly and iteratively according to performance (adaptive). You could make a big-bet investment in something that you can directly control, like a family business or interest (visionary). You could try pooling funds and collaborating with others to develop a new opportunity for returns (shaping). Or you could focus on cutting unnecessary expenditure and creating a strict spending budget to free up resources for saving (renewal).

Another thought experiment is to ask yourself which thinking path is most appropriate. You can then mentally simulate different approaches when confronted with a challenge—will you plan, adapt, envision, shape, or renew? You will develop intuition for which problems are attacked best with which approach, and you will likely derive different and complementary insights as you carry out this series of thought experiments.

Remind yourself that the strategy palette is not just for strategizing but for the whole cycle of thought and action toward creating a desired outcome. Therefore, apply the thinking to the whole cycle of your actions, and make sure that you are using information and are innovating, organizing, and leading in a manner consistent with your chosen approach.

Diversifying Your Experience

You should try to work in different types of businesses so that you can gain hands-on experience with each style. Deploy yourself in different situations, even if they do not play to your natural strengths. You will be able to do this without becoming a career butterfly since any large company comprises multiple businesses that are very different in character, and any individual business requires different approaches in different geographies and at different stages of its life cycle. Furthermore, every product or function within a business will face strategic challenges of a different nature. Many Japanese companies have a tradition of the "horizontal fast track" to broaden the experience of promising employees by rotating them through different parts of the business. Consider developing your own career plan along the same lines.

Setting the Context for Others

You should develop your strategic leadership capabilities by building and managing teams to deploy each approach. In particular, think about selecting individuals with the right traits and capabilities for the desired approach or approaches. Do you need an analyst or an entrepreneur? A visionary or a follower?

You should also practice asking the questions noted in chapter 8 to set the context for each style. Developing your own repertory of such questions is one of the most powerful moves you can make to improve your leadership skills.

Keep your eye on changing conditions, and help connect your team with that changing reality and help them modulate their approach accordingly. Remind yourself that you are trying to manage an artful disequilibrium, not perfect an unchanging recipe. Constantly ask and observe what needs to change, and then be the agent of this change.

The digital technology revolution, globalization, and other drivers of change look set to continue: the diversity of conditions that business faces will likely persist or even increase for some years to come. Gone are the days when a manager could start and end a career with one firm, in one relatively unchanging business, rising through the ranks while accumulating and deploying a static set of knowledge and skills. Managers who master the strategy palette will surely generate more value for their companies and be advantaged themselves in developing their careers successfully.

Now, let's get painting!

Self-Assessment

What Is Your Approach to Strategy?

This short self-assessment is designed to assess the fit between your environment, your intended approach to strategy, and your strategic practices.

Your Current Strategizing Practices

Please select one statement that __best__ describes your current strategizing practices.

A. We set a clear goal and plans, which do not change frequently, and we execute to achieve them.

B. We strive to realize an imagined end state, and we react flexibly to obstacles that we encounter along the way.

C. We identify opportunities to reduce costs and preserve capital, guided by detailed plans, so that we can eventually identify a new path to growth.

D. We constantly scan the environment for signals of change, which we use to guide a portfolio of experiments to remobilize our resources around successful ones.

E. We actively engage other stakeholders and companies in our industry, create a shared long-term vision, and build platforms to enable collaboration.

Circle your answer above, and write it down here:

Your Perceived Business Environment

Please select one statement that <u>best</u> describes your perceived business environment.

F.   Our industry or company has been shaken by an internal or external shock or has become misaligned with a shifting business environment.

G.   Our industry is ripe for disruption by an imaginative new player.

H.   Our industry is marked by a high degree of dynamism and unpredictability, driven by shifting customer demand, technologies, or competitive structure.

I.   Our industry has a stable, predictable pattern of demand and competitive structure.

J.   Our industry can be shaped or reshaped by a coalition of players acting in coordination.

Circle your answer above, and write it down here:

Your Intended Approach to Strategy

Please select one statement that <u>best</u> describes the strategy you currently intend to pursue.

K.   We continuously renew our competitive edge, leveraging our agility and flexibility.

L.   We build sustainable competitive advantage through superior scale or capabilities.

M.   We succeed by seeing and realizing new possibilities, leveraging our imagination, speed, and persistence.

N.   We succeed by building and maintaining platforms to orchestrate the activities of other companies and stakeholders.

O.   We are focused on ensuring short-term viability as a prelude to reigniting growth by realigning our strategy.

Circle your answer above, and write it down here:

Results: Are You Using the Right Approach to Strategy?

Please circle the quadrants that best reflect your answers regarding strategizing practices, perceived environment, and intended style:

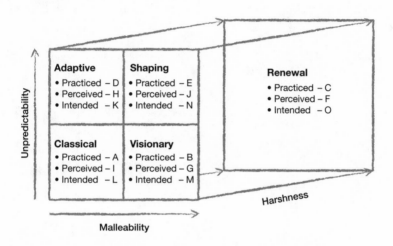

Looking at the results, reflect on the following questions:

- Are our current strategizing practices in line with our intended approach to strategy?

- Does our intended approach to strategy match our perceived environment?

- What are the reasons for any mismatch, and how could we address them?

Further Reading

Chapter 1: Introduction

Freedman, Lawrence. *Strategy: A History.* Oxford: Oxford University Press, 2013.

Ghemawat, Pankaj. "Competition and Business Strategy in Historical Perspective." *Business History Review* 76, no. 1 (2002): 37–74.

Reeves, Martin, Claire Love, and Philipp Tillmanns. "Your Strategy Needs a Strategy." *Harvard Business Review*, September 2012.

Wiltbank, Robert, Nicolas Dew, Stuart Read, and Saras D. Sarasvathy. "What to Do Next? The Case for Non-Predictive Strategy." *Strategic Management Journal* 27, no. 10 (2006): 981–998.

Chapter 2: Classical: Be Big

Ansoff, Igor H. *Corporate Strategy. An Analytic Approach to Business Policy for Growth and Expansion.* New York: McGraw-Hill, 1965.

Barney, Jay. "Firm Resources and Sustained Competitive Advantage." *Journal of Management* 17, no. 1 (1991): 99–120.

Henderson, Bruce. "The Experience Curve." *BCG Perspectives*, 1968.

———. "The Product Portfolio." *BCG Perspectives*, 1970.

———. "The Rule of Three and Four." *BCG Perspectives*, 1976.

———. "Strategic and Natural Competition." *BCG Perspectives*, 1980.

Lafley, A. G., and Roger L. Martin. *Playing to Win: How Strategy Really Works.* Boston: Harvard Business Review Press, 2013.

Lochridge, Richard. "Strategy in the 1980s." *BCG Perspectives*, 1981.

Peters, Thomas J., and Robert H. Waterman Jr. *In Search of Excellence.* New York: Warner Books, 1982.

Porter, Michael. "How Competitive Forces Shape Strategy." *Harvard Business Review*, March–April 1979, 137–145.

———. "What Is Strategy?" *Harvard Business Review*, November 1996.

Prahalad, C. K., and Gary Hamel. "The Core Competence of the Corporation." *Harvard Business Review*, May–June 1990.

Stalk, George, Philip Evans, and Lawrence E. Shulman. "Competing on Capabilities: The New Rules of Corporate Strategy." *Harvard Business Review*, March–April 1992.

Wernerfelt, Birger. "A Resource-Based View of the Firm." *Strategic Management Journal* 5 (1984): 171–180.

Chapter 3: Adaptive: Be Fast

Darwin, Charles. *The Origin of Species*. London: John Murray, 1859.

Eisenhardt, Kathleen M., and Donald N. Sull. "Strategy as Simple Rules." *Harvard Business Review*, January 2001.

Fine, Charles. *Clockspeed: Winning Industry Control in the Age of Temporary Advantage*. New York: Basic Books, 1999.

McGrath, Rita G. *The End of Competitive Advantage: How to Keep Your Strategy Moving as Fast as Your Business*. Boston: Harvard Business Review Press, 2013.

Mintzberg, Henry. "Patterns in Strategy Formation." *Management Science* 24, no. 9 (1978): 934–948.

Nelson, Richard, and Sidney Winter. *An Evolutionary Theory of Economic Change*. Cambridge: Belknap Press, 1985.

Reeves, Martin, and Mike Deimler. *Adaptive Advantage: Winning Strategies for Uncertain Times*. Boston: Boston Consulting Group, 2012.

———. "Adaptability: The New Competitive Advantage." *Harvard Business Review*, August 2011.

Stalk, George. "Time: The Next Source of Competitive Advantage." *Harvard Business Review*, July–August 1988.

Chapter 4: Visionary: Be First

Bower, Joseph L., and Clayton M. Christensen. "Disruptive Technologies: Catching the Wave." *Harvard Business Review*, January–February 1995.

Hamel, Gary and C. K. Prahalad. *Competing for the Future*. Boston: Harvard Business Review Press, 1996.

Johnson, Mark, Clayton Christensen, and Henning Kagermann. "Reinventing Your Business Model." *Harvard Business Review*, 2008.

Kim, W. Chan, and Renée Mauborgne. "Blue Ocean Strategy: How to Create Uncontested Market Space and Make the Competition Irrelevant." *Harvard Business Review*, October 2004.

Lindgardt, Zhenya, Martin Reeves, George Stalk, and Mike Deimler. "Business Model Innovation: When the Going Gets Tough." *BCG Perspectives*, December 2009.

Moore, Geoffrey A. *Crossing the Chasm: Marketing and Selling High-Tech Products to Mainstream Customers*. New York: Harper Business Essentials, 1991.

Reeves, Martin, George Stalk, and Jussi Lehtinen. "Lessons from Mavericks: Staying Big by Acting Small." *BCG Perspectives*, June 2013.

Chapter 5: Shaping: Be the Orchestrator

Brandenburger, Adam M., and Barry J. Nalebuff. *Co-opetition.* New York: Currency Doubleday, 1996.

Chesbrough, Henry. "Open Innovation: The New Imperative for Creating Profit from Technology." *Academy of Management Perspectives* 20, no. 2 (2006): 86–88.

Evans, Philip, and Tom Wurster. *Blown to Bits: How the New Economics of Information Transforms Strategy.* Boston: Harvard Business School Press, 1999.

Freeman, R. Edward. *Strategic Management: A Stakeholder Approach.* Boston: Pitman, 1984.

Henderson, Bruce. "The Origin of Strategy." *Harvard Business Review,* November 1989.

Iansiti, Marco, and Roy Levien. *The Keystone Advantage: What the New Dynamics of Business Ecosystems Mean for Strategy, Innovation, and Sustainability.* Boston: Harvard Business School Press, 2004.

Levin, Simon. *Fragile Dominion: Complexity and the Commons.* New York: Basic Books, 2000.

Moore, James F. *The Death of Competition: Leadership and Strategy in the Age of Business Ecosystems.* New York: Harper Business Press, 1996.

Prahalad, C. K., and Venkat Ramaswamy. *The Future of Competition: Co-creating Unique Value with Customers.* Boston: Harvard Business School Press, 2004.

Reeves, Martin, and Alex Bernhardt. "Systems Advantage." *BCG Perspectives,* 2011.

Reeves, Martin, Thijs Venema, and Claire Love. "Shaping to Win." *BCG Perspectives,* 2013.

Chapter 6: Renewal: Be Viable

Burrough, Brian, and John Helyar. *Barbarians at the Gate: The Fall of RJR Nabisco.* New York: HarperBusiness, 1990.

Duck, Jeanie D. *The Change Monster: The Human Forces That Fuel or Foil Corporate Transformation and Change.* New York: Three Rivers Press, 2001.

Hammer, Michael, and James A. Champy. *Reengineering the Corporation: A Manifesto for Business Revolution.* New York: HarperCollins, 1993.

Hout, Tom M., and George Stalk. *Competing Against Time: How Time-Based Competition Is Reshaping Global Markets.* New York: Free Press, 1990.

Kaplan, Robert S., and William J. Bruns. *Accounting and Management: A Field Study Perspective.* Boston: Harvard Business Review Press, 1987.

Kotter, John P. *Leading Change.* Boston: Harvard Business School Press, 1996.

Reeves, Martin, Kaelin Goulet, Gideon Walter, and Michael Shanahan. "Lean, but Not Yet Mean: Why Transformation Needs a Second Chapter." *BCG Perspectives,* October 2013.

Reeves, Martin, Knut Haanæs, and Kaelin Goulet. "Turning Around a Successful Company." *BCG Perspectives,* December 2013.

Chapter 7: Ambidexterity: Be Polychromatic

Birkinshaw, Julian, and Christina Gibson. "Building Ambidexterity into an Organization." *MIT Sloan Management Review*, summer 2004.

March, James G. "Exploration and Exploitation in Organizational Learning." *Organization Science* 2, no. 1 (1991): 71–87.

Reeves, Martin, Knut Haanæs, James Hollingsworth, and Filippo L. Scognamiglio Pasini. "Ambidexterity: The Art of Thriving in Complex Environments." *BCG Perspectives*, February 2013.

Reeves, Martin, Ron Nicol, Thijs Venema, and Georg Wittenburg. "The Evolvable Enterprise: Lessons from the New Technology Giants." *BCG Perspectives*, February 2014.

Tushman, Michael L., and Charles A. O'Reilly III. "Ambidextrous Organizations: Managing Evolutionary and Revolutionary Change." *California Management Review* 38, no. 4 (1996): 8–30.

Chapter 8: Lessons for Leaders: Be the Animator

The Boston Consulting Group. "Jazz vs. Symphony—A TED Animation," *BCG Perspectives*, October 24, 2014.

Clarkeson, John. "Jazz vs. Symphony." *BCG Perspectives*, 1990.

Torres, Roselinde, Martin Reeves, and Claire Love. "Adaptive Leadership." *BCG Perspectives*, December 13, 2010.

von Oetinger, Bolko. "Leadership in a Time of Uncertainty." *BCG Perspectives*, 2002.

Multi-Armed Bandit (MAB) Simulation Model

We researched the characteristics and effectiveness of each of the approaches to strategy in the strategy palette by simulating how they perform in different business environments. We modeled environments as a so called multi-armed bandit (MAB) problem, which is able to richly capture the economics of decisions under uncertainty. Different algorithmic solutions to this problem then represent the strategic approaches in the palette.

The MAB problem is named after a well-known problem in decision theory. A gambler is faced with choosing which of several slot machines to play. After having played, the gambler will have some knowledge about the payout of some machines but no knowledge of others and will therefore be forced to choose between partial knowns and unknowns. The problem is therefore ideal for modeling trade-offs between exploitation of known options and exploration of unknown options, and for testing strategies under high degrees of ignorance and uncertainty.

More technically, each slot machine, or bandit, is modeled as a probability distribution, with a given mean value and standard deviation. These two parameters may change over time, both independently (e.g., to model exhaustion over time or environmental dynamism) and in response to choices made by one or more gamblers (e.g., to model competition or environmental shaping). The probability distribution is, of course, unknown to the gamblers, but may be learned over time as more and more values are drawn from each bandit. In our model, the bandits correspond to a set of investment options, with payoffs that are independent from each other and unknown to the strategy being tested.

By changing model parameters such as the uncertainty of the payout distributions, the rate and uncertainty by which the means of the distributions change, the degree to which the distributions change in response to investment behavior, and the costs of making investments, we can richly model a set of business environments. Specifically, unpredictability is modeled by uncertainty in the shifts in payout distributions over time. Malleability is modeled as payouts' shifting in response to repeated investments. Harshness is modeled as a cost imposed on shifting between options against an overall resource constraint. In this way classical, adaptive, visionary, shaping, and renewal environments can all be modeled.

The strategies that compete in these various environments can also be modeled as the choices the fictional gambler or strategist makes, according to the information he or she has about payoffs from previous investments. The algorithms driving these choices can be varied with respect to how much information from previous investments is retained, how that information is weighted, how much effort and time is devoted to exploration of new options, how beliefs about the payouts of the investment arms are updated, and how quickly the strategy converges and settles on a preferred investment option. In this way, it is possible to model the behaviors of search, adaptation, shaping, and resource conservation, which underpin the five strategies of the strategy palette.

Specifically, classical strategies are modeled as a limited period of exploration followed by convergence on a preferred investment option. An adaptive strategy is modeled by a continued allocation of a portion of investments to exploration of random options. A visionary strategy is modeled as a deep (multiround) exploration of multiple options followed by convergence on a preferred option, and a shaping strategy is simulated as a periodic, ongoing, deep exploration of multiple options. A renewal strategy is simulated as a rapid convergence on the best option discoverable within a limited period of exploration.

We simulated which strategies performed best in each environment by allowing them to compete with each other in the various environments

FIGURE C-1

Simulation of five core strategies (schematic view)

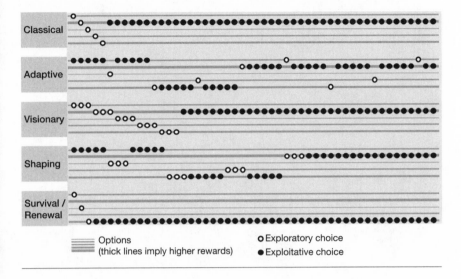

Options
(thick lines imply higher rewards)

o Exploratory choice
● Exploitative choice

represented in the strategy palette, and validated that the canonical strategies of the palette were indeed the ones best fitted for their respective environments (figure C-1).

For ease of visual representation, we compared each strategy against a baseline strategy of moderate exploration: this strategy invests in exploration by testing new options—one out of every ten rounds. For the rest of the time, it settles on the best option found so far, which is determined by average rewards gathered over the past ten rounds in which any one option was pursued.

The same simulation model forms the analytical core of the companion app for this book. With this app, readers have a chance to build muscle memory of the different approaches to strategy by running a lemonade stand in a series of environments that correspond to those of the strategy palette.

NOTES

Chapter 1

1. Rita G. McGrath, *The End of Competitive Advantage: How to Keep Your Strategy Moving as Fast as Your Business* (Boston: Harvard Business Review Press, 2013).

2. Martin Reeves, Claire Love, and Philipp Tillmanns, "Your Strategy Needs a Strategy," *Harvard Business Review*, September 2012.

3. The discussion of Mars throughout this book comes from Paul S. Michaels (Mars CEO), interview with authors, April 2014, and is supplemented by other sources where indicated.

4. Tata Consultancy Services, "Corporate Facts," About TCS, accessed May 7, 2014, www.tcs.com/about/corp_facts/Pages/default.aspx; Times Internet Limited, "Circuit of Glory," "Times of Tata," *Economic Times*, May 14, 2014, http://economictimes.indiatimes.com/timesoftata.cms. The discussion of Tata Consultancy Services (TCS) throughout this book comes from Natarajan Chandrasekaran (TCS CEO), interview with authors, June 2014, and is supplemented by other sources where indicated.

5. "Quintiles Named Preferred Provider in Phase I Market Report," *Wall Street Journal*, August 9, 2013, http://online.wsj.com/article/PR-CO-20130809-908208 .html. The discussion of Quintiles throughout this book comes from Dennis Gillings (Gillings founder) and Tom Pike (Gillings CEO), interviews with authors, February–March 2014, and is supplemented by other sources where indicated.

6. Liu Jie, "Paying Price for Success in Commerce," *China Daily*, Biz Updates, February 3, 2014, www.chinadaily.com.cn/beijing/2014-02/03/content_17272245.htm.

7. Sara Lepro, "American Express to Cut 7,000 Jobs," *Huffington Post Business*, November 25, 2011, www.huffingtonpost.com/2008/10/30/american-express-to-cut-7_n_139476.html. The discussion of American Express throughout this book comes from Ken Chenault (Amex CEO), interview with authors, April 2014, and is supplemented by other sources where indicated.

Chapter 2

1. David A. Kaplan, "Mars Incorporated: A Pretty Sweet Place to Work," *Fortune*, January 17, 2013, http://fortune.com/2013/01/17/mars-incorporated-a-pretty-sweet-place-to-work/.

2. For brand values, see Mars, "How We Work," Mars website, accessed May 8, 2014, www.masterfoodsconsumercare.co.uk/global/careers/how-we-work.aspx. For U.S. ranking, see "Mars," *Forbes*, May 12, 2014, www.forbes.com/companies/mars/.

The discussion of Mars throughout this book comes from Paul S. Michaels (Mars CEO), interview with authors, April 2014, and is supplemented by other sources where indicated.

3. Sebastian Joseph, "Cadbury and Mars Push to Boost Chocolate Sales in Slow Summer Months," *Marketing Week: News*, July 13, 2013, www.marketingweek.co.uk/news/ cadbury-and-mars-push-to-boost-chocolate-sales-in-slow-summer-months/4007375 .article.

4. Bruce D. Henderson, "The Product Portfolio," *BCG Perspectives*, 1970, www .bcgperspectives.com/content/classics/strategy_the_product_portfolio/.

5. BCG Strategy Institute, "Average Operating Margin 2007–2012." Analysis based on Compustat and CapitalIQ data.

6. David J. Lynch, "Thousands of Layoffs by DHL, ABX Air Hit Wilmington, Ohio," *USA Today*, December 15, 2008, http://usatoday30.usatoday.com/money/ economy/2008-12-15-wilmington-dhl-abx-air-layoffs_N.htm.

7. Igor H. Ansoff, *Corporate Strategy. An Analytic Approach to Business Policy for Growth and Expansion* (New York: McGraw-Hill, 1965).

8. Bruce D. Henderson, "The Experience Curve," *BCG Perspectives*, 1968, www .bcgperspectives.com/content/classics/strategy_the_experience_curve/.

9. Henderson, "The Product Portfolio."

10. Richard Lochridge, "Strategy in the 1980s," *BCG Perspectives*, 1981, www .bcgperspectives.com/content/classics/strategy_strategy_in_the_1980s/.

11. Michael Porter, "How Competitive Forces Shape Strategy," *Harvard Business Review*, March–April 1979, 137–145.

12. Birger Wernerfelt, "A Resource-Based View of the Firm," *Strategic Management Journal* 5 (1984): 171–180; Jay Barney, "Firm Resources and Sustained Competitive Advantage," *Journal of Management* 17, no. 1 (1991): 99–120; C. K. Prahalad and Gary Hamel, "The Core Competence of the Corporation," *Harvard Business Review*, May–June 1990.

13. George Stalk, Philip Evans, and Lawrence E. Shulman, "Competing on Capabilities: The New Rules of Corporate Strategy," *Harvard Business Review*, March–April 1992.

14. Bob Cramer, "With Developed Markets Reaching Maturity and Emerging Markets Slowing Down, What Will Drive Future Growth?" *Bidness Etc.*, February 5, 2014, www.bidnessetc.com/business/the-household-and-personal-products-industry-dark-clouds-on-the-horizon/.

15. Ivan Marten and Andrew Mack, "The European Power Sector: Only the Nimble Will Survive," *BCG Perspectives*, March 2013, www.bcgperspectives.com/content/ articles/energy_environment_european_power_sector_only_nimble_will_thrive/.

16. Frank Klose and Jonas Prudlo, "Flexibilization: The New Paradigm in Power Generation," *BCG Perspectives*, June 2013, www.bcgperspectives.com/content/articles/ energy_environment_flexibilization_new_paradigm_in_power_generation/;

Cornelius Pieper et al., "Solar PV Plus Battery Storage: Poised for Takeoff," *BCG Perspectives*, July 2013, www.bcgperspectives.com/content/articles/energy_ environment_solar_pv_plus_battery_storage_poised_for_takeoff/; Deutsche Telekom, "QIVICON Wins Innovation Prize and Gains New Partners," Qivicon: Media Information, September 7, 2014, www.qivicon.com/en/meta/media-relations/ qivicon-wins-innovation-prize-and-gains-new-partners/.

17. Jack Welch, *Winning* (New York: Harper Business, 2004).

18. William Reed Business Media SAS, "Inside Quintiles: The World's Largest CRO," *Outsourcing Pharma*, July 29, 2013, www.outsourcing-pharma.com/Clinical-Development/Inside-Quintiles-The-World-s-Largest-CRO. The discussion of Quintiles throughout this book comes from Dennis Gillings (Quintiles founder) and Tom Pike (Quintiles CEO), interviews with authors, February–March 2014, and is supplemented by other sources where indicated.

19. Michael Porter, "What Is Strategy?" *Harvard Business Review*, November 1, 1996.

20. Deutsche Bahn, "Competition Report 2013," 2013, 6–23.

21. Diageo, "Reserve: Leading Growth in Luxury Spirits," investor conference transcript, November 2013, www.diageo.com/en-row/investor/Pages/resource .aspx?resourceid=1600.

22. The discussion of Huawei throughout this book comes from Guo Ping (Huawei CEO), interview with authors, March 2014, and is supplemented by other sources where indicated.

23. Nathaniel Ahrens, "China's Competitiveness: Myth, Reality, and Lessons for the United States and Japan: Case Study: Huawei," Center for Strategic and International Studies, Washington DC, 2013.

24. Michael J. Silverstein et al., *The $10 Trillion Prize: Captivating the Newly Affluent in China and India* (Boston: Harvard Business Review Press, 2012).

25. Will Connors and Devon Maylie, "Nigeria Gives Huawei a Place to Prove Itself," *Wall Street Journal*, September 12, 2011, http://online.wsj.com/news/articles/SB10 001424053111904279004576524742374778386.

26. Henderson, "The Product Portfolio"; Bruce D. Henderson, "The Rule of Three and Four," *BCG Perspectives*, 1976, www.bcgperspectives.com/content/ Classics/strategy_the_rule_of_three_and_four/; Martin Reeves, Mike Deimler, and George Stalk, "BCG Classics Revisited: The Rule of Three and Four," *BCG Perspectives*, December 2012, www.bcgperspectives.com/content/articles/ business_unit_strategy_the_rule_of_three_and_four_bcg_classics_revisited/.

27. John A. Byrne, "How Jack Welch Runs GE," *BusinessWeek*, June 8, 1998, www .businessweek.com/1998/23/b3581001.htm.

28. Henderson, "The Experience Curve."

29. Barney Jopson, "P&G Chief AG Lafley Promotes Four Executives to Head Major Units," *Financial Times*, June 5, 2013, www.ft.com/intl/cms/s/0/d0579dc2-ce2e-11e2-8313-00144feab7de.html?siteedition=intl#axzz3DUT2FjD3.

30. The discussion of Mahindra throughout this book comes from Anand Mahindra (Mahindra CEO), interview with authors, June 2014, and is supplemented by other sources where indicated.

31. Shell International BV, "Chairman's Message," Annual Report 2012: Our Business, accessed May 7, 2014, http://reports.shell.com/annual-report/2012/businessreview/ourbusinesses/chairmansmessage.php.

32. Shell International, "Introduction from the CEO," Sustainability Report 2012, accessed May 7, 2014, http://reports.shell.com/sustainability-report/2012/introduction.html.

33. The discussion of Mylan throughout this book comes from Heather Bresch (Mylan CEO), interview with authors, April 2014, and is supplemented by other sources where indicated.

34. Diageo, "Diageo Opens Its New Customer Collaboration Centre," Diageo, Our Brands website, accessed May 12, 2014, www.diageo.com/en-row/ourbrands/infocus/Pages/CustomerCollaborationCentre.aspx.

35. Goodreads, "Peter F. Drucker," *Quotes*, May 8, 2014, www.goodreads.com/author/quotes/12008.Peter_F_Drucker.

36. MastersInDataScience.org, "Data Science in Retail," May 17, 2014, www.mastersindatascience.org/industry/retail/; James L. McKenney and Theodore H. Clark, "Procter & Gamble: Improving Consumer Value Through Process Redesign," Case 195126 (Boston: Harvard Business School, March 31, 1995).

37. Quintiles, "Where We Are: Locations," May 8, 2014, www.quintiles.com/locations/.

38. Amir Hartman, "The Competitor: Jack Welch's Burning Platform," *Financial Times Press*, September 5, 2003, www.ftpress.com/articles/article.aspx?p=100665&seqNum=5.

39. Kaplan, "Mars Incorporated."

40. The discussion of Pfizer throughout this book comes from Ian Read (Pfizer CEO), interviews with authors, February–March 2014, and is supplemented by other sources where indicated.

41. Andrew Ward, "Pfizer Break-up May Follow AstraZeneca Deal," *Financial Times*, May 4, 2014, www.ft.com/intl/cms/s/0/ba383d00-d399-11e3-b0be-00144feabdco.html?siteedition=intl#axzz31X8zJqbT.

42. Jim Collins, "The 10 Greatest CEOs of All Time," Jim Collins website, July 21, 2003, www.jimcollins.com/article_topics/articles/10-greatest.html.

Chapter 3

1. The discussion of Tata Consultancy Services (TCS) throughout this book comes from Natarajan "Chandra" Chandrasekaran (TCS CEO), interview with authors, June 2014, and is supplemented by other sources where indicated.

2. See the following Tata Consultancy Services documents, all accessed May 7, 2014: "Corporate Facts," www.tcs.com/about/corp_facts/Pages/default.aspx; "Innovation Brochure," www.tcs.com/SiteCollectionDocuments/Brochures/ Innovation-Brochure-0513-1.pdf; Tata Consultancy Services Facebook page, www .facebook.com/Corporate.Learnings/posts/571975139536810?stream_ref=5.

3. Natarajan Chandrasekaran, e-mail message to authors, May 20, 2014.

4. Chaitanya Kalbag and Goutam Das, "The Whole Organisation Is Pumped Up and I Have to Keep That Going," *Business Today*, November 10, 2013, http://businesstoday. intoday.in/story/bt-500tcs-ceo-natarajan-chandrasekaran-interview/1/199788.html.

5. Tata Consultancy Services, "Annual Report 2009–10," accessed May 6, 2014.

6. Shishir Prasad, "TCS' N Chandrasekaran: Planet of the Apps," *Forbes India*, October 10, 2012, http://forbesindia.com/printcontent/33871.

7. Saritha Rai, "India's TCS Becomes the World's Second Most Valuable IT Services Firm," *Forbes*, September 13, 2013, www.forbes.com/sites/saritharai/2013/09/13/ indias-tcs-is-second-most-valuable-it-services-firm-globally/.

8. Daniel Pantaleo and Nirmal Pal, *From Strategy to Execution: Turning Accelerated Global Change into Opportunity* (Berlin: Springer, 2008), 10.

9. The discussion of Zara and Inditex throughout this book comes from Zara senior management, correspondence with authors, June 2014.

10. Greg Petro, "The Future of Fashion Retailing: The Zara Approach, Part 2 of 3," *Forbes*, October 25, 2012, www.forbes.com/sites/gregpetro/2012/10/25/the-future- of-fashion-retailing-the-zara-approach-part-2-of-3/; Unique Business Strategies, "The Story of Zara: The Speeding Bullet," *The Strategist's Choice*, May 12, 2014, www .uniquebusinessstrategies.co.uk/pdfs/case%20studies/zarathespeedingbullet.pdf.

11. Nelson M. Fraiman, "Zara," Columbia Business School, Case 080204, New York, May 13, 2014.

12. Seth Stevenson, "Polka Dots Are In? Polka Dots It Is!: How Zara Gets Fresh Styles to Stores Insanely Fast—Within Weeks," *Slate: Operations*, June 21, 2012, www .slate.com/articles/arts/operations/2012/06/zara_s_fast_fashion_how_the_company_ gets_new_styles_to_stores_so_quickly_.html.

13. Henry Mintzberg, "Patterns in Strategy Formation," *Management Science* 24, no. 9 (1978): 934–948.

14. Richard Nelson and Sidney Winter, *An Evolutionary Theory of Economic Change* (Cambridge, MA: Belknap Press, 1985); George Stalk, "Time: The Next Source of Competitive Advantage," *Harvard Business Review*, July–August 1988.

15. Charles Fine, *Clockspeed: Winning Industry Control in the Age of Temporary Advantage* (New York: Basic Books, 1999); Kathleen M. Eisenhardt and Donald N. Sull, "Strategy as Simple Rules," *Harvard Business Review*, January 2001; Rita Gunther McGrath and Ian C. MacMillan, "Discovery Driven Planning: Turning Conventional Planning on Its Head," *DeepCanyon*, August 1999.

16. Martin Reeves and Mike Deimler, "Adaptability: The New Competitive Advantage," *Harvard Business Review*, August 2011; Reeves and Deimler, *Adaptive Advantage*.

17. BCG Strategy Institute analysis, "Increasing Unpredictability of Returns 1950–2010," calculated as average five-year rolling standard deviation of percent firm market capitalization growth by sector, weighted by firm market capitalization for all public US companies, based on Compustat data.

18. Paul Bjacek, "Commodities Volatility: It May Not Go Away Soon!" *Accenture*, February 10, 2012, www.accenture.com/us-en/blogs/cnr/archive/2012/02/10/Commodities-volatility.aspx.

19. Informa Australia, "BHP Billiton: Flexibility Needed in Mining Industry," *Mining and Resources*, September 27, 2013, http://informaaustralia.wordpress.com/2013/09/27/bhp-billiton-flexibility-needed-in-mining-industry/.

20. Nathan Bennett, "What VUCA Really Means for You," *Harvard Business Review*, January–February 2014.

21. Martin Reeves et al., "Signal Advantage," *BCG Perspectives*, February 2010.

22. James Sterngold, "New Japanese Lesson: Running a 7-11," *New York Times*, May 9, 1991, www.nytimes.com/1991/05/09/business/new-japanese-lesson-running-a-7-11.html.

23. Donald Rumsfeld, "Donald Rumsfeld Unknown Unknowns!" YouTube, August 7, 2009, www.youtube.com/watch?v=GiPe1OiKQuk.

24. Standing Committee to Review the Research Program of the Partnership for a New Generation of Vehicles, *Review of the Research Program of the Partnership for a New Generation of Vehicles* (Washington, DC: National Academy Press, 2001).

25. Toyota Motor Sales USA, "Worldwide Sales of Toyota Hybrids Top 6 Million Units," news release, January 14, 2014, http://corporatenews.pressroom.toyota.com/releases/worldwide+toyota+hybrid+sales+top+6+million.htm; Henk Bekker, "Most-Popular Japanese Passenger Vehicle Brands and Cars," 2009 Full Year List of Top 10 Best-Selling Cars in Japan, June 20, 2011, www.best-selling-cars.com/japan/2009-full-year-list-of-top-10-best-selling-cars-in-japan/.

26. Andy Serwer, "Larry Page on How to Change the World," *Fortune*, April 29, 2008, http://archive.fortune.com/2008/04/29/magazines/fortune/larry_page_change_the_world.fortune/index.htm.

27. Josh Halliday, "Google+ Launch: Search Giant Closes 10 Products," *Guardian* (London and Manchester), September 5, 2011, www.theguardian.com/technology/2011/sep/05/google-plus-launch-closes; Bharat Mediratta, "The Google Way: Give Engineers Room," *New York Times*, October 21, 2007, www.nytimes.com/2007/10/21/jobs/21pre.html?_r=0.; Christopher Mims, "Google's '20% Time,' Which Brought You Gmail and AdSense, Is Now as Good as Dead," *Quartz*, August 16, 2013, http://qz.com/115831/googles-20-time-which-brought-you-gmail-and-adsense-is-now-as-good-as-dead/.

28. Miltiadis D. Lytras, Ernesto Damiani, and Patricia Ordóñez de Pablos, *Web 2.0: The Business Model* (Berlin: Springer, 2008); Martin Reeves, Henri Salha, and

Marcus Bokkerink, "Simulation Advantage," *BCG Perspectives*, August 4, 2010, https://www.bcgperspectives.com/content/articles/strategy_consumer_products_ simulation_advantage/.

29. Halliday, "Google+ Launch."

30. The discussion of Telenor throughout this book comes from Jon Fredrik Baksaas (Telenor CEO), interview with authors, June 2014, and is supplemented by other sources where indicated.

31. Lillian Goleniewski, *Telecommunications Essentials: The Complete Global Source for Communications Fundamentals, Data Networking and the Internet, and Next-Generation Networks* (Boston: Addison-Wesley Professional, 2002).

32. Telenor Group, "Telenor Digital," Our Business, accessed June 5, 2014, www .telenor.com/about-us/our-business/telenor-digital/.

33. Randall Stross, "So You're a Good Driver? Let's Go to the Monitor," *New York Times*, November 25, 2012, www.nytimes.com/2012/11/25/business/seeking-cheaper-insurance-drivers-accept-monitoring-devices.html?_r=1&adxnnl=1&adxnnlx=1410959757-PWjgA23/ PwV/7Lj2mrSMgA.

34. Morningstar, "Q1 2012 Earnings Call Transcript," Morningstar, June 14, 2012, www.morningstar.com/earnings/39922695-progressive-corporation-pgr-q1-2012.aspx.

35. Leslie Brokaw, "In Experiments We Trust: From Intuit to Harrah's Casinos," *MIT Sloan Management Review*, March 3, 2011, http://sloanreview.mit.edu/article/ in-experiments-we-trust-from-intuit-to-harrahs-casinos/.

36. Erik Brynjolfsson and Michael Schrage, "The New, Faster Face of Innovation: Thanks to Technology, Change Has Never Been So Easy or So Cheap," *New York Times*, August 17, 2009, http://online.wsj.com/news/articles/SB10001424052970204830 30457413082018426034o.

37. Halliday, "Google+ Launch."

38. Martin Reeves, Yves Morieux, and Mike Deimler, "People Advantage," *BCG Perspectives*, March 2010, www.bcgperspectives.com/content/articles/strategy_ engagement_culture_people_advantage.

39. Hal Gregersen, "How Intuit Innovates by Challenging Itself," *Harvard Business Review Blog Network*, February 6, 2014, http://blogs.hbr.org/2014/02/how-intuit-innovates-by-challenging-itself/.

40. Robert I. Sutton and Huggy Rao, "When Subtraction Adds More," *BusinessWeek*, February 11, 2014, www.businessweek.com/articles/2014-02-11/when-subtraction-adds-more.

41. Robert Safian, "The Secrets of Generation Flux," *Fast Company*, November 2012, www.fastcompany.com/3001734/secrets-generation-flux.

42. Seth Weintraub, "Apple Acknowledges Use of Corning Gorilla Glass on iPhone, Means Gorilla Glass 2 Likely for iPhone 5," *9to5Mac*, March 2, 2012, http://9to5mac .com/2012/03/02/apple-acknowledges-use-of-corning-gorilla-glass-on-iphone-means-gorilla-glass-2-likely-for-iphone-5/.

43. Reed Hastings, "Netflix Culture: Freedom and Responsibility," *Slideshare*, August 1, 2009, www.slideshare.net/reed2001/culture-1798664.

44. Yahoo!, "Netflix: Historical Prices," *Yahoo! Finance*, May 20, 2014, https://uk.finance.yahoo.com/q/hp?s=NFLX&a=00&b=01&c=2009&d=11&e=31&f=2009&g=d&z=66&y=198; Tom Huddleston Jr., "Netflix Is Gobbling Up Internet Traffic, Study Finds," *Fortune*, May 14, 2014, http://fortune.com/2014/05/14/netflix-is-gobbling-up-internet-traffic-study-finds/.

45. Hastings, "Netflix Culture," 80.

46. 3M, "McKnight Principles," 3M Company website, History page, accessed May 11, 2014, http://solutions.3m.com/wps/portal/3M/en_US/3M-Company/Information/Resources/History/?PC_Z7_RJH9U52300V200IP896S2Q3223000000_assetId=1319210372704.

47. Alec Foege, "The Trouble with Tinkering Time," *Wall Street Journal*, January 18, 2013, http://online.wsj.com/news/articles/SB10001424127887323468604578246070515298626.

48. Eric von Hippel, Stefan Thomke, and Mary Sonnack, "Creating Breakthroughs at 3M," *Harvard Business Review*, September 1999.

Chapter 4

1. The discussion of Quintiles throughout this book comes from Dennis Gillings (Quintiles founder) and Tom Pike (Quintiles CEO), interviews with authors, February–March 2014, and is supplemented by other sources where indicated. See also Matthew Herper, "The Next Billionaire: A Statistician Who Changed Medicine," *Forbes*, May 8, 2013, http://www.forbes.com/sites/matthewherper/2013/05/08/the-next-billionaire-a-statistician-who-changed-medicine/.

2. Quintiles, "Investor Overview," May 8, 2014, http://investors.quintiles.com/investors/investor-overview/default.aspx; Matthew Herper, "Money, Math and Medicine," *Forbes*, November 3, 2010, www.forbes.com/forbes/2010/1122/private-companies-10-quintiles-dennis-gillings-money-medicine.html.

3. TED Conferences, "Alan Kay," TED Speaker, May 17, 2014, www.ted.com/speakers/alan_kay.

4. Gary Hamel, "Bringing Silicon Valley Inside," *Harvard Business Review*, September 1999.

5. The discussion of 23andMe throughout this book comes from Anne Wojcicki (23andMe founder and CEO), interview with authors, February 2014, and is supplemented by other sources where indicated.

6. Genomeweb, "23andMe Raises $50M in Series D Financing," Genomeweb, December 11, 2012, www.genomeweb.com/clinical-genomics/23andme-raises-50m-series-d-financing.

7. Aaron Krol, "J. Craig Venter's Latest Venture Has Ambitions Across Human Lifespan," *Bio IT World*, March 4, 2014, www.bio-itworld.com/2014/3/4/j-craig-venters-latest-venture-ambitions-across-human-lifespan.html.

8. Ibid.

9. Anita Hamilton, "1. The Retail DNA Test," Invention of the Year, *Time*, October 29, 2008, http://content.time.com/time/specials/packages/article/0,28804,1852747_1854493,00.html.

10. Elizabeth Murphy, "Inside 23andMe Founder Anne Wojcicki's $99 DNA Revolution," *Fast Company*, October 14, 2013, www.fastcompany.com/3018598/for-99-this-ceo-can-tell-you-what-might-kill-you-inside-23andme-founder-anne-wojcickis-dna-r.

11. Jemima Kiss, "23andMe Admits FDA Order 'Significantly Slowed Up' New Customers," *Guardian* (London and Manchester), March 9, 2014, www.theguardian.com/technology/2014/mar/09/google-23andme-anne-wojcicki-genetics-healthcare-dna.

12. Robert Langreth and Matthew Herper, "States Crack Down on Online Gene Tests," *Forbes*, April 18, 2008, www.forbes.com/2008/04/17/genes-regulation-testing-biz-cx_mh_bl_0418genes.html; Andrew Pollack, "F.D.A. Orders Genetic Testing Firm to Stop Selling DNA Analysis Service," *New York Times*, November 25, 2013, www.nytimes.com/2013/11/26/business/fda-demands-a-halt-to-a-dna-test-kits-marketing.html; US Food And Drug Administration, "23andMe, Inc. 11/22/13," Inspections, Compliance, Enforcement, and Criminal Investigations, November 22, 2013, www.fda.gov/ICECI/EnforcementActions/WarningLetters/2013/ucm376296.htm.

13. Alison Sander, Knut Haanæs, and Mike Deimler, "Megatrends: Tailwinds for Growth in a Low-Growth Environment," *BCG Perspectives*, May 2010, www.bcgperspectives.com/content/articles/managing_two_speed_economy_growth_megatrends/.

14. W. Chan Kim and Renée Mauborgne, "Blue Ocean Strategy: How to Create Uncontested Market Space and Make the Competition Irrelevant," *Harvard Business Review*, October 2004; Gary Hamel and C.K. Prahalad, *Competing for the Future* (Boston: Harvard Business Review Press, 1996); Joseph L. Bower and Clayton M. Christensen, "Disruptive Technologies: Catching the Wave," *Harvard Business Review*, January–February 1995; Martin Reeves, George Stalk, and Jussi Lehtinen, "Lessons from Mavericks: Staying Big by Acting Small," *BCG Perspectives*, June 2013.

15. United Parcel Service of America, "About UPS," UPS website, accessed May 15, 2014, www.ups.com/content/us/en/about/index.html?WT.svl=SubNav.

16. United Parcel Service of America, "1991–1999: Embracing Technology," History, UPS website, accessed May 15, 2014, www.ups.com/content/ky/en/about/history/1999.html?WT.svl=SubNav.

17. Martin Reeves, "UPS: Big Bet Vision," case study of the US freight market, India Strategy Summit, Mumbai, August 22, 2014.

18. United Parcel Service of America, "Enabling E-Commerce," Business Solutions, UPS website, accessed May 15, 2014, www.ups.com/content/us/en/bussol/browse/ebay.html.

19. Reeves, "UPS: Big Bet Vision."

20. Eric T. Wagner, "Five Reasons 8 out of 10 Businesses Fail," *Forbes*, September 12, 2013, www.forbes.com/sites/ericwagner/2013/09/12/five-reasons-8-out-of-10-businesses-fail/.

21. Murphy, "Inside 23andMe founder Anne Wojcicki's $99 DNA Revolution."

22. Stephen Nale, "The 100 Greatest Steve Jobs Quotes," Complex, October 5, 2012, www.complex.com/pop-culture/2012/10/steve-jobs-quotes/.

23. Intuitive Surgical, "Company Profile," Intuitive Surgical website, accessed May 11, 2014, www.intuitivesurgical.com/company/profile.html. The discussion of Intuitive Surgical throughout this book comes from an interview by the authors in April 2014 with the company's management; and BCG, "Meet the Mavericks," joint seminar at Strategic Management Society Conference, Geneva, March 2013, and is supplemented by other sources where indicated.

24. Intuitive Surgical, "Annual Report 2013."

25. Jay P. Pederson, *International Directory of Company Histories: General Electric Company*, vol. 137 (Detroit: St. James Press, 2012).

26. Trevor Butterworth, "The Fifth Wave of Computing," *Forbes*, June 6, 2010, www.forbes.com/2010/06/29/computing-technology-internet-media-opinions-columnists-trevor-butterworth.html. The discussion of Mobiquity throughout this book comes from Scott Snyder (Mobiquity cofounder and president), interview with authors, February 2014, and is supplemented by other sources where indicated.

27. Peter Cohan, "Mobiquity's Founder and CEO Bill Seibel Is Unstoppable," *Forbes*, July 17, 2013, www.forbes.com/sites/petercohan/2013/07/17/mobiquitys-founder-and-ceo-bill-seibel-is-unstoppable/.

28. Cohan, "Mobiquity's Founder and CEO."

29. The Henry Ford, "Henry Ford's Quotations," March 12, 2013, http://blog.thehenryford.org/2013/03/henry-fords-quotations/.

30. Michael Karnjanaprakorn, "Take a Bill Gates-Style 'Think Week' to Recharge Your Thinking," *Lifehacker*, October 22, 2012, http://lifehacker.com/5670380/the-power-of-time-off.

31. Adrian Covert, "Facebook Buys WhatsApp for $19 Billion," *CNN Money*, February 19, 2014, http://money.cnn.com/2014/02/19/technology/social/facebook-whatsapp/.

32. Kevin Baldacci, "7 Lessons You Can Learn from Jeff Bezos About Serving the Customer," *Salesforce Desk*, June 6, 2013, www.desk.com/blog/jeff-bezos-lessons/.

33. Jim Davis, "TiVo Launches 'Smart TV' Trial," *CNET*, December 22, 1998, http://news.cnet.com/TiVo-launches-smart-TV-trial/2100-1040_3-219409.html.

34. Dominic Gates, "Seattle's Flexcar Merges with Rival Zipcar," *Seattle Times*, October 30, 2007, http://community.seattletimes.nwsource.com/archive/?date=20071030&slug=flexcar31; Bernie DeGroat, "Hitchin' a Ride: Fewer Americans Have Their Own Vehicle," *Michigan News*, January 23, 2014, http://ns.umich.edu/new/releases/21923-hitchin-a-ride-fewer-americans-have-their-own-vehicle.

35. Jay P. Pedersen, *International Directory of Company Histories: Groupe Louis Dreyfus S.A. History*, vol. 60 (Detroit: St. James Press, 2004); BCG, "Meet the Mavericks," joint seminar at Strategic Management Society Conference, Geneva, March 2013.

36. Clare O'Connor, "Amazon's Wholesale Slaughter: Jeff Bezos' $8 Trillion B2B Bet," *Forbes*, May 7, 2014, www.forbes.com/sites/clareoconnor/2014/05/07/amazons-wholesale-slaughter-jeff-bezos-8-trillion-b2b-bet/.

37. Richard Harroch, "50 Inspirational Quotes for Startups and Entrepreneurs," *Forbes*, February 10, 2014, www.forbes.com/sites/allbusiness/2014/02/10/50-inspirational-quotes-for-startups-and-entrepreneurs/4/.

Chapter 5

1. Novo Nordisk, "The Blueprint for Change Programme: Changing Diabetes in China," *Sustainability*, February, 2011, www.novonordisk.com/images/Sustainability/PDFs/Blueprint%20for%20change%20-%20China.pdf. The discussion of Novo Nordisk throughout this book is from written correspondence by the authors in July 2014 with Novo Nordisk senior management and is supplemented by other sources where indicated.

2. PharmaBoardroom, "Interview with Lars Rebien Sørensen, CEO, Novo Nordisk," *PharmaBoardroom*, April 30, 2013, http://pharmaboardroom.com/interviews/interview-with-lars-rebien-s-rensen-president-ceo-novo-nordisk.

3. China Daily Information, "Diabetes in China May Reach Alert Level," *China Daily USA*, September 4, 2013, http://usa.chinadaily.com.cn/china/2013-09/04/content_16941867.htm; International Diabetes Federation, "IDF Diabetes Atlas," accessed May 16, 2014, www.idf.org/sites/default/files/DA6_Regional_factsheets_0.pdf.

4. Novo Nordisk, "Changing Diabetes," Novo Nordisk School Challenge, accessed May 17, 2014, http://schoolchallenge.novonordisk.com/diabetes/novo-nordisk-changing-diabetes.aspx.

5. Novo Nordisk, "Blueprint for Change Programme," 8.

6. PharmaBoardroom, "Interview with Lars Rebien Sørensen."

7. Novo Nordisk, "Blueprint for Change Programme."

8. Ibid.; Novo Nordisk, "Novo Nordisk Expands R&D Centre in China," Novo Nordisk News, August 3, 2004, www.novonordisk.com/press/news/chinese_r_and_d.asp.

9. Novo Nordisk, "Blueprint for Change Programme," 3.

10. PharmaBoardroom, "Interview with Lars Rebien Sørensen."

11. Bruce D. Henderson, "The Origin of Strategy," *Harvard Business Review*, November 1989.

12. Edward R. Freeman, *Strategic Management: A Stakeholder Approach* (Boston: Pitman, 1984).

13. James F. Moore, *The Death of Competition: Leadership and Strategy in the Age of Business Ecosystems* (New York: Harper Business Press, 1996); Marco Iansiti and Roy

Levien, *The Keystone Advantage: What the New Dynamics of Business Ecosystems Mean for Strategy, Innovation, and Sustainability* (Boston: Harvard Business School Press, 2004); Simon Levin, *Fragile Dominion: Complexity and the Commons* (New York: Basic Books, 2000); Adam M. Brandenburger and Barry J. Nalebuff, *Co-opetition* (New York: Currency Doubleday, 1996).

14. Philip Evans and Tom Wurster, *Blown to Bits: How the New Economics of Information Transforms Strategy* (Boston: Harvard Business School Press, 1999); Martin Reeves and Alex Bernhardt, "Systems Advantage," *BCG Perspectives*, June 2011, www .bcgperspectives.com/content/articles/future_strategy_strategic_planning_systems_ advantage/; Martin Reeves, Thijs Venema, and Claire Love, "Shaping to Win," *BCG Perspectives*, October 2013, www.bcgperspectives.com/content/articles/business_unit_ strategy_corporate_strategy_portfolio_management_shaping_to_win/.

15. Henry Chesbrough, "Open Innovation: The New Imperative for Creating Profit from Technology," *Academy of Management Perspectives* 20, no. 2 (2006): 86–88; C. K. Prahalad and Venkat Ramaswamy, *The Future of Competition: Co-creating Unique Value with Customers* (Boston: Harvard Business School Press, 2004).

16. Christopher Null, "The End of Symbian: Nokia Ships Last Handset with the Mobile OS," *PC World*, June 14, 2013, www.pcworld.com/article/2042071/the-end-of-symbian-nokia-ships-last-handset-with-the-mobile-os.html.

17. Nathan Ingraham, "Apple Announces 1 Million Apps in the App Store, More than 1 Billion Songs Played on iTunes radio," *Verge*, October 22, 2013, www.theverge .com/2013/10/22/4866302/apple-announces-1-million-apps-in-the-app-store.

18. BBC, "Nokia at Crisis Point, Warns New Boss Stephen Elop," *BBC News: Technology*, February 9, 2011, www.bbc.co.uk/news/technology-12403466; Chris Ziegler, "Nokia CEO Stephen Elop Rallies Troops in Brutally Honest 'Burning Platform' Memo? (Update: It's Real!)," *Endgaget*, February 8, 2011, www.engadget .com/2011/02/08/nokia-ceo-stephen-elop-rallies-troops-in-brutally-honest-burnin/.

19. Mark Scott, "Nokia Announces New Strategy, and a New Chief to Carry It Out," *New York Times*, April 29, 2014, www.nytimes.com/2014/04/30/technology/ nokia-announces-new-strategy-and-chief-executive.html?_r=0.

20. Justin Smith, "Facebook Platform Payment Providers Report Strong Growth in Q1," *Inside Facebook*, April 14, 2009, www.insidefacebook.com/2009/04/14/ facebook-platform-payment-providers-report-strong-growth-in-q1/.

21. Julie Bort, "It's Official: Red Hat Is the First Open Source Company to Top $1 Billion a Year," *Business Insider*, March 28, 2012, www.businessinsider.com/its-official-red-hat-becomes-the-first-1-billion-open-source-company-2012-3. The discussion of Red Hat throughout this book comes from Jim Whitehurst (Red Hat CEO), interview with authors, February 2014, and is supplemented by other sources where indicated.

22. Red Hat, "Our Mission," Red Hat website, accessed September 18, 2014, www.redhat.com/en/about/company.

23. Yahoo!, "Red Hat Inc.," *Yahoo! Finance*, September 18, 2014, https://uk.finance. yahoo.com/q/hp?s=RHT&b=11&a=00&c=2008&e=16&d=11&f=2008&g=d.

24. Facebook, "Facebook Platform Migrations," Facebook website, accessed May 23, 2014, https://developers.facebook.com/docs/apps/migrations.

25. Apple, "iTunes Charts," Paid Apps, accessed September 18, 2014, www .apple.com/uk/itunes/charts/paid-apps/; Greg Kumparak, "Apple Announces Top 10 iPhone App Downloads of 2008," *Tech Crunch*, December 2, 2008, http://techcrunch .com/2008/12/02/apple-announces-top-10-iphone-app-downloads-of-2008/.

26. Ian Urbina and Keith Bradsher, "Linking Factories to the Malls, Middleman Pushes Low Costs," *New York Times*, August 7, 2013, www.nytimes.com/2013/08/08/world/ linking-factories-to-the-malls-middleman-pushes-low-costs.html?_r=0; Fung Group, "Supply Chain Management," Fung Group Research, accessed September 18, 2014, www .funggroup.com/eng/knowledge/research.php?report=supply; Fung Group, "Who We Are," Fung Group website, September 3, 2014, www.funggroup.com/eng/about/.

27. "The World's Greatest Bazaar: Alibaba, a Trailblazing Chinese Internet Giant, Will Soon Go Public," *Economist*, May 23, 2013, www.economist.com/news/ briefing/21573980-alibaba-trailblazing-chinese-internet-giant-will-soon-go-public- worlds-greatest-bazaar. The discussion of Alibaba throughout this book comes from Ming Zeng (Alibaba CSO), interview with authors, March 2014, and is supplemented by other sources where indicated.

28. Alexa Internet, "The Top 500 Sites on the Web," Alexa website, accessed September 18, 2014, www.alexa.com/topsites.

29. Stephen Gandel, "What Time Is the Alibaba IPO?" *Fortune*, September 17, 2014, http://fortune.com/2014/09/17/what-time-is-the-alibaba-ipo/.

30. "The World's Greatest Bazaar."

31. Christina Bonnington, "Apple's Developer Conference, WWDC, Has Grown into a Disaster," *Wired*, April 29, 2013, www.wired.co.uk/news/archive/2013-04/29/ wwdc-is-too-big.

32. Google, "Google I/O 2013," Developers home page, accessed May 5, 2014, https://developers.google.com/events/io/.

33. Adam Bryant, "The Memo List: Where Everyone Has an Opinion," *New York Times*, March 10, 2012, www.nytimes.com/2012/03/11/business/jim-whitehurst-of-red- hat-on-merits-of-an-open-culture.html?pagewanted=all.

Chapter 6

1. HSN Consultants, Inc., "Global Cards," *Nilson Report*, 2008, http://www .nilsonreport.com/publication_chart_and_graphs_archive.php. The discussion of American Express throughout this book comes from Ken Chenault (American Express CEO), interview with authors, April 2014, and is supplemented by other sources where indicated.

2. Michael Barbaro and Louis Uchitelle, "Americans Cut Back Sharply on Spending," *New York Times*, January 14, 2008, www.nytimes.com/2008/01/14/business/14spend .html?pagewanted=all&_r=0.

3. Sara Lepro, "American Express to Cut 7,000 Jobs," *Huffington Post Business*, November, 25, 2011, www.huffingtonpost.com/2008/10/30/american-express-to-cut-7_n_139476.html.

4. Peter Eichenbaum, "American Express Marketing Cuts May 'Cheat' Brand (Update2)," *Bloomberg*, August 6, 2009, www.bloomberg.com/apps/news?pid= newsarchive&sid=a2Y3p_tL_J1A.

5. Yahoo!, "Historical Prices: American Express Company," *Yahoo! Finance*, May 21, 2014, http://finance.yahoo.com/q/hp?s=AXP&a=11&b=1&c=2009&d=00&e=2&f=2010&g=d.

6. Ibid.

7. Kenneth I. Chenault, "American Express Chairman & CEO Key Remarks," Bank of America Merrill Lynch 2009 Banking and Financial Services Conference, New York, November 10, 2009.

8. Ibid.

9. Peter Eavis, "Kenneth Chenault's Crisis Years," *New York Times*, December 18, 2012, http://dealbook.nytimes.com/2012/12/18/kenneth-chenaults-crisis-years/?_ php=true&_type=blogs&_r=0.

10. American Express Company, "American Express Announces 2008 Membership Rewards(R) Program Partner Lineup," Investor Relations, May 22, 2008, http:// ir.americanexpress.com/Mobile/file.aspx?IID=102700&FID=6134500.

11. Chenault, "Key Remarks."

12. Robert S. Kaplan and William J. Bruns, *Accounting and Management: A Field Study Perspective* (Boston: Harvard Business Review Press, 1987); Michael Hammer and James A. Champy, *Reengineering the Corporation: A Manifesto for Business Revolution* (New York: HarperCollins, 1993); Tom M. Hout and George Stalk, *Competing Against Time: How Time-Based Competition Is Reshaping Global Markets* (New York: Free Press, 1990).

13. Ron Nicol, "Shaping Up: The Delayered Outlook," *BCG Perspectives*, October 2004, www.bcgperspectives.com/content/articles/strategy_shaping_up_the_delayered_ look/.

14. John P. Kotter, *Leading Change* (Boston: Harvard Business School Press, 1996); Jeanie D. Duck, *The Change Monster: The Human Forces That Fuel or Foil Corporate Transformation and Change* (New York: Three Rivers Press, 2001).

15. Clifford Krauss and John Schwartz, "BP Will Plead Guilty and Pay Over $4 Billion," *New York Times*, November 15, 2012, www.nytimes.com/2012/11/16/business/ global/16iht-bp16.html.

16. Martin Reeves, Sandy Moose, and Thijs Venema, "BCG Classics Revisited: The Growth Share Matrix," *BCG Perspectives*, June 2014, www.bcgperspectives.com/content/ articles/corporate_strategy_portfolio_management_strategic_planning_growth_ share_matrix_bcg_classics_revisited/.

17. The discussion of Bausch & Lomb and Forest Laboratories throughout this book comes from Brent Saunders (Bausch & Lomb CEO), interviews with authors, March 2014, and is supplemented by other sources where indicated.

18. Matthew Herper, "$9 Billion Bausch & Lomb Sale Mints New Turnaround Artist," *Forbes*, May 27, 2013, www.forbes.com/sites/matthewherper/2013/05/27/9-billion-bausch-lomb-sale-mints-new-turnaround-artist/; United Securities and Exchange Commission, Form S-1 Registration Statement (Washington, DC: 2013).

19. Bausch & Lomb, "Investor Relations," Our Company, August 5, 2013, www.bausch.com/our-company/investor-relations#.VByPDstOW70.

20. Martin Reeves et al., "Lean, but Not Yet Mean: Why Transformation Needs a Second Chapter," *BCG Perspectives*, October 2013, www.bcgperspectives.com/content/articles/transformation_growth_why_transformation_needs_second_chapter_lean_not_yet_mean/. Note: For our study we looked closely at transformation programs using a method of paired historical comparison, an approach that eliminates interesting but irrelevant details and zeroes in on the key factors that separate success from failure. We looked at a dozen pairs of companies, each in the same industry and facing similar challenges at similar times.

21. Ibid.

22. Martin Reeves, Knut Haanæs, and Kaelin Goulet, "Turning Around the Successful Company," *BCG Perspectives*, December 2013, www.bcgperspectives.com/content/articles/transformation_large_scale_change_growth_turning_around_successful_company/.

23. This discussion of Kodak comes from a series of interviews and e-mail correspondence by the authors between May and June 2014 with leaders of Kodak's corporate communications department and is supplemented by various other sources such as Giovanni Gavetti, Rebecca Henderson, Simon Giorgi, "Kodak and the Digital Revolution (A)," Case 705448 (Boston: Harvard Business School, 2005); Robert J. Dolan, "Eastman Kodak Co.," Case 599106 (Boston: Harvard Business School, 1999); A. Cheerla, "Kodak—A Case of Triumph & Failure" (2010), http://www.managedecisions.com/blog/?p=444; and Steve Hamm, Louise Lee, and Spencer E. Ante, "Kodak's Moment of Truth," *BusinessWeek*, February 18, 2007, http://www.businessweek.com/stories/2007-02-18/kodaks-moment-of-truth.

24. "Marc Faber: We Could Have a Crash Like in 1987 This Fall! Here's Why," *Before It's News*, May 12, 2012, http://beforeitsnews.com/gold-and-precious-metals/2012/05/marc-faber-we-could-have-a-crash-like-in-1987-this-fall-heres-why-2129176.html.

25. "Fortune 500: 2008," *Fortune*, September 18, 2014, http://fortune.com/fortune500/2008/wal-mart-stores-inc-1/. The discussion of AIG throughout this book comes from Peter Hancock (AIG CEO), interview with authors, April 2014, and is supplemented by other sources where indicated.

26. Matthew Karnitschnig, "U.S. to Take Over AIG in $85 Billion Bailout; Central Banks Inject Cash as Credit Dries Up," *Wall Street Journal*, September 16, 2008, http://online.wsj.com/news/articles/SB122156561931242905; Leslie P. Norton, "The Man

Who Saved AIG," *Barrons*, August 11, 2012, http://online.barrons.com/news/articles/SB50001424053111904239304577575214205090528#articleTabs_article%3D1.

27. Jody Shenn and Zachary Tracer, "Federal Reserve Says AIG, Bear Stearns Rescue Loans Paid," *Bloomberg*, June 14, 2012, www.bloomberg.com/news/2012-06-14/new-york-fed-says-aig-bear-stearns-rescue-loans-fully-repaid.html.

28. American International Group, "Annual Report," 2013, 5.

29. Stuart Read et al., *Effectual Entrepreneurship* (New York: Routledge, 2011).

30. BCG, "DICE: How to Beat the Odds in Program Execution," August 2014.

31. Perry Keenan et al., "Strategic Initiative Management: The PMO Imperative," *BCG Perspectives*, November 2013, www.bcgperspectives.com/content/articles/program_management_change_management_strategic_initiative_management_pmo_imperative/.

32. Mike Sager, "What I've Learned: Andy Grove," *Esquire*, May 1, 2000, www.esquire.com/features/what-ive-learned/learned-andy-grove-0500.

33. For One AIG identity, see Bloomberg, "AIG's Bob Benmosche Memo to Employees," *Newsarchive*, September 17, 2014, www.bloomberg.com/bb/newsarchive/aWbEUgKiZLNM.html. For return of brand name, see American International Group, "AIG Returns Core Insurance Operations to AIG Brand, Reveals New Brand Promise," *Business Wire*, November 11, 2012, www.businesswire.com/news/home/20121111005039/en/AIG-Returns-Core-Insurance-Operations-AIG-Brand#.VBypRMtOW71.

Chapter 7

1. Hugh Johnston, "Geared for Growth," PepsiCo website, February 21, 2013, www.pepsico.com/Download/CAGNY_Webdeck.pdf. The discussion of PepsiCo throughout this book comes from Indra Nooyi (PepsiCo CEO), interview with authors, April 2014, and is supplemented by other sources where indicated.

2. Ted Cooper, "PepsiCo Shows Why Frito-Lay and Pepsi Are Better Together," Investing Commentary, *Motley Fool*, January 15, 2014, www.fool.com/investing/general/2014/01/15/heres-why-pepsico-is-positioned-better-for-2014-th.aspx; PepsiCo, "Quick Facts," PepsiCo website, August 22, 2013, www.pepsico.com/Download/PepsiCo_Quick_Facts.pdf.

3. PepsiCo, "Annual Report 2012," 2012, 24.

4. James G. March, "Exploration and Exploitation in Organizational Learning," *Organization Science* 2, no. 1 (1991): 71–87; Michael L. Tushman and Charles A. O'Reilly III, "Ambidextrous Organizations: Managing Evolutionary and Revolutionary Change," *California Management Review* 38, no. 4 (1996): 8–30.

5. Julian Birkinshaw and Christina Gibson, "Building Ambidexterity into an Organization," *MIT Sloan Management Review*, summer 2004.

6. Martin Reeves et al., "The Evolvable Enterprise: Lessons from the New Technology Giants," *BCG Perspectives*, February 2014, www.bcgperspectives.com/

content/articles/future_strategy_business_unit_strategy_evolvable_enterprise_
lessons_new_technology_giants/; Martin Reeves and Jussi Lehtinen, "The Ingenious
Enterprise: Competing Amid Rising Complexity," *BCG Perspectives*, May 2013, www
.bcgperspectives.com/content/articles/growth_business_unit_strategy_ingenious_
enterprise_competing_amid_rising_complexity/.

7. Martin Reeves, Claire Love, and Nishant Mathur, "The Most Adaptive
Companies 2012: Winning in an Age of Turbulence," *BCG Perspectives*, August
2012. Adaptive companies are defined as outperforming in 75 percent of turbulent
and stable periods or 30 percent of all turbulent quarters. Outperformance
calculation is based on market cap growth relative to industry-average growth.
The analysis looked at US public companies between 1960 and 2011 and is based
on Compustat data.

8. Martin Reeves et al., "Ambidexterity: The Art of Thriving in Complex
Environments," *BCG Perspectives*, February 2013, www.bcgperspectives.com/content/
articles/business_unit_strategy_growth_ambidexterity_art_of_thriving_in_
complex_environments/.

9. Lockheed Martin, "Skunk Works® Origin Story," *Aeronautics*, May 7, 2014,
www.lockheedmartin.com/us/aeronautics/skunkworks/origin.html.

10. Joe Clifford, "Toyota's Skunkworks Plug-in Hybrid Sports Car," *Toyota* (blog),
January 28, 2014, http://blog.toyota.co.uk/toyotas-skunkworks-plug-in-hybrid-
sports-car#.VCBnsstOW7o.

11. This discussion of Towers Watson comes from John Haley (Towers Watson
CEO), interview with authors, February 2014, and is supplemented by other sources
where indicated.

12. Julia Cooper, "Towers Watson, Mercer Lead Largest Benefits Consulting Firms,"
San Francisco Business Times, July 11, 2014, www.bizjournals.com/sanfrancisco/subscriber-
only/2014/07/11/benefits-consulting-firms-2014.html.

13. Towers Watson, "Annual Report 2012," 2012, 15.

14. Christopher Lawton, "TV Sellers Are Thinking Big," *Wall Street Journal*,
November 20, 2007, http://online.wsj.com/news/articles/SB119551914597698572.

15. Corning, "CEO: 'Corning Is Built for Longevity,'" press release, April 29, 2014,
www.corning.com/news_center/news_releases/2014/2014042901.aspx.

16. Ben Dobbin, "Gorilla Glass, 1962 Invention, Poised to Be Big Seller for
Corning," *Huffington Post*, February 10, 2010, www.huffingtonpost.com/2010/08/02/
gorilla-glass-1962-invent_n_667416.html.

17. Seth Weintraub, "Apple Acknowledges Use of Corning Gorilla Glass on iPhone,
Means Gorilla Glass 2 Likely for iPhone 5," *9to5Mac*, March 2, 2012, http://9to5mac
.com/2012/03/02/apple-acknowledges-use-of-corning-gorilla-glass-on-iphone-means-
gorilla-glass-2-likely-for-iphone-5/; Bryan Gardiner, "Glass Works: How Corning
Created the Ultrathin, Ultrastrong Material of the Future," *Wired*, September 24, 2012,
www.wired.com/2012/09/ff-corning-gorilla-glass/all/.

18. Corning corporate communications department, e-mail message to authors, July 29, 2014.

19. Corning, "Corning Launches Ultra-Slim Flexible Glass," press release, June 4, 2012, www.corning.com/news_center/news_releases/2012/201206040l.aspx.

20. Haier Group, "Haier Ranked the #1 Global Major Appliances Brand for 4th Consecutive Year—Euromonitor," *Reuters*, December 24, 2012, www.reuters.com/article/2012/12/24/haier-ranked-first-idUSnPnCN34281+160+PRN20121224. This discussion of Haier comes from written correspondence by authors with Haier senior management in June 2014 and is supplemented by other sources where indicated.

21. Haier Group, "Haier: The Evolution of You," Haier website, accessed May 8, 2014, www.haier.com/us/about-haier/201305/P020130512352743920958.pdf.

22. Lao-Tzu, "The Tao-te Ching," May 11, 2014, http://classics.mit.edu/Lao/taote.1.1.html.

23. Ruimin Zhang, "Raising Haier," *Harvard Business Review*, February 2007.

24. Ibid.

25. Haier corporate communications department, e-mail message to authors, June 13, 2014.

26. Lance Whitney, "iPhone 6 Images Reportedly from Foxconn Reveal Larger Body," *CNET*, May 12, 2014, www.cnet.com/news/iphone-6-renders-reportedly-from-foxconn-reveal-larger-body/; Allan Yogasingam, "Teardown: Inside the Apple iPhone 5," *EDN Network*, September 21, 2012, www.edn.com/design/consumer/4396870/Teardown--Inside-the-Apple-iPhone-5.

Chapter 8

1. Pfizer, "To Our Shareholders," CEO letter, February 28, 2014, www.pfizer.com/files/investors/financial_reports/annual_reports/2013/letter.htm; Pfizer, "Annual Report 2011," 2011, and "Annual Report 2013," 2013; Simon King, "The Best Selling Drugs Since 1996: Why AbbVie's Humira Is Set to Eclipse Pfizer's Lipitor," *Forbes*, July 15, 2010, www.forbes.com/sites/simonking/2013/07/15/the-best-selling-drugs-since-1996-why-abbvies-humira-is-set-to-eclipse-pfizers-lipitor/; Yahoo!, "Historical Prices: Pfizer Inc. (PFE)," *Yahoo! Finance*, September 17, 2014, https://uk.finance.yahoo.com/q/hp?s=PFE&a=00&b=1&c=2000&d=11&e=30&f=2000&g=d&z=66&y=66.

2. Pfizer, "Annual Report 2013," 2, 8.

3. Pfizer, "R&D Collaborations," Annual Review 2013, May 13, 2014, www.pfizer.com/files/investors/financial_reports/annual_reports/2013/assets/pdfs/pfizer_13ar_i_collaborate.pdf.

4. Pfizer, "To Our Shareholders"; Pfizer, "To Our Stakeholders," CEO letter, February 28, 2013, www.pfizer.com/files/investors/financial_reports/annual_reports/2012/letter.html; Andrew Ward, "Pfizer Break-up May Follow AstraZeneca Deal," *Financial Times*, May 4, 2014, www.ft.com/intl/cms/s/0/ba383d00-d399-11e3-b0be-00144feabdco.html?siteedition=intl#axzz31X8zJqbT.

5. Bruce Henderson, "Why Change Is So Difficult," *BCG Perspectives*, 1968, www
.bcgperspectives.com/content/Classics/why_change_is_so_difficult/.

6. Dow Jones Newswires, "AIG's Benmosche Pushes on Bid to Buy Bonds," *Wall
Street Journal*, March 23, 2011, http://online.wsj.com/news/articles/SB1000142405274870
4050204576218401104973260.

7. US Department of the Treasury, "Treasury Sells Final Shares of AIG Common
Stock, Positive Return on Overall AIG Commitment Reaches $22.7 Billion," Press
Center, November 12, 2011, www.treasury.gov/press-center/press-releases/Pages/
tg1796.aspx.

8. Erik Holm, "Hoping to Strike Profit Gold, AIG Ramps Up in Data Mining,"
Wall Street Journal, October 15, 2012, http://online.wsj.com/news/articles/SB1000087239
63904447999045780525918608972244.

INDEX

Page numbers followed by *f* refer to figures and page numbers followed by *t* refer to tables.

ACKNOWLEDGMENTS

This book has been a true collaborative effort of many within and beyond our firm, The Boston Consulting Group, and we sincerely thank all of those who have contributed in many ways.

Special credit is due to Kaelin Goulet and Thijs Venema, ambassadors to the BCG Strategy Institute, who worked tirelessly and selflessly over a one-year period to help develop the ideas, examples, interviews, and analyses that constitute the foundation of the book and without whose great dedication and partnership the project could not have come to fruition.

Thanks are also due to other Strategy Institute ambassadors who contributed significantly to the ideas in this book. Claire Love cowrote the original *HBR* article "Your Strategy Needs a Strategy," which was the trigger for writing the book and which forms its conceptual foundation. Georg Wittenburg developed the simulation model for testing the effectiveness of different strategies in different environments and conceived and designed the companion app, which experientially simulates different approaches to strategy. Amin Venjara ran the development process for the app. Tomasz Mrozowski, Lisanne Pueschel, and Caroline Guan developed the illustrations and analyses for the book, and Bastian Bergmann ran the time-consuming permissions, editing, and finishing process. Other SI ambassadors helped lay the conceptual foundations for the book; they include Jussi Lehtinen (algorithmic strategy); Nishant Mathur, Charles Hendren, Matt Stack, Peter Goss, Eugene Goh, and Sofia Elizondo (adaptive strategy); Akira Shibata (strategy styles survey and analytics); Alex Bernhardt (shaping strategy); Filippo Scognamiglio (experience curve revisited); Judith Wallenstein (social dimensions of strategy); and Maya Said (adaptive strategy capabilities).

We also thank our academic collaborators, who guided our thinking throughout the process. Professor Simon Levin of Princeton University helped us understand and learn from biological strategies and evolutionary processes and supported us in developing an index of adaptive advantage for US companies. Mihnea Moldoveanu of the Rotman School, Toronto University, inspired us with his thinking on metaheuristics; and an algorithmic conception of strategy was the trigger for the simulation model. Philip Tillmans, University of Aachen, was also a coauthor on the original *HBR* article. Thomas Fink of the London Institute of Mathematical Sciences; Luciano Pietronero, Rome University; and Can Uslay, Rutgers University, also contributed significantly to our thinking.

We are especially indebted to the CEOs and other leaders who agreed to be interviewed for this book and who shared their experiences and reflections on different approaches to strategy under different circumstances: Tom Pike (CEO, Quintiles), Dennis Gillings (Chairman and Founder, Quintiles), Anne Wojcicki (CEO, 23andMe), Jim Whitehurst (CEO, Red Hat), Scott Snyder (CEO, Mobiquity), Ian Read (Chairman and CEO, Pfizer), Kenneth Chenault (CEO, Amex), Ming Zeng (CSO, Alibaba), Heather Bresch (CEO, Mylan), John Haley (CEO, Towers Watson), Indra Nooyi (CEO, PepsiCo), Natarajan Chandrashekaran (CEO, Tata Consulting Services), Peter Hancock (CEO, AIG), Brent Saunders (CEO, Forest Labs), Guo Ping (CEO, Huawei), Paul Michaels (CEO, Mars), Anand Mahindra (CEO, Mahindra), and Jon Fredrik Baksaas (CEO, Telenor).

We are grateful to our BCG partners and former partners who contributed to various publications that paved the way for this book, including Mike Deimler, Ron Nicol, Rachel Lee, Yves Morieux, Ted Chan, Roselinde Torres, Mike Shanahan, Philip Evans, George Stalk, Gideon Walter, Marcus Bokkerink, Rob Trollinger, Sandy Moose, and Wolfgang Thiel. Also to those who opened doors to their clients to support our research: Andrew Toma, Tom Reichert, Francois Candelon, Dag Bjornland, Craig Lawton, Achim Schwetlick, Grant Freeland, Sharon Marcil, Vikram Bhalla, and Roselinde Torres. We thank our former and current CEOs for encouragement and help in removing obstacles throughout the process: Carl Stern, Hans Paul Buerkner, and Rich Lesser.

Thanks are due to our friends at Harvard Business Review Press for both their encouragement and for managing the project so professionally and smoothly, especially to Melinda Merino, our editor.

We are grateful to Bernadette Hertz for tireless administrative support.

Finally, we dedicate this book to BCG's founder, Bruce Henderson, who was an early pioneer in business strategy and strategy consulting and who shaped the intellectual foundations of strategy at BCG and beyond. We celebrate the hundredth anniversary of his birth on April 30, 2015, which roughly coincides with the publication date for this book. We hope that our effort proves worthy of this coincidence and renews and adds in a small way to his inestimable legacy.

ABOUT THE AUTHORS

MARTIN REEVES is a senior partner and managing director in BCG's New York office and leads the Bruce Henderson Institute, BCG's vehicle for research and translation of ideas from beyond the world of business into practical frameworks and tools for business strategy.

Martin has devoted a significant part of his career to developing and applying new ideas in business strategy. He was named a BCG Fellow in 2008, and he has published and spoken widely on strategy issues. He splits his time equally between research and client service. His interests include self-tuning organizations, corporate longevity, commoditization, strategy and sustainability, new bases of competitive advantage, the economics of trust, adaptive strategy, and managerial heuristics.

Martin joined BCG in London in 1989 and later moved to Tokyo, where he led the firm's Japan Health Care practice for eight years and was responsible for BCG's business with global clients. He has led numerous strategy and organizational assignments, both for individual companies and for industry associations across the globe.

Martin lives in New York City with his wife Zhenya. He is the proud father of five: Thomas, Morris, Alexandra, Anastasia, and Ekaterina.

KNUT HAANÆS is a senior partner and the global leader of BCG's Strategy practice. He also leads the BCG Geneva office and has previously been office administrator of BCG Oslo.

Knut consults widely on strategy with clients across multiple industries and sectors, focusing on value creation and growth. Knut also has a deep passion for sustainability and has worked for international organizations such as the World Economic Forum (WEF) and the World Wide Fund for Nature (WWF). In particular, he is interested in how sustainability can drive innovation and new business models. Knut is also co-responsible for the collaboration between BCG and *MIT Sloan Management Review* in the area of strategies for sustainability.

Knut has published more than twenty articles on strategy and sustainability in journals such as *Harvard Business Review, MIT Sloan Management Review, Business Strategy Review, Journal of Applied Corporate Finance, European Management Review, Scandinavian Management Review*, and has authored a number of BCG reports.

Previously, Knut was executive director of the Research Council of Norway. He has also been an associate professor at the BI Norwegian Business School and a research associate at IMD in Switzerland. His first job was as a trainee at the trade council in the Norwegian Embassy in Paris. Knut holds an MSc in economics from the Norwegian School of Economics and a PhD in strategy from Copenhagen Business School. He was subsequently a visiting scholar at Stanford University, sponsored by the Scandinavian Consortium for Organizational Research (SCANCOR).

Knut is married to Sabine and has two children, Nora and Maxim.

JANMEJAYA SINHA is chairman of BCG's Asia Pacific practice. He is also a member of BCG's global Executive Committee.

Janmejaya works extensively with clients in the United States, United Kingdom, Asia, Australia, and India over a range of issues encompassing large-scale organization transformation, strategy, governance, and family business issues. He has been a member of various committees set up by the government of India, the Reserve Bank of India (RBI), and the Indian Banks' Association (IBA). He is currently chairman of the Confederation of Indian Industry's (CII) Committee on Financial Inclusion.

Janmejaya writes extensively for the press and is a regular speaker at the World Economic Forum, the Confederation of Indian Industry (CII), the Indian Banks' Association (IBA), the Federation of Indian Chambers of Commerce and Industry (FICCI), the Reserve Bank of India (RBI), and other media events. He is a coauthor of the book *Own the Future: 50 Ways to Win from The Boston Consulting Group*. Janmejaya has presented a TED talk on "What's Really Happening in Emerging Markets" as part of a series of talks curated by TED and BCG. In 2010 *Consulting* magazine named him one of the Top 25 most influential consultants in the world.

Prior to joining The Boston Consulting Group, Janmejaya worked for the Reserve Bank of India for several years in various departments. He also worked briefly for the World Bank.

He holds a PhD from the Woodrow Wilson School of Public and International Affairs, Princeton University, a BA and an MA in economics from Clare College, Cambridge University, and a BA and an MA in history from St. Stephen's College, Delhi University.

Janmejaya lives with his wife Malvika in Mumbai and has two sons, Amartya and Advait.